The GREATNESS In YOU

Presented By The World's Greatest Motivator
LES BROWN and "The Connector,"
JON TALARICO

© 2022 Jon Talarico
Book Cover Design: Dr. Shadaria Allison

Interior Book Design & Formatting: TamikaINK.com
Editor: Heather Duma, TamikaINK.com
Consulting Services: Dawn Lieck, Finally Free, LLC
Project Management by Nichol Perricci @ DNP

ALL RIGHTS RESERVED. No part of this book may be reproduced in any written, electronic, recording, or photocopying without written permission of the publisher or author. The exception would be in the case of brief quotations embodied in critical articles or reviews and pages where permission is specifically granted by the publisher or author.

LEGAL DISCLAIMER. Although the author has made every effort to ensure that the information in this book was correct at press time, the author do not assume hereby disclaim any liability to any party for loss, damage, or disruption caused by errors or missions, whether such errors or omissions result from negligence, accident, or any other cause.

Published By: Igniting The Flame Publishing

Library of Congress Cataloging-in-Publication Data has been applied for

ISBN: 979-8-218-05686-5

PRINTED IN THE UNITED STATES OF AMERICA

Table of Contents

Introduction By Les Brown 1
Discover The Million in YOU By Jon Talarico 6
Awaken the Great Giant By Fernanda Castañeda 14
Realize You're the Difference When "Greatness Is in YOU!"
By Deborah Allen 21
Answer the Call By Dr. Pamela Henkel 30
A Little Chat With Myself By Brian Dawkins 37
Pioneering Greatness II- Be Ballast by David D. Archer Jr. .46
Get Up, Get Up, Get Up! By Alicia Lyttle 54
Fearfully and Wonderfully Made By Dawn Lieck 61
From Near Death to Hollywood By Sam Humphrey 66
Adornami By Andrea Edwards Adams 76
Growing Into Your Voice by Jodie Solberg 84
1983 By Carmen Cadena 91
The Most Important Game By Dan Gomer 98
Are You Prepared for Greatness?
By Dr. Jacquelyn Hadnot 105
Expect Great Things in Your Life
By Carolyn Brooks-Collins 114
Embrace The Wilderness by Angela Bennett 121
Transform Your Mind, Believe, And Receive What You Ask
For By Carrie Watson 131
Playing the Cards You're Dealt By Donato Perricci 138
Million In You By Andre Notice 145
From Pain to Power By Dr. Chris Leininger 152
Live a Life You Love and Find Greatness Within You
By Dominika Schwarc 159

The Boy Who Never Stopped Dreaming
By Barry Overton 168

Enough Is Enough! Empower Yourself to Help (Your)
Children and Teenagers Discover Their Greatness!
By Ellen Wulfert 175

Destiny Unleashed By Kelisha Worrell 185

My Pain Got Me Here! By Michelle Alston 193

Potential Greatness And Your Participation In It
By Rodney Lucero 199

Position of Power By Shirley Brown Danzy 207

From Cancer to Courageous - There Is Greatness Still in Me!
By Lisa Yvette Jones 215

The Greatness In You By Sylvia Tsui 224

Take Your Life Back by Angie Osorio 230

Seven Ways To Maintain, Manage and Multiplying Assets
For The Greatness In You By Dr. Steven D. Davis 239

Finding Peace By Dr. Sarita Graham 250

Shoot for the Moon. If You Miss, Grab the Stars
By Linda Ellison 259

What Will Your Story Be By Dr. Shirlee Turner 266

My Story By Tonya Flowers 273

Recognize the Greatness in You By Stephon Suggs 280

Perseverance During Uncertainty: Victory at the End
By Tara Nicole Green 287

Saving Souls for Jesus By Irma Matos 294

Introduction
By Les Brown

My mother, Mamie Brown, was one of the most important people in my life. She instilled greatness in me and asked me to always remember to instill greatness in others. She showed me that no matter what the odds were, you had to push through.

My mother also showed me that greatness is not just an idea; greatness is action. When she adopted my brother and me, she didn't know how to be a mother. She didn't know how to raise us or even how she was going to feed and clothe us. What she did know, however, was that she loved us the moment that she saw us.

My birth mother, who I've never met, made Mamie Brown promise never to separate my twin brother Wesley and me, and she didn't. I held on to a lot of resentment toward my birth mother until I read a quote one day by Kahlil Gibran:

"Our parents bring us into the world, but in the end, we are responsible for what we become."

The message to me was clear; I was my own person, and the person who gave birth to me wasn't the one who was to decide who I was or who I was to become.
I also awakened to the idea that my real mother, Mamie Brown, chose to love us. She didn't have to.

To this day, I carry that love and determination into everything I do with a soaring spirit of hope and possibility. I owe a lot of my success to the values that the great Mamie Brown instilled in me. I am honored and proud to be her son.

Even with all the love and support of Mamie, I wasn't successful right in the beginning. I experienced many hard times and was kept prisoner by my own limitations. I was blessed to have great mentors over the years, and thankfully, Mr. Leroy

Washington started me on my path to greatness with his powerful words.

Mr. Washington told me that these "limitations" existed only in other people's projections and that someone's opinion of you didn't have to become your reality.

I didn't have the advantage and opportunities most people had growing up but what I did have was a resolve to create my own greatness within myself and then in my life. With the help of studying and mastering the principles that guided the success of those I wanted to be like, I was able to believe in my dreams and see them become a reality. I stayed persistent and positive, and if you know me, I stayed very "Hungry!"

I didn't take NO for an answer, and I was not going to be denied success, and neither are you!

When you stay HUNGRY for your goals and dreams, you set in motion an unstoppable human spirit that can alter the course of humanity.

The greatness in YOU is right there, ready to be activated in your life so that you can start to make an immediate impact in your own life and in the lives of others.

As much as I would love to come to each and every one of you and make sure you bring out your greatness, ultimately, it's up to YOU to make the decision to be great. Greatness is a decision, and I want you to decide right now that you will settle for nothing less!

The level of success you want to achieve in all areas of your life is up to only one person, YOU!

Where you are right now in life depends completely on YOU. By accepting 100% responsibility for the decisions you've made and the results you've achieved, you create confidence and certainty that if greatness is to be, it is surely and solely up to me!

You have the power to choose greatness, and you have the power to change the path and trajectory of your life starting from today. Right now, as you read through this powerful book and hear these amazing stories of overcoming insurmountable pain, hardship, and difficulties, know that you, too, can break through and break free of those things holding you back in the past.

You must believe that your dream life is not only possible but it's necessary because your greatness needs to be shared with the world. This book is going to inspire you to step into your full potential and live life with renewed enthusiasm, excitement, and commitment to excellence.

Greatness isn't handed to anyone. It is CHOSEN!

I want you to find YOUR greatness and decide right now to be great.

I want to remind you that the clock of your life is ticking. Each second you delay on your greatness is another moment in time that an opportunity to help, heal and impact others is lost.

We've lost enough time already. The world needs you right now!

For the past 47 years, I have worked with hundreds of thousands of students all over the world to help them discover their greatness. The ones who succeed are the ones who are coachable, act, and then stay focused and determined on their mission and purpose.

You've already taken the first step to discovering your greatness by picking up this book. You made the decision to change your life, and you said I'm going to take action.

This is your time. Don't wait until the end of this book to get moving. When one of these amazing and inspiring stories speaks to you, get going!

This book is the answer to creating more happiness, joy, and love in your life, and most importantly, it's the blueprint to bringing out the *Greatness in You*.

I believe in you. Mamie Brown's boy believes that YOU can discover your greatness.

It's time for YOU to believe as well!

You have something special in you, GREATNESS, and a whole lot more. *Bring it out!*

LES BROWN

About Visionary - Les Brown

Les Brown helps business owners and leaders from all sectors of society expand towards new opportunities. He is the author of the highly anticipated book, *You've Got to be Hungry,* where he skillfully weaves his compelling life story into the fabric of our daily personal and professional lives.

After mistakenly being declared "educable mentally retarded" in elementary school, teachers did not recognize the true potential of little Les Brown. However, he used determination, persistence, and belief in his ability to go beyond being a sanitation worker to unleash a course of amazing achievements, including broadcast station manager, political commentator, and multi-term state representative in Ohio. For three decades, he has not only studied the science of achievement but he's also mastered it by interviewing hundreds of successful business leaders and collaborating with them in the boardroom, translating theory into bottom-line results for his clients.

Revered as an icon by his colleagues, Brown received the National Speakers Association coveted Council of Peers Award of Excellence (CPAE), the prestigious Golden Gavel Award for achievement and leadership in communication, and a Chicago-area Emmy® for his unsurpassed fundraising pledge drive for the Public Broadcasting System. Toastmasters International also voted him one of the Top Five Outstanding Speakers.

Discover The Million in YOU
By Jon Talarico

*Don't ask yourself what the world needs. Ask yourself what makes you come alive, and go do that, because **what the world needs is people who have come alive.**"*
- Howard Thurman

I believe we're all given a specific mission to complete while we're here on Earth. To achieve our mission, I also believe it's vital that we discover our inner greatness - or what I like to call, *The Million in You.*

The Million in You is a phrase that has gone through several iterations over the years before settling on the current one. I feel this short and memorable phrase is an accurate encapsulation of all the right ingredients of what's needed to live a more abundant, successful, and happy life. These key ingredients include your passion, your purpose, your superpower, and your "why" for living.

I believe The Million in You applies to every human being on the planet. Every person is priceless. Every person is 100% unique. And I truly believe that every person has unlimited greatness inside of them - no matter who they are or their life circumstance. The secret is being able to tap into this greatness and share it with the world.

To awaken the greatness within ourselves and to become truly alive, we must first discover The Million in You that resides deep inside of all of us. But with the ongoing chaos and distractions that bombard us in today's modern world, it can be harder than ever to tap into this part of ourselves. To put it more simply, we've lost our way. The path to The Million in You is now covered with doubts, confusion, uncertainty, negativity, and nonsense.

So how can this path to The Million in You finally be cleared? What's needed is a new path combined with an accurate blueprint that will guide those who have given up or lost their way.

Thankfully, I've not only been able to figure out how to create this new path to The Million in You for myself, but I've been able to show others how to do the same with massive success. Now I want to share *exactly* what I've discovered with you so you can transform your life in ways you can't possibly imagine.

Before I dive into more details on what you can do, first, let's turn back the clock on Father Time.

Having grown up in a broken home within a blue-collar town, the idea of achieving greatness didn't even exist in my mind. What I witnessed early on in my life were hard-working people simply trying to survive, put food on the table, and pay the bills.

Luckily, I had that one person in my life that was an angel on earth. A person who inspired me, pushed me to exceed the invisible limitations of my mind, and to keep pushing forward. That living angel was my grandmother. I believe we all have that one person in our lives that believes and supports us. It could be a family member, a co-worker, or even a close friend.

My grandmother was a guiding light in my world. She pushed me to read books, to study and closely listen to those who spoke about what's possible, and to understand how any dream could be turned into reality. She was an eternal optimist, and it rubbed off on me in many profound ways.

As I got older and began to dive deeper into my understanding of people, the universe, success, and how the world works, I had a rude awakening when it came to my first success in life. I realized that my success was short-lived. I'd get excited about a new venture, and then it would fizzle out nearly as soon as it started. I'd then start a new project – and the same cycle would repeat. I couldn't create lasting change. *I was stuck.*

This repeated cycle lasted for decades. The roller coaster ride of life's ups and downs never yielded any consistent (or lasting) results in my life. I also found myself living a double life. On one side of the coin, everyone knew they could rely on good ol' Jon to get anything done for them. I was a loyal friend who could make anything happen. On the other side of the coin, my inner life was in turmoil. I couldn't look at myself in the mirror.

I'd numb myself to the pains and disappointments of life with alcohol, drugs, unhealthy relationships, and other needless drama.

Then one day, I came across a person who would not only help me turn my life around in a very positive way, but he also became my mentor and a dear friend of mine. That person was the now legendary Mr. Bob Proctor. He shared with me a huge insight that I'd never realized before. He noticed that I'd created a false self-image and dialogue inside my mind that was running the show of my life.

Mr. Proctor told me that even though I thought I was in 100% control of all the decisions, I wasn't. He said that many of the decisions I'd made in life were running on autopilot thanks to decades of mental conditioning. Even though I thought I was running the show, my subconscious mind was the one who was really in charge. This new way of thinking didn't sink in right away for me at first, but when it did – my entire life changed. It felt like a bolt of lightning had not only run through my body, but it was at that moment I finally felt liberated.

I'd finally discovered why I'd been stuck in life. Why every new project I started never took off. Why I could never achieve the goals I wanted. I knew that if I wanted to finally break free of these pre-programmed subconscious patterns, I had to change the way I was thinking and the way I was doing things.

Thanks to Mr. Proctor and the other amazing mentors I found along my way in life, I've been able to change the trajectory of my own success and happiness in many remarkable ways. Looking back, I now realize that was the moment that I discovered the very beginnings of The Million in ME. I was able to clearly see that I'd created an image of myself that was full of shame, guilt, anger, blame, and self-pity. I was the ultimate victim at the hands of a very well-known captor – *myself*.

The first step in discovering your own Million in You is to recognize that your results up to this point in your life are a *direct result of a false self-image.* By developing this awareness, you can take the first step to come alive again. You can create a new self-image of yourself - one that's overflowing with self-confidence, one that experiences mental clarity and certainty in who you are, what you want, and how you're going to accomplish exactly what you desire.

The next step that I discovered, and one you can apply as well, to achieve complete and total freedom is to realize that the inner flame that burns bright in all of us when we were just born is still there. It's always been there and has never been extinguished. Sure, it may have been dimmed to a mere flicker of light during trying times in our lives, but it's always remained steadfast.

If you want to reignite your inner spirit and ramp up the intensity of the flame that resides deep inside of you, then it requires a new way of behaving. In my past, I'd been trying to achieve success using the same failed system over and over again. It never worked.

What I realized by studying other influential and inspirational leaders throughout the course of history was they all had one trait in common: they'd developed and nurtured a burning flame of desire inside of them that was focused on exactly what they wanted. This required a radical shift in their thoughts, behaviors, and actions. And this is exactly what I began doing in my own life.

When I made this initial positive shift to my own thoughts, behaviors, and actions, it felt uncomfortable at first. But the results that started to come to fruition in my life were not only shocking but unimaginable.

- I started to think from a place of abundance vs. lack. I imagined having my own wishes and desires already accomplished in my life right now, not in the future.
- I started to act like the person that I'd always wanted to become. This was something I learned from one of my favorite authors, Neville.
- I was reminded that I had the greatest gift I'd ever been given, just as you have – and that's your imagination. Your imagination and thoughts hold the power to shape your world.

You have the ability to learn, to dream, and make the choice to close your eyes and imagine whatever it is in your life that you want to become naturally drawn to you.

When I began to focus on the things I wanted in life vs. focusing on the things I didn't want, everything started to change. And here's the most important part that I want to emphasize with you – all you need to do is focus on your WHAT, not the HOW. By this, I mean first, you need to focus on what you want in life. You don't need to have any worry or concern for how these things will occur. Those doors will open for you in a short time.

As you begin to think differently, removing any limitations or doubts from your mind, you'll find yourself opening to an exciting and exhilarating future. The Million in You will come to you. It's the one thing you can do better than anyone else on the planet. It's your spiritual gift that, once revealed, will make an immediate impact in your life and the lives of those that cross your path.

As you begin to come alive, it's important to master the third and final step, which is the ability to be disciplined in your thinking and in your behaviors as you pursue your new path forward. *This is critical to your success.* Your old habits and subconscious programming will try their hardest to resurrect themselves and steer you back to the path of conformity and comfortability. Don't fall for this sneaky mental trap.

What's worked for many of my students and for me to safeguard against this common trap is *accountability*. Accountability is your insurance policy to success. And it's something many people completely overlook or underestimate.

What I've found is your chance of keeping your dream alive will become much greater when you have someone who's there guiding you along the way, pushing you, and holding you to a higher standard of excellence that accepts zero excuses.

The seed of success is rooted in the pivotal moments when you don't want to do the things you know are necessary to help you get what you want. But with the right amount of accountability and commitment, you'll achieve exactly what it is that you desire.

There's very little difference between good and great. But true greatness is achieved by developing the winning habits that most people simply don't want to do. Most people tiptoe through life, never waking up to their own goals and dreams. The greatness in you demands not only that you wake up but that you act in the face of any adversity, fear, or apprehension.

To discover the Million in You requires a consistent commitment and dedication to yourself. A commitment that means you'll no longer settle for a mediocre life of simply existing but instead demand an exceptional life that's filled with excitement, joy, abundance, and happiness.

JON TALARICO

About Visionary - Jon Talarico

Considered among the world's foremost experts in building successful relationships, Jon Talarico has directly worked with thought leaders, celebrities, entrepreneurs, and of course, countless individuals just like yourself, looking to create an impact and a flourishing, prosperous life.

Jon has spent decades researching and testing out the chemistry of self-discovery and opportunities, developing a simple-to-understand system that anyone can apply and yield meaningful results.

Having endured a difficult life growing up and seeing many distressing facets of life, Jon understands and knows what it's like to have a difficult life. Your experience may be different, but the pain remains the same. His experience paved a path to help transform lives, which he has been doing for over a decade.

Jon's message of hope in immense possibilities beyond common imagination formed the foundation of many success stories to date.

"I truly believe we can change the world by connecting and creating one relationship at a time."
– Jon Talarico

What Jon teaches through his coaching programs is the same fundamental mindset that he himself practices every single day. This same mindset brought a lifestyle that was once beyond his wildest dreams.

Today, Jon has traveled to over 38 countries and five continents, including some of the most exclusive and beautiful places one can think of. Jon has also helped produce two Hollywood films and became co-owner of a $25 million dollar sports franchise. More importantly, Jon had the privilege of helping bring the gift of hearing to over 1,600 hearing-impaired patients in the Caribbean. Be his life as dreamy as it can be, Jon remains a humble, down-to-earth human being.

Connect with me:
IG: @jontalarico
FB: https://www.facebook.com/groups/millioninyou
Web: Jontalarico.com
Jon@jontalarico.com

FERNANDA CASTAÑEDA

Awaken the Great Giant
By Fernanda Castañeda

It is not what happens to you but how you react to it that matters.
– Epictetus

All of us have had challenges. Situations that have nearly knocked us out of the game or have totally knocked us out of the game. Those challenges shake you to the core. I have had a few of these myself and what I have come to realize is that it is out of hardships that we grow and that we learn about the magnificent power that lies dormant, waiting for the master to regain its place in consciousness.

The first of these experiences I can remember came in the form of a "new beginning," which at the time felt more like "the end" of my life. Shortly after turning 13, my mom sat me down and told me that in six months, we were going to uproot, leave everything we had ever known as familiar behind, including my father, and seek a better future in a foreign land.

Up to this time in my life, I had grown up with a lot of consistency as I lived in the same house for 13 years, went to the same Catholic, girls-only school from Pre-K - 9th grade, and had the same group of friends.

This is a drastic change in anyone's life, and in my 13-year-old mind, the unknown created a lot of anxiety and also a lot of expectations.

As soon as we got to the United States, everything seemed magical. Everything was so clean and modern, and English sounded so cool. However, two months after our arrival, I had to start school, and that is when the real shock began. From one day to the next, I was the odd one out due to being the only Colombian in the school. This meant that I was a target for bullies, which was a new experience in my life.

I also couldn't communicate, which was frustrating and limited me to only ESL classes, which are not the best in the level of education. On other occasions, I was also at the receiving end of racist comments and rants while out and about with my children. Furthermore, because of my legal status, I was also very limited in what I could do, where I could work, and where I could go.

As I was adjusting and starting a new life, I found myself with a boyfriend at 16. He came to be my second biggest experience in the form of me becoming a mother on January 12, 2006, just 22 days after my 18th birthday. At this point in my life, I was still not fluent in English as I found myself not needing it due to still being in those ESL classes. I was still undocumented, working at a minimum wage job, and without the support of my son's father or my family or friends.

I still remember standing in the middle of the hallway, shortly after I had shared the news of my pregnancy with my parents and my brother, and overhearing my family saying hurtful things, one of them being that I had my fun and now they were going to be the ones responsible for raising and paying for my child's needs. It was at that moment that I felt a very deep pain inside, and it was also at that moment that I made a promise to myself to never depend on anyone to provide my children or me with everything needed and more. This is a promise that I have kept since.

The third of the life-changing events in my life came in 2018 while burying my brother, who was 37 at the time, after a four-year battle with heart failure. Just two months prior, I had been at my grandmother's bedside pronouncing her dead, and now I was repeating the story, but now it was with the body of my beloved brother, Juan Miguel.

Three days before, on December 31, 2017, at 11:40 pm, I received a call from my dad in Colombia letting me know that my brother, who also lived in Colombia, had suffered a massive heart attack and was dead. They were waiting for the medics to get to his apartment, which caused a delay of about 20 minutes in which he was totally dead. Although the medics were able to get a very weak pulse back, and he was kept alive for three days on life support, it was clear to all of us that this was the end of his journey on Earth.

I flew to Colombia on January 2 and was the first one in the hospital on the 3rd. I still believe that he waited for me to say goodbye, and I believe that he is still with me every step of the way. My brother was such a big love and light in my life, and his departure left a big void in my life.

Each of those events taught me how to find the greatness in me, and perhaps it could help you too.

The first event showed me that either we are walking in faith, or we are walking in fear. Being a mom of two children myself, I cannot imagine moving our entire lives to a foreign country where we don't speak the language. My mom's courage and faith kept us moving day after day because she "knew" that all her sacrifices would pay off.

Most of the time, we become paralyzed with fear because of not knowing what awaits on the other side of the HARD decisions we must make. When we listen to fear more than move in faith, we start living in survival, under the emotions of stress, and soon, we find ourselves living a life we don't like, working at a job we hate, and settling for what we have already because we can't see the magnificence, the opportunities, the growth, the transformation that lives on the other side of fear.

The second life event showed me that having a goal is crucial to getting anywhere in life. Before finding out that I was pregnant, I was mainly focused on working so I could have fun, hanging out with friends and my boyfriend, and passing school. I had no bigger plans for my life because I didn't think I could do anything significant due to my immigration status. What I came to find out years later is that when I stood in that hallway and I made a decision that I was going to amount to something in life, I didn't allow fear, doubt, or worry about coming in between my desire and my decision, I had sealed my faith. I had a goal and a why, and I was determined to make it in life. Another lesson my early pregnancy taught me was that, in the words of Les Brown, "Other people's opinions of you don't have to become your reality." In the eyes of my family and society, I was going to end up as another low-income minority on government support. And based on statistics, my probability of doing something with my life was almost nonexistent, yet I did not allow their opinions and comments to become my future. I made my own decision from an elevated desire of love for my son and for wanting to provide for him a better life.

The third event taught me the ultimate truth and the biggest lesson that helped me discover the greatness in me. This is that we are spiritual beings having a human experience. This discovery that completely changed my life is important for the following reason.

As spiritual beings, we are also limitless beings in our purest form. This means that every single one of us, and no one is so special to be excluded, can tap into our true self or spirit and instantly feel whole.

This is the place where intuition lives. This is the place you can tap for ideas and inspiration. This is the place where limitless abundance and love exist, and we can all access it by first discovering who we truly are at our core.

I have since read many books on the subject, studied it, and currently meditate daily to reconnect with the magnificence and the greatness that is me. However, it is not easy to stay connected to ourselves because it is usually easier to not do the work and blame the conditions and environment for our results.
However, if we are able to get past all distractions and really have that deep connection with ourselves, we realize then that we can fully transform our lives. We can change every aspect of our lives; we are the painters creating our masterpiece called life. Blaise Pascal, who was a French philosopher in the 1600s, said, "All of humanity's problems stem from our inability to sit quietly in a room alone." If what we want is to have the capacity to solve any issues with ease, create a brighter future, send love out into the world, become better human beings, live a happier, healthier, and fulfilled life, all that is needed is to sit quietly until you find the great giant that lies dormant inside yourself, and then you wake the giant up and change your life from a life of existence, suffering, drama, and hatred to one of bliss, joy, freedom, love, kindness, lightness and expansion.

When we walk by faith instead of fear, we have a clear goal, and a strong why, discover our true self, and become unstoppable. It is time to change your life and live the greatness in you, and the time is now. The only time to make a choice, the only time to feel and act, the only time that matters is the present. We cannot create in the past or in the future. We can only create from where we are right now and see how our life unfolds before our eyes. The only time we have is right now to manifest the greatness in you.

About the Author
Fernanda Castañeda

In a time when symptoms are treated and root causes ignored, Fernanda Castañeda is on a global mission to educate people on what is necessary to achieve physical, mental, and emotional wellness. As an Advanced Practice Registered Nurse, she is inspiring others to take control of their lives using a comprehensive mind, body, and soul approach.

FERNANDA CASTAÑEDA

She believes that people really need to understand it's not just what they eat that is as equally important to their health as what is eating them in terms of their thoughts and emotions. She is also bilingual and currently the COO of The Million in You, an educational company dedicated to personal and professional transformation. She also coaches and teaches others how to develop a powerful mindset and skill set to create permanent change and lasting results.

Fernanda has participated in several medical missions abroad in some of the most remote areas of Africa and Asia, providing life-saving care to those most in need. She is also the founder and creator of Positive Blueprints, a graduate of the Les Brown Power Voice Speaker Program, a Motivational Speaker, and a best-selling author.

Connect with me:
IG: @_fernanda_castaneda
FB: https://www.facebook.com/FernandaCastaneda01
tiktok: @castaneda.fernanda
Web: positiveblueprints.com
positiveblueprints@gmail.com

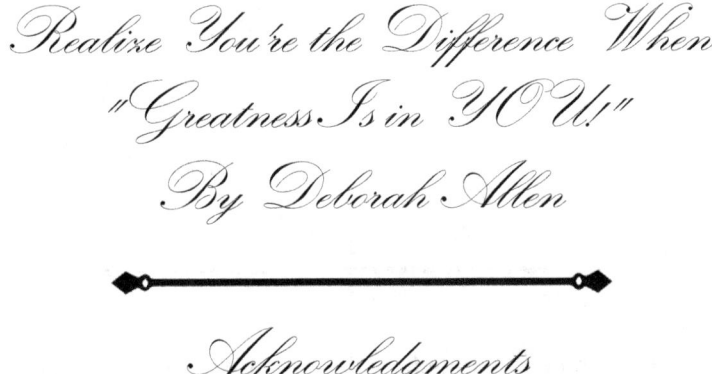

Realize You're the Difference When "Greatness Is in YOU!"
By Deborah Allen

Acknowledgments

I want to express heartfelt gratitude to my mentors: Les Brown and Jon Talarico, who helped set ablaze and ignite the greatness again back inside of me! Thank you for allowing me to share and participate in this great vision!

Special thanks to my husband, Apostle Glen Allen Sr, who I serve in ministry with and who has embraced the fierceness in me. Lighthouse Apostolic Ministries of God Church, a sincere thank you for always being a place of advancement, change, purpose, vision, love even dreams.

Wondrously, I have birthed six children, but I'm the mother of nine. Our children have been a blessing to my very existence. I'm so awed by my support from family, friends, and clients. All your love has been priceless. You have been the "why" inside of me!

Thank you, Jesus, for the purpose and destiny that you have decreed upon my life. You alone have positioned me to take part in this mighty project that has allowed me and others to birth out GREATNESS!

Apostle Deborah Allen

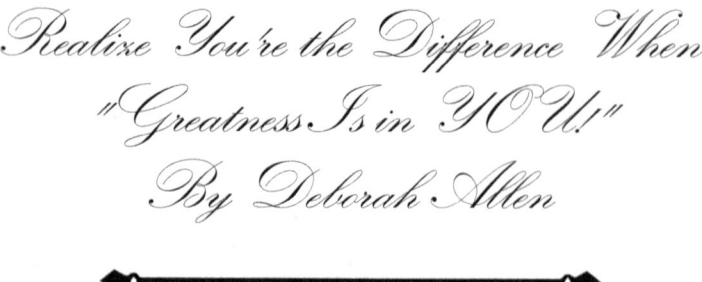

Realize You're the Difference When "Greatness Is in YOU!"
By Deborah Allen

Undisputedly, people will remember the greatness and impact you leave on this magnificent world! Everyone can do something to be a part of the change but realize you make the ultimate difference. This is your time to become the most phenomenal version of yourself and release your greatness. Now is the moment to reach deep down and bring forth your gifts and worth for all to see. Ultimately life is better because you have graced it. You bring change in every situation because you are different, unique, and brilliant. There is nobody else like you or the wealth of knowledge that has been learned by fire within you. Realize you are born different, and you are needed for such a time as this. You are of great value in this space called creation. I can hear you say, "Are you sure I have a purpose?" Do not be so surprised, but yes, purpose is your portion. You were born to stir up the atmosphere and even the universe all around you.

I was someone born in the inner city of St. Louis, Missouri. The area was and still is rough, with deadly statistics all around. I was born two months premature, weighing 2lbs 3 oz, and was destined to live! We didn't have much, but I knew greatness was inside of me. I lived in a community full of violence, gangs, addictions, brokenness, and more. Yet, everything in the universe lined up for me to be born and thrive. I have to admit life was hard but yet I still had dreams. When I was younger, I didn't understand that I had the power to determine my destiny. For this cause, I went along with the crowd and, at times, did what everyone else did.

Not surprisingly, I became a teenage mother because I didn't realize I was destined to be the difference. These were crucial years, and I had to decide and even realize that I was the only one who could be the difference my son and I needed. I could have chosen to quit because I was young, and it was so much chaos and pressure in my life. Yet, I refused to lose, and I fiercely battled to finish high school and college and mature into a woman of purpose. Those years birthed out of me the understanding that I was the difference and there was greatness in me!

Through the process of life in my thirties, I was graced to make a lot of money in the childcare arena, about 2 million dollars. The center allowed me to be a help and change my own community. Realize you make the difference and are graced to make wealth! Life is blessed because you have so much to contribute. You have been blessed because there are only certain things that you alone can perform. Celebrate because despite it being billions of people, there are things only you can achieve. Recognize that you are full of your dreams, goals, and causes and are wonderful. I know you will not believe me, but everything about you is important. You are extremely valuable. Do not allow somebody else's opinion of you to devalue you or make you feel like you are nothing.

I had such success for ten years, and I thought that would never change. Regretfully, because I did not build with the right people or mindset, I burned out and walked away from everything, my center, and especially my dreams. I thought my life was over because I had not yet realized I was still the difference. I want to be a witness that the hardest thing I ever had to do was get back up again. There was a time about four years ago that I decided to dream again after I truly realized I was the difference and created "The FIERCE System" that I used to reinvent myself. I had to search deep inside of me and discover my voice again, even realize I'm the difference when "Greatness Is in YOU!" It took everything inside of me to kill the fear that was inside me and believe in myself again. I had to trust and realize that I was the gift. Not only that, but I would not die with my dreams inside of me.

I shifted from a successful but stressful entrepreneurial career and returned to corporate America about seven years ago. Man, that put fear in me to walk back into a field I had been away from for a decade. See, over the years, I had forgotten what I really wanted. Now my why had to be bigger than my fear, and I went through the steps of The FIERCE System, and I climbed the corporate ladder again. I am speaking faith into your life and building you up again. It can seem as if we have been beaten down by so many things. We could feel defeated by disappointments, setbacks, failures, relationships, or even ourselves. It is ok that you have made mistakes. Forgive yourself about those things. Life is different because you are here. The world, your children, your family, your coworkers, as well as other people, would notice your absence. Everything around you would miss you. Nothing about you is unoriginal—your DNA, face, voice, and fingerprints are not copies.

Nobody else has DNA that matches yours exactly. Priceless and rare is what you are. No one else could ever be you. That's how precious you are, and I celebrate you. I lift a toast to your every accomplishment. I salute your life, honor all that you have brought to light and celebrate your voice. I cheer your story, tenacity, and you. Even when you thought you were weak, you held on, for you are strong. I can hear some of you say, "Yeah, but there have been times I barely held on." However, you are the gift, and you make the difference, and you did endure.

I love being able to play a part in your life to push you into your next and encourage you to achieve your greatness. The FIERCE System will make you aware of the remarkable changes you need as well as what you are implementing. Realize you make the difference, and your very presence can bring a solution and even calm some of the storms in others' life. Realize you make a difference through your kindness and smile, which bring so much joy to others. You make a difference by displaying character and integrity. You are an encouragement and have allowed your strength to be a phenomenal example. Really understand you make a difference in a room by being a conduit of power. Continue to change the flow and be a positive vibe. This System helps you to remember you make a difference. World changers speak affirmation of power, not of doom and gloom. Speak into your life about what you want, and need, and get up every day with expectations. Make sure you read your goals and dreams every day, 2-3 times a day. Repetition is what changes and shift our mind to the correct thinking and get rid of the stinking thinking. I want you to practice speaking positive words. You must be able to speak into existence what you do not see. Everything you are seeking is already seeking you. Before I created The FIERCE System, I was stuck in a rut for four years, and I remember being laid out on the floor at church and crying because I felt so weary, even defeated. Life had not been going the way I imagined or according to my plan. I felt like I had done nothing but lost. God spoke to me and assured me that my life was not over. That life was a process, and to not quit in the middle of living. Finally, he told me to get back again and run after my dreams. He also said that I mattered and made all the difference. He told me to dream and believe again. Wow, that put a fire back down in my belly. My mind began to see new possibilities, and I recognized that life was not over! Realize you make the difference when greatness is in you, even if you were born from rape, incest, on an abandoned floor, or put up for adoption. I am charging everyone that read this book to realize you make a difference and work what you have in your hand to succeed. You have everything inside of you to win.

Push until everything you visualize is manifested. Be relentless and strong because it is shaping us to be lions of destiny. Realize you make the difference, so roar, hunt, and enlarge your territory. Elite people are called to walk to a different drummer. Do not die or quit with your dreams unfulfilled. Leave here empty don't take your dreams with you. These last four years, I've fought to live and even bring forth my voice, dreams, goals, and purpose. You guys, this is my gift of greatness which is to cheer for you. You are well able to do mighty exploits in this season. You are winning by leaps and bounds. Be encouraged, ignited even fiercely roar! Be the lion that you are created to be. Be who you are, and that is mighty. Realize you're the difference when "Greatness Is in YOU!"

The Fierce System

- F – Find yourself. Find your true self and be true to your own voice, dreams, and goals.
- I – Indeed, be independent. Indeed be independent, for you are the difference maker in your life and the entire world.
- E– Evaluate your life and story. Evaluate your story and life with clear eyes and not the eyes of your past and of unlearned you.
- R – Realize you make the difference. Realize life is better because you are here and have purpose to fulfill.
- C – Create opportunity through purpose. Create opportunity through purpose with the gift in your hand that will bring you before great men and allows you to make wealth.
- E – Evolve into the greatest version of you. Evolve into the greatest version of you that the process of time has allowed you to become who you were born to be.

About Deborah Allen

    Finding one's *inner voice* can be a liberating, awe-inspiring, and transformational experience. Fashioned to help the masses find their "fierce"; is the dynamic professional Deborah Allen.

    Deborah Allen is a 17X best-selling author & 7X international speaker, certified life coach, cleric, and CEO and creative founder of **The Fierce System**, a multifaceted liaison specialty centered around helping women to both find and develop their voice. Having been trained by world-renowned NSA motivational speaker Mr. Les Brown, Deborah understands the importance of strategy, development, and credible mentorship, traits she seamlessly translates to her growing clientele.

Deborah's mantra is simple: Her one and only goal is to motivate clients, helping them to create the life they were meant to live.

Refusing mediocrity on all fronts, Deborah has trailblazed a credible path for those she serves. She has served as Senior Pastor of Lighthouse Apostolic Ministries of God Church for the last 22 years; and is the Executive Director of the nonprofit organization, L.A.M. Ministries, Inc.

Matching servant leadership with incredible respect for higher learning, Deborah holds licenses as an RMA/CDA & Certified Life Coach; and is a member of the National Speaker Association Speaker (NSA) and a Black Speakers Network (BSN) Speaker. Her conglomerate, The Fierce System, comprises many platforms, including Fierce TV, Radio, and blog, as well as the Fierce Voices of Destiny Program, where she mentors, develops, and creates strategic alignment between clients and their true life's calling. She is the Founder and CEO of Igniting The Flame Publishing, Visionary Coaching & Consulting Group LLC, and Deborah Allen Enterprise.

Deborah proudly attests that women are at the heart of all she does and that her desire is to see them be strong and fierce and know that they can truly achieve their dreams and walk in purpose. When she is not out helping women to come alive, rebuild, shift and find themselves again, Deborah is a valued asset to her communal body and a loving member of her family and friendship circles.

Deborah Allen. Energizer. Organizer. Servant Leader

Deborah Allen ~ Contact Information

Facebook: https://www.facebook.com/deborahallenfierce
Instagram: https://www.instagram.com/deborahallenfierce/
Twitter: https://twitter.com/deborahallenfie

Periscope: https://www.pscp.tv/ladydeborahallen/follow

LinkedIn: https://www.linkedin.com/in/prophetessdeborahallen/

YouTube: https://www.youtube.com/channel/UCTOf0igcAxlVaneH2ZOo_Zg

1st Website: https://deborahallenfierce.com/

2nd Website: https://deborahallenspeaker.com/

The Fierce, Ignition & Activation Show/Podcast:
https://envisionedbroadcasting.com/fierceignition%26activation?fbclid=IwAR03g_k7RO44QE1Ybahy2poVzktBDv08wX07e1X4N0yPF0Spi_MEataMG-o

Email: deborahallenfierce@gmail.com

DR. PAMELA HENKEL

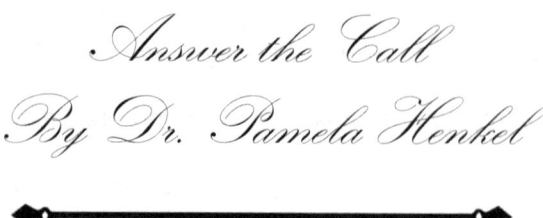

Answer the Call
By Dr. Pamela Henkel

When God is ready to do something in the Earth, He shifts the atmosphere; when God is ready to do something in us, He shifts our company.

One of the most impactful opportunities afforded to us by God is the opportunity to be enthused by our faith and guided by the instincts of our organic purpose. Helping us in the navigation of such is a unique power found in the hearts and counsel of divine mentorship.

There has not been a moment in my life where the reality of my next level wasn't preceded by the leadership and guidance of mentors. There is no greater value to the acceptance of achieving our dreams and walking in the alignment of who God called us to be, like the understanding that great vision becomes even greater destiny, when we involve helping hands. God has always sent my help in *two's*. For as long as I can remember, I've had the honor of having two mentors aiding me to birth, attain, and sustain the calling on my life. It has been in the presence of their influence that I have been able to humbly execute projects, experience growth in my character, and maintain powerful transformations in my perception and overall mindset.

It is of significant importance that we pay close attention to the cues of life arriving through the appearance of who shows up, for our *glow up*. I can remember experiencing a point of heartfelt transition in my life, where I experienced the personal loss of both of my mentors while simultaneously feeling the unction of the Lord's pressing on my life for more. I was given a vision of a stage, and from the crowd, I was able to observe two pairs of men's shoes. Perplexed by the elucidation of the vision, I had no idea that God was preparing me for my next assignment and, more importantly, the next candidates of mentorship that would energize my purpose and take my life to the next level. Not long after, heaven collided with my reality in the form of an introduction of two of the most prolific mentors I've had to date; the insightful guru, Mr. Jon Talarico, and world-renowned motivator, Mr. Les Brown.

The proof of God's intention for mentorship in our lives has shown its quintessential stretch; throughout Biblical history. We saw it clearly through the rise and fall of Israelite leaders in the wilderness. We observed the impression that Elijah's mentoring left on Elisha. In one of our greatest examples, we observed the triune relational mentorship between Jesus, God, and the Holy Spirit, displayed in his daily walk. Mentorship is important to God. He designed its necessity in our lives to better steer the effectiveness of our calling so that we may reflect His goodness in a broken world. Subsequently, when I connected with Mr. Les Brown at the Next Conference and then, later through that affiliation, was introduced to Mr. Jon Talarico, I knew that God was setting me up to serve, grow, and illuminate His purpose on the Earth.

Like so many of the mentors before them, Les and Jon would challenge everything I thought I knew about functioning in purpose, for purpose, on purpose.

There is a metamorphosis that takes place when we submit to the process of mentorship, a trade of wills for the exchange of a future far richer than we could observe in our previous seasons. **At every new level of our personal journey, mentors reflect the standard for our *next*.** It is with this recollection that I came to terms with the realization that Mr. Les Brown, along with Mr. Jon Talarico's presence in my life, meant that it was time for me to stop playing small, to expand my capacity for personal excellence, and to develop a global perspective for the possibility of tangible success in my life. I did just that.

I went from running a developing podcast to expanding in the realms of television and radio. I went from blogging to becoming an International bestselling visionary author. I went from pastoring a few to leading in the world of international mentoring. In short, I developed a propensity for the same success and achievements of those God placed in leadership over my life.

This is the evidence of a life willingly molded by the impression of effective mentorship.

Perhaps the greatest observation from my personal experience is not how essential mentorship is to achieve great things but rather how important our purpose is to timely submission. My personal mantra has always been that we are here on purpose with a purpose by design, not by default. We have to make the most of our time here on Earth. When we show God that we are serious enough to invest and submit to credible mentorship, we also display a seriousness for His calling on our lives. I didn't know that with one welcome of mentorship in my life, I was, in turn, touching the potential of my future, a calling so progressive that I now need a telescope to see how far I've come.

Activating Your Now

The greatest virtue found in my success isn't in the accomplishments but rather in the fact that it is contagious. If you find yourself sitting on the sidelines of your destiny, I implore you to act now! What God made possible in my story is not a measure of exclusivity or secret formulas but rather a will to connect my faith to His plan; in the hopes of a better future now.

> *"Now faith is confidence in what we hope for and assurance*
> *about what we do not see."*
> *- Hebrews 11:1*

When we yield to the motivation of God's voice, combined with the provisions of our *"now"* faith, we become a magnet for achieving our life's true purpose. While some may marry fulfilling their life's calling to various accolades, purpose-enthused leaders understand that in fulfilling the call, they are responsible for generational preservation, spiritual maturity, and world change. The road will not always be easy, but it will be worth it. I cannot express how many days of uncertainty I survived, how many pitfalls I've faced, or the number of significant losses I endured along the journey, but I can attest that when I made up my mind to invest in answering His call on my life, God did the rest; and He will do the same for you.

Today you might be faced with the sting of past failures; perhaps you've had mentors in the past, only to find yourself a little further from your life's original intent, or perhaps you are still wrestling with the fact that God chose you to do something great. Wherever you are in your journey, I'd like to exhort you to get up again. Take your current situation, transition, and placement as a context clue that God is fully invested in the intention of your significance and is pushing you toward destiny.

Get up. Get plugged in. Believe again. Live again. Answer the call.

Mr. Brown and Mr. Talarico, thank you for answering your call and for pushing me forward into mine.

DR. PAMELA HENKEL

Acknowledgments

First, I would like to thank Jesus. He is The Greatness in me!

Next, I would like to thank my wonderful husband, James. For being my constant source of joy. Team Henkel, our six beautiful children, and granddaughter. My mother, Constance, for always demonstrating true strength. Because of her, I know what it means to endure like a soldier. My earthly father and my "mother in love" are cheering me on from heaven. My business coach, great encourager, and 'father in love' Bob.

Norman Vincent Peale said ***imagination is the true magic carpet***. Thank you, Mr. Les Brown and Mr. Jon Talarico, for taking all of us on this ride!

I would like to thank each of the contributing authors. Your stories have touched my heart and empowered my soul. It is an honor to be represented on the pages of this book with you! Together we will change the world!

A BIG Thank You to the entire Anthology Team - Fernanda Castañeda, Apostle Deborah Allen, Nichol Perricci, Dawn Lieck, Shadaria Alison, Tamika Hall, and Renee Huffman. Thank you for making this entire journey seamless.

This book has a mantra, "When personal God-given greatness is discovered, a world changer is born!" Get ready, world; change has come! I LOVE YOU ALL.

<blockquote>
To Your Greatness
BLESSINGS,
Dr. Pamela Henkel
</blockquote>

About Dr. Pamela Henkel

Individuals seasoned with generous amounts of charisma, compassion, and undeniable essence, possess the kind of ingenuity; that shifts the world into its own greatness. Stewarding these traits in unyielding measure; is the spirited professional, Dr. Pamela Henkel.

Dr. Pamela Henkel is an International Best-Selling Author, multifaceted compere, speaker, elite coach, CEO, and Founder of both Purpose with Pamela and Pamela Henkel

Ministries. Her multifaceted production and International radio conglomerate fashioned to enthuse women, entrepreneurs, authors, and diverse professionals to take hold of their life's purpose.

Dr. Pamela Henkel's mission is to add value to as many lives as possible - reminding them that they are here on purpose with a Purpose by Design and not by default.

Partnering her passions with sincere regard for higher learning, community, and achievement. Dr. Pamela Henkel's career remains a reflection of creative grace, captivating the hearts and minds of many. She holds a doctorate in Philosophy, Christian Leadership, and Business. Living life as one dedicated to the service of people.

Hosting a myriad of professional skill sets without compromising her dedication to humanity, Dr. Henkel has maintained a nonpareil presence in the modern business world. As the creative founder of Purpose TV, The Pamela Show, and more, she extends her podcast, International radio, and social platforms to promote the voices of many on a global scale. Her propensity for success in her field has led her to award-winning achievements, such as the nomination as one of the Top 50 Women of Business, an elite membership of the Power Voice, as well as a personal mentorship from the world-renowned speaker and mentor Les Brown. Dr. Henkel's trusted expertise has yielded her various leadership positions, such as Client Enrichment Program Director at the Million in You Lifestyle and Head Coach for the Inner Circle.

Dr. Pamela Henkel calls Minnesota home, where she is wife, mother, and grandmother to her loving family and always encourages people to be the salt and the light everywhere they go.

Dr. Pamela Henkel. Leader. Energizer. Philanthropist.

www.purposewithpamela.com
https://linktr.ee/Purposewithpamela

A Little Chat With Myself
By Brian Dawkins

Narrator, I HAVE GREAT NEWS. God never makes mistakes! He never experiments! That means that everything He created has a purpose. And yes, that includes you. So, everything that was created was designed by the Creator to succeed in its area of gifting or functioning.

A seed in hand is just a seed. That same seed in the ground has a forest inside. So the greatness that is in you now is waiting on the right belief systems, environments, and actions taken to birth your fruit to this world. So your greatness is not ahead of you; it's in you. NOW!

I thought it best, to allow you to eavesdrop in on a conversation between the younger me (Scooter) and me at 48 (BDawk).

BDawk - Scooter, can we chop it up for a sec?

Scooter - That's cool.

Narrator - So Bdawk and Scooter took a seat on the swings at Yancy Park on the North Side of Jacksonville, FL. Right around the corner from their house. Scooter was slumped down as if this would be a boring conversation.

It is a nice sunny day out with the smell of someone barbecuing in the air.

BDawk - No matter what it looks like currently or where you may find yourself now, it will not always be. There is much more in you that will allow you to see far more than you can see with your eyes.

Scooter -- Pst...Whatever, Pops! I'm one of the smallest, often overlooked, and since we are being honest, afraid to do what others are doing around me to get cash now. But I might as well get mine now too. I want spending money to get some fresh new Fila's.

BDawk - Glad you brought that up. Because of your size and feeling overlooked, it pushes you to outwork all around you. It pushes you to have the mindset that when it comes to conditioning, you'll be the last person standing. Which, in turn, brought the best out of you.

So, you went from someone who didn't look the part to becoming the prototype for the safety position for a lot of GM's around the NFL.

Now, you are not so small because of a late growth spurt. But the way you fight, is just as tenacious as when you fought in the neighborhood backyards because of your desire to outwork anyone. No matter the size.

So that tough environment, in those dark spaces, combined with your willingness to fight whomever, brought out of you a level of greatness that you now have a bust in the Pro Football HALL OF FAME!!

As for being afraid to cross the line into stealing and selling drugs, that's called Being Smart!! It's also called delayed gratification. Your willingness to say no to the quick shortcut helped you build the character that allows you to now speak in front of children, adults, churches to companies. Mainly because of the name you have built. With your Faith, character, and integrity being the cornerstones.

But it is also why you respected what your parents and other authority figures told you.

Scooter - OK, what about getting cut my 11th-grade year AAU Summer league & only being brought back last minute to play spot defense and only play garbage time. Oh, and getting the scholarship taken back by the U of Florida?

BD - The embarrassment of getting cut would have been bad enough, but the fact that you were let on the team only to play in garbage time really placed another log on your fire to burn. So that would be the last team you would ever be cut from!!
Regarding the scholarship being taken back, it gave you a choice that all face to some degree, to sink into a pit of self-pity and perhaps take up your neighborhood get-rich-fast schemes. Or swim by asking for help. And you chose to ask your DB coach. Coach Black, to help tutor you so you could get your 1.6 GPA up. And he not only tutored you, but he taught you how you best learned.

He taught you that your slow processing was not the issue. It was how you were trying to learn material that was the issue. I know that was taught to you by other teachers along the way, but it did not work for you as it doesn't work for you as it does for all.

And when you got it, YOU GOT IT, JACK!! You made 4.0 every 9 nine weeks. You even become the type of kid that actually asked for extra credit. Yeah, mind-blowing, right?

Scooter - Now I know you lying. There ain't no way I'm asking for more work.

BD - Yet, there you were, completing extra credit to help make the Honor Roll for the first time since like kindergarten. And with that newfound belief, you would go on to college and kill it.

Scooter - College? Hard to go to college without a scholarship where I'm from!

BDawk BD - Oh, I forgot to mention, you do get a scholarship. From Clemson!

BRIAN DAWKINS

Scooter - , What the heck is a Clemson?
BD - It's a school in South Carolina. That offers you a scholarship late in the game. In fact, it was the last scholarship given.

Scooter - I must have balled out my Senior year.

BDawk BD - I could say yes and no, but as you stated earlier, we are being honest. It was more about Clemson wanting your High School teammate, Patrick Sapp, so much that they took you in.

Scooter - I don't get it.

BDawk BD - Long story short, they wanted him so bad, that they were willing to have you two to come as a package deal.

Scooter - So I went there knowing that they really didn't want me?

BD - Not exactly. You and Pat would have a conversation a week or so before signing day, and you would inform him that you were trying to get in touch with the only college that offered you, South Carolina. You called all day and could not get in contact with anyone. Scooter, me knowing what I know, if a team stops taking your calls, you are no longer on their radar.
So Pat asked you if you would go to Clemson, and you said if they give you a scholarship, without question. So he called Rick Stockstill, the recruiter from Clemson for our area, on Thursday night. We flew to Clemson Friday evening for a last-minute visit, and we both signed letters of intent that weekend.

Scooter - So that thing about surrounding yourself with QP Quality People, is not just a thing older people say to get us young folk so that we do the right stuff, huh?

BD - Nope. It's real. It's true, and it works, no matter the age of the person that does it.

It also doesn't matter how you get your foot in the door, and it's what you do with the opportunity. And you killed it!!

And looking back, had you gone to Florida on the initial scholarship, you would not have asked for and received help. You would not know in your heart of hearts that you could do it, because you would have continued to study in ways that did not benefit your learning style. So there is an excellent chance that you would have struggled greatly.

Scooter - I just don't see how any of this fits me with what I see around me every day. People work hard, and most never really make ends meet.
BD - It's because of a vision that you cemented in your mind around your 11th-grade year. This fixed in your thoughts a way you wanted to live. Even though you didn't have anything really around you, that would suggest you could do it.

Narrator - At this point, Scooter is now sitting up, with his shoulders facing B Dawk as much as they could be without him not falling.

Scooter - Vision? Now you trippin, but I'm listening.

BD- The summer right before your 12 12th-grade year. You also were blessed by someone to attend an FCA basketball camp in NC.

Scooter - Was it free, because my pops worked hard for what we had, but we didn't have no summer camp for a week money.

BD- That's why I said blessed to go. Someone you will never meet paid for you to go to a camp there. It was there you would not only strengthen your relationship with the Lord. You'd also be introduced to journaling, a practice you do every day now.

But you'd also see neighborhoods that you said you and your family would live in. Where, as you put it, "Where Oreo cookies never run out. Or you don't have to hide them in your room."

You made the declaration that you would be a professional something. You didn't 100 percent know what yet, but you wanted that lifestyle you saw there.
Scooter - OK. Now we talkin'. You got me reeled in. What happens next.
BD- A couple of thoughts back, QP. After that trip, if there were people you still hung around that would hurt your chances of being a Pro, you politely begin to distance yourself from them.

You began to write out your autograph over and over, saying, "One day, folk gon pay for this right here!"

And guess what... They actually do.

Scooter - WOW!! That's crazy!

BDawk - You are also an inspirational speaker.

Scooter - Just when I started believing you, you drop this bomb on me. Ain't no way in the world, I'm purposefully getting up in front of folk and talking. You must've forgot about my stutter and fear of speaking in front of people.

BD- Nope. How could I forget? The countless ways we tried to get out of leading anything where I had to speak. But, that which we saw as a significant weakness has become one of our greatest giftings & strengths. You are now able to share your story with different walks of life. From the church to the boardroom, from kids to adults, your level of triumph against the odds resonates.
And we've only chopped it up about some of the things you've grown through.

Scooter - Grown through? What do you mean grown through?

BD- The things in your life that would have derailed others, that didn't have your willingness to fight. Brought out something different in you. Because you refused to stay down and out. You figured out that setbacks, were not STAY BACKS. That in them there will be feedback, so we can get back, and then some!

THE GREATNESS IN YOU

Narrator - It's often said that hindsight is 20/20. That looking back on a thing, one can usually see areas to be done differently. And on the other side of the coin, it is said to look ahead. And don't get me wrong, both of these are powerful ways to thrive in life.

But what if we've been so focused on those two, putting our focused creative prowess at the wrong ends of the equation systemically, without blinking. What if we have been looking in good areas but not the best area to find your greatness ultimately. Because it's not behind you, it's not ahead of you.

Doggone it... Your Greatness Is Inside Of You! And only the Creator of the thing knows the real functions for it.
So submit yourself to the Lord, Seek, and you shall find Him, Knock and keep knocking if need be, and doors will be opened.

And remember, God doesn't make junk, and you and I are His proudest achievement. Not water. Not the sun. Not even the ever-expanding universe He created. It was you and I that were created in His image and likeness. So let's go live, like God told the truth about us... Because He did, I mean, HE IS!!

"No eye has seen, no ear has heard, and no mind has imagined what God has prepared for those who love him."
1 Corinthians 2:9 NLT

About Brian Dawkins

Brian Dawkins is an NFL Hall of Fame legend, Founder of the Brian Dawkins Impact Foundation, Author, Inspirational Speaker, Mindset Coach, husband, father & Blessed man of God.

  Drafted by the Philadelphia Eagles in 1996, Dawkins fought to elevate his own game and that of his entire team. He dominated through sixteen seasons in the NFL all the way into the

Hall of Fame. A nine-time Pro Bowler, Dawkins was named All-Pro and All-NFC five times. In addition to being named to the NFL's All-Decade Team of the 2000s, Dawkins is a member of the Eagles 75th Anniversary Team and the only player in NFL history with 25+ Interceptions, 25+ sacks, and& 25+ Forced Fumbles. Brian was inducted into the NFL Hall of Fame in 2018.

In 2019, he launched the Brian Dawkins Impact Foundation. Leveraging the values and knowledge Brian gained over his lifetime, the Foundation is on a mission to help disadvantaged young people, families, and communities while promoting spiritual, cerebral, and physical wellness. With an initial focus in Jacksonville and Philadelphia — the communities that made Brian into the person he is today – the Foundation supports those who may be impacted by hardship in their lives but retain the drive and passion for succeeding.

Brian's first book, Blessed By The Best: My Journey to Canton and Beyond, is an inspirational journey that follows Dawkins' trials to train his mind and Faith along with his skill. He is also a successful Mindset Coach who teaches strategies and tools he has learned through these trials to those seeking to unleash the better version of themselves ongoing!

Pioneering Greatness II - Be Ballast By David D. Archer Jr.

Do You See What I See? I Am Driven by Your Success!

The tools that I impart through this medium are inspired by an amalgamation of ancient teachings and learnings from leaders of successful nations. These rulers triumphed in times when defending kingdoms was necessary to save ancestral history. These tools are also motivated by the words, thoughts, and actions of great modern-day businesspersons, successful athletes, and other everyday leaders like yourself, regardless of age. I have used this zeitgeist of positive thinking to inspire my own thoughts on success, which I proudly share here in this book.

So, who am I? I am a messenger for positivity and an architect of successful solutions. My passion is deeply rooted in seeing persons reach their fullest potential and achieve what is rightfully theirs. Another person's success is my reward for the time, energy, and skills that I put into writing, speaking, and breathing hope into their lungs. My vision is to have nations of people who are positively influenced by the way they think and live their lives and do the same to others. When persons are positively influenced, they influence and inspire others. They then teach others, and their success yields even more success. When this is consistently repeated, it becomes a movement that builds successful nations.

A movement of positively influenced people is the foundation for world peace, the elimination of hunger, and the physical and mental freedom of people who live in nations that suppress them.

My vision is, therefore, simple. Through your reading of this book, you will be inspired by the inspiration of great leaders. By learning from people who have themselves penned positive solutions and built a nation of people who are wired to fend for themselves, you too will discover solutions and be eager to share these in your life. In doing so, you will help build successful nations.

I am not alone in this quest because I read (and so should you!) of others who pack their bags daily and work towards positively influencing people. Every time you read a line in one of these thoughts, you too have joined the movement. You simply have to continuously engage yourself in a mental state of positive reinforcement, remembering your right to be successful and achieve greatness. Let us never stop teaching another until our vision of positively influencing people and building succession nations becomes the vision of the world. I'm ready - are you?

Decipher the Complexity of the Human Mind
If our paths are always at risk of being hampered by unforeseen barriers, is it not in your best interest to always create paths of lesser resistance? I think, yes - a complex mind is kept running smoothly by always finding the optimum way of operation. This is the rhythm of your inner soul - it will define your direction and your outcome.

In this way, we should not be perplexed by the nuances of life's challenges, for they are gifts. They build up our strength despite being disguised as hurdles. The sprinter might miss the call, while the calm, methodical, and patient runner will benefit from all of life's joys. After all, you are not alone in your quest for greatness. You are merely one of many strategically positioned to receive gifts. For it is your persistence that will reap bountiful rewards - and I hope you will share these rewards and build a nation of successors.

To find your optimum mode of operation, do not hold back your growth with misguided thoughts. Rather, leap with a spring in your step and capture life's marvels through focused thoughts and ingenious strategies always crafted for the good of others.

Second, smile not at others. Rather, smile with yourself and with others. This creates the blueprint for cordial relationships, the hallmark of successful and permanent dynasties.

Third, consider your voice. Is it loud enough? Are your cries personal or in service of others in their plight, with an innate sense that their success will equate to yours? Let the free mind not be restricted by poisonous verbiage. Replace it with the language of "can do" and "will do."

Finally, if success is not your drive, pull over, and allow the lanes to be occupied by drivers and passengers who are questing for greatness without bounds. They are ignited by growth and are headed to the ends of the universe on a fast-moving train to slow dance with stars and bounce on planets. If you want to join them, void the ticket of hesitation and trade it for positive yielding and growth.

Apply these basic rules to your mind and share them with others in your life out of love, passion, and a desire to see others become greater than they are right now. You cannot be great by yourself; you must bring others along with you! In this way, you can positively influence people and build successful nations - by conquering the complexity of your mind.

I Don't Have a Plan B, and Neither Should You

I can hear it now - the comments of my professional and financial advisors as they prepare me for the best and worst-case scenarios of my future. They help me rigorously plan for success - and yet also tell me that I should prepare for the worst!

This is the advice many people receive - to always have a "Plan B." I would never in my life advise anyone to develop a Plan B - it only sets you up to fail. What if you have a dream of being a great doctor, but your Plan B, if you don't make it through medical school, is to be a nurse? With this thinking, you will most likely become a nurse - because you have already made up your mind that you could fail.

What about the Plan B thinker who plans for their Plan A companion but expects to end up with a second-choice marriage? Where else could they end up besides lonely or in a relationship where they are simply waiting to exhale?

My belief is simple. You should painstakingly plan and commit to your Plan A. Do not settle and make excuses for your failure by hiding behind a Plan B. The clear power of positive planning and thinking should never be muddied with other plans of failure. Your mind is powerful, and when receiving messages for success, they must be just that and nothing else. Otherwise, you trick your brain into believing that the positive plans that you have conceived are not good enough - and your brain will execute Plan B for you. A powerful and successful brain works with clear and precise instructions. You must feed your brain the right words of positive affirmation in order to receive its full potential.

I can hear some of you right now disagreeing with me, ready to fight the notion of needing a Plan B in life. But let us consider this.

If you plan an outdoor concert, a Plan B should be to have a plan in case of rain. In my view, your Plan A should either be to not have the concert outdoors because it can rain or erect tents from the beginning! This means no scrambling on the day of the concert -
all is going according to plan.

You might argue if you don't get the job you applied for, your Plan B would be to apply for another. But what about making your Plan A to pursue a profession or career - so that several jobs and opportunities are available to you? This means you will always have options, even if you need to move to France for the perfect job!

This idea is controversial, but I do not care - as I am here to help build a higher, more robust, and dynamic YOU. Close your eyes and say "Plan A." Then say, "Plan B." Do this a few times and concentrate on the emotion your brain generates when you say the two words. You should feel a difference in the message remitted through your brain. One (Plan A) is boundless, and the other (Plan B) is limiting. Already here, you can see how to be kinder to your neurons - you don't need a degree in neuroplasticity to understand what happens when you feed your brain with positivity and excellence! Go for your Plan A. Encourage others to become Plan A thinkers. In doing so, you can positively influence people and build a nation of positive, successful people.

There Must Be Something That Would Make You Fight

Life without passion is death. Ok, maybe that is a bit harsh. What I mean is that a life without passion is close to death - which is to say, within each of us is a component of our humanity that makes us react with passion. That is the key to life.

When I say passion, I am not referring to the ability of someone to motivate anger within you for a physical fight. My reference is to your soul and the armies within it that you will put on the line to defend or champion a cause or ignite a change.

In other words: what will you fight for? A friend of mine became pregnant in the midst of a bad relationship. She made a choice to give birth to her beautiful baby girl. I have often thought of her and commended her for her decision and bravery – and am equally amazed at how her beautiful girl is now her passion. She provides, protects, plans, and breathes life into the best opportunities for her daughter. She had choices, but her decision to have her little girl sparked a new passion in her life. That passion resulted in something that she will fight for! She is achieving greatness.

I am increasingly amazed by the story of a successful woman I know whose passion was so great for humanity and its care that she traveled to a remote country in deplorable conditions to feed, teach and nurture homeless children. Away from her fancy clothes and luxury amenities, she immersed herself in a new life of philanthropy without comforts and amidst extreme difficulties. Yet, her passion for helping the needy overshadowed a world that, on a daily basis, is extremely far removed from her own. She found something to fight for, and she is to be called amazing for it. Philanthropy is now a part of her innate being. She is achieving greatness.

Another story of excellence is about a young girl from a prominent family who, at an early age, became pregnant without hope and direction for her life. She was forced to leave school and work for pennies. But her choices led to newfound responsibility. A quest for a better life and the resurgence of her dignity became her passion. It became something for which she would fight. Armed with a new responsibility (her son), she forged through many of life's obstacles, became educated, and the ability to become a Judge is now within her reach. She is achieving greatness!

To be a complete human being, we must have things that we believe in - beliefs that are innate, strong, and indescribable. These beliefs are the core of our passion. I encourage people to at least find one thing they can call their passion. Something that motivates them and affords them a sense of fulfillment, which is rewarding. It must be something that defines their action and propels them to the highest pinnacle. I am innately passionate about positively influencing people, businesses, and governments and building successful nations - and I will fight for it. What will you fight for?

I invite you to continue pioneering greatness by never giving up on your quest to become the best version of yourself.

DAVID D. ARCHER JR.

About David D Archer Jr.

Mr. David D. Archer Jr. is a global adviser, leader, author, motivational speaker, and performer. His love for people and their growth is the motivation behind his Pioneering Greatness movement of written books and speaking engagements.

David helps to build people, businesses, governments, and nations. He currently serves as the Deputy Governor of the Virgin Islands while he impacts the world with his Pioneering

Greatness movement. He is also the author of the books *Pioneering Greatness I - The Empowerment Experience and Pioneering Greatness II - Be Ballast.*

David is married to Dr. Allison Flax-Archer and has two children, Alexia Monae Archer and Prince-David Archer. He is an active member of several service organizations, including *Rotary*, and exercises his entrepreneurial spirit in businesses related to *arts, entertainment, hospitality, and real estate.*

Learn more about David by visiting www.daviddarcher.com or by emailing david@daviddarcher.com

@daviddarcherjr on Facebook, Instagram, Twitter

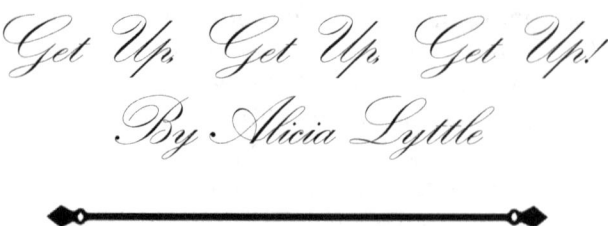

Get Up, Get Up, Get Up!
By Alicia Lyttle

August 17th, 2010, I walked out on my husband, and Les Brown made me do it.

Les called me early one morning after hearing the disturbing news that I was battling cancer again. I was first diagnosed with ovarian cancer one year after marriage and quickly underwent surgery and treatments. Unfortunately, 18 months later, it returned, and this cycle would repeat itself throughout my marriage. A mutual friend had told Les that I was battling it again for the 5th time. When I answered Les's phone call, he said, "Alicia, I know why this is happening to you, and there's something that I need you to do for me. The next time your husband walks toward you, I need you to tell me how your body feels on the inside." "On the inside?" I asked. "Yes, Alicia, on the inside," Les Brown said.

Les then began to teach me about a term he coined relationship illness, and he asked me if I'd ever heard the statement, "That person makes me sick." I uttered, "Yes, I have heard that term before; what are you trying to get at?" "Well, it's true. People really can make you physically sick. Your relationship, how he treats you, and the stress he puts you in is the root cause of your cancer. You are in a toxic relationship. " I need you to tell me how your body feels the next time you see him walking towards you and then call me back," he said as he abruptly hung up the phone.

Shortly after, I saw my husband parading towards my office as I peeped out the back window towards the pool house he converted into his office and studio. He was so unpredictable that I wasn't sure if he would yell at me for something, laugh and tell a joke, or rattle off instructions for me to do something for him.

Following Les's instructions, I connected with my inner self, closed my eyes, and shockingly witnessed that my body was boiling on the inside. How could I have not noticed this before?

Once he arrived in my office, he spewed off a few complaints about his breakfast not being hot enough. Then, he interrogated me on when I would be delivering lunch to his office. Then reminded me to check his emails for him and not to disturb him while he was playing his video games.

He had an obscenely loud alarm on his phone that went off two times a day at 12 noon and 7 pm, and if his meals were not delivered at those exact times, pandemonium would break loose in the house. I hired a woman to help me cook his meals and take them to him on time, but unfortunately, she was out that day.

As soon as he left my office, I called Les Brown and said to Les, "I was boiling on the inside!" Les said calmly, "Get out as quickly as you can. If you want to live, you must muster up the courage to leave."

The business was a super successful multi-million dollar company; we lived in a huge mansion, drove luxury cars, and only traveled first class. Although I had thought about leaving dozens of times, I had spent the last ten years of my life building a business with him, and I feared the repercussions that might fall on our staff and our clients if I left.

The opportunity to leave would come soon enough. A few weeks later, I got a call from my husband's assistant saying she found out he was going on a trip with another woman. I asked her not to say anything, and I used this as my opportunity to get out.

While he was on vacation with his mistress, I packed up, took my suitcase, laptop, and cell phone, and drove away. Once he returned home and noticed I was gone, he threatened me, saying if I didn't return, he'd make my life a living hell. He worked hard to deliver on that promise and locked me out of our business, the bank accounts, credit cards, and the house, and kept me from ever seeing any of my five dogs ever again. My sister and mother also worked in the business, and he locked them out of everything because I left. I was 34 years old and at one of the lowest points in my life.

I ended up sleeping on my sister's sofa, down on myself for the situation I was now facing. One day while lying on that sofa wallowing in self-pity, my phone rang, and it was Les Brown. "Alicia, what are you doing?"

"Les, I'm lying on the sofa." Then I started my pity party by telling him how I worked every day in the business and was left with nothing; he would not even give me one of the five dogs we had and how this was so unfair.

As one might expect, Les stopped me mid-conversation and said, "Alicia, you've landed on your back, but you can look up, so GET UP" then he said, "GET UP," and his voice got louder, and he repeated it, "GET UP," and then in that deep Les Brown power voice he said, "GEEEETTTTT UUUUUPPPPPP!" You have greatness within you; tap into it right now, and he once again abruptly hung up the phone!

I jumped off the sofa, went to my sister's room, and said, "You know what, we're going to start over. We must have something of value that someone else would be willing to pay us for." And at that moment, my sister and I launched our new business, which has gone on to make millions of dollars.

When faced with something that seems like destruction, you can become bitter and sour and let that poison the rest of your life.

It's not easy but keep moving forward. You might have to dig down deep. Know that there are good days ahead, and you get to choose how to live your life every day. Are you going to stay on the sofa or GET UP?

Today, my core business is teaching people how to tap into that greatness within, pull out their skills and talents, and turn them into an online business. I teach people that no matter what situation they are in right now, they have the opportunity to change it by pulling out the greatness within them.

That day, I was forced to get up, so I started a side hustle that became so successful that I started teaching others how to start a side hustle online. I conduct free workshops on my website www.freelancinggenius.com that have changed so many lives it brings me pure joy! My sister and I have been blessed to have traveled all over the world, from Nigeria and South Africa to Australia, New Zealand, Singapore, Malaysia, the United

Kingdom all over the Caribbean, and the United States, teaching others to leverage the power of the Internet to create financial freedom.

What do you have within you that you can turn into an online business and transform your future? Let's walk through 3 steps to get you on the right path. The first step is to identify what skills and talents you already have that others would be willing to pay you for. Most people go through life without really tapping into their skills and talents. One of my favorite authors, Erma Bombeck, said, "When I stand before God at the end of my life, I would hope that I would not have a single bit of talent left, and could say, I used everything you gave me." Are you using everything you have?

The next step is to identify what skills you've always wanted to learn that people would be willing to pay you for. Every skill you acquire increases your ability to level up. Today we have YouTube and Google, and the knowledge is out there when we search for those things we want to learn. Have a deep hunger for acquiring new talents and skills that if you don't fill up daily with the knowledge, you feel the emptiness in your stomach as you starve for more.

The last step is putting yourself on social media and sites like fiverr.com, upwork.com, and freelancer.com. Self-promotion has never been easier than today in the era of social media. You have to get out there and give it everything you've got! Push yourself. There will never be a better time to start, so push yourself; the world is waiting for you.

So, what are you going to do with that greatness you have? Whatever your greatness is, what are you going to do with it?

We all have seeds of greatness, skills, and talents that others would be willing to pay us for. Nelson Mandela said, "There is no passion to be found playing small — in settling for a life that is less than the one you are capable of living." Today you are in the position to make a living around what you are passionate about, so have the courage to live a life that is true to yourself.

Yes, I'm cancer free and in a fantastic relationship, and my new business with my sister has far surpassed the old business. The one thing I want to leave you with is that when you need to talk yourself into your greatness, remember these words by Les Brown, get up, get up, GET UP!

If there is anything that you feel I could do to help you on your journey, I invite you to reach out to me on social media, on my website www.alicialyttle.com, or check out my workshop at www.freelancinggenius.com.

About Alicia Lyttle

Business owner, Business Coach, International Speaker & Trainer.

Before jumping into entrepreneurship, Alicia was enrolled in the Ph.D. program at the University of Michigan, pursuing a career in Environmental Science and Policy. She worked with some notable organizations, including The White House, The United States Environmental Protection Agency (USEPA), and The City of New Orleans in the Mayor's Office.

ALICIA LYTTLE

In the year 2000, she was introduced to how to build a business via the Internet and left her Ph.D. behind. In 2010 she experienced several setbacks from battling cancer and walking away from a marriage that left her from being a millionaire to being flat broke. She bounced back, and with hard work and dedication, today she is a self-made millionaire through her online ventures.

Alicia has traveled the world to places such as Singapore, China, Australia, the United Kingdom, New Zealand, South Africa, and throughout the United States as a well-sought-after speaker and trainer. Not only does she speak on stage, but she is a regular guest on podcasts, radio shows, local news stations, and more, all emphasizing how to leverage the Internet to work from anywhere, be your own boss and build the lifestyle you deserve and desire.

Alicia is the founder of Pow Social, a Digital Marketing Agency based on the island of Jamaica with clients such as the National Commercial Bank and Hertz. She also produces a weekly segment on Jamaica's public broadcasting channel (PBCJ) called The Digital JamPrenuer that teaches everyday people how to use the Internet to improve their lives.

Alicia's goal is to help others recognize their brilliance and turn that brilliance into profits by leveraging the power of the Internet. Alicia believes that the Internet is the great equalizer allowing people from all backgrounds to build wealth regardless of their past.

Images:
https://drive.google.com/drive/folders/1QUgxwor15hvDQTAkQruxMSVvdC3M9s-F?usp=sharing

Social Media Links:
Facebook: https://www.facebook.com/aliciarosettalyttle
Instagram: https://www.instagram.com/alicialyttle/
Clubhouse: https://www.clubhouse.com/@alicialyttle
LinkedIn: https://www.linkedin.com/in/alicialyttle/

Website Link: www.alicialyttle.com

Fearfully and Wonderfully Made
By Dawn Lieck

Most of us, as we grow older, create a preconceived notion of what our lives will be. I know I certainly did! I would be married to a wonderful man, have the house with the white picket fence, and have six beautiful children!

Sometimes when we set these plans up for ourselves and things don't go as planned, we are disappointed and feel that somehow we have failed. This often happens because we fail to realize it's not for us to plan. It's God's plan and will.

Now I'm not saying that God planned my life the way it played out in those early years. I can now take responsibility for my own decisions. Decisions that were not part of the plan, but I thought I knew better at the young age of 17.

I had lost my dad the year before, a devastating blow as I was the epitome of a "daddy's girl." The loss and grief sent me into a defiant tailspin: drinking, drugs, and unwed sex.

I thought that the older man I was with was great, we had so much fun together! That is until I ended up pregnant. Of course, I immediately stopped drinking and abusing drugs, and I was going to be a mom! He, however, did not. I very quickly learned that he was a full-blown alcoholic with no desire to change his ways. There would be no perfect husband and certainly no white picket fence.

Even though I was only 17, I knew that the baby I was carrying was my blessing from God. I was beyond scared because I knew I would be on this journey of parenthood on my own, but I refused to have my gift raised in a home with substance abuse and alcoholism.

When I told my family the news of my blessing, I was shamed by some and supported by others. However, there was a resounding; "You've ruined your life," "You'll never amount to anything now," and "Congratulations, you've just become another statistic."

Hearing these actual words being said to me by the people I loved the most was a very formative thing in my life. I mean, they said it, so it must be true, right?

I began to live that narrative. The single teen mom with no plan and no future. There were some very rough times for us in those early years. I went and signed up for public assistance. A monthly check that was $50 short of my rent and $120.00 per month in food stamps for the two of us.

Some nights my son would ask why I wasn't eating dinner with him. I would tell him I wasn't hungry or that I had already eaten. He never knew that the .25 can of vegetable soup he was eating was all I could afford. If I had eaten a can with him, I would've been short a dinner for him that week. I was too proud to ask anyone for help because that would have validated to me that I really was a statistic.

I accepted this life for the first five years of my son's life. I felt what everyone had said was true. This was it. I was a young unwed single mother on public assistance. This was my fate. I was a statistic.

Because my assistance didn't come close to covering all of my expenses just to live, I worked cleaning other people's houses to make ends meet. It was very hard work at very low pay. I would clean and daydream about having a nice home like the one I was cleaning. My son really needed his own room. It all seemed so absolutely impossible to me.

Then it happened. My sister got a new job and talked me into applying as well. I got that job, and at $8.00 an hour, I was elated! I found out that I was very good at telemarketing and was shortly the #1 appointment setter in the department! What a boost of confidence for me; maybe I was capable of more!

I worked hard and was promoted time and time again. I was finally shown that I wasn't what they said. I was a momma with a beautiful son, and I was capable of whatever I set my mind to.

With no high school diploma or college education, within five years, I was running that hundred-million-dollar business as the general manager to the tune of a quarter million dollar a year salary!

I tell this story to say to you, "FORGET WHAT THEY TOLD YOU!"

God gives each of us gifts and talents. He gives us all a specific purpose. Last but certainly not least, He will open our eyes and show us the path to our greatness. It's our responsibility to walk the path shown to us in faith. It is inevitable that those who are obedient, follow the Word, and walk in faith will prosper.

Where we falter is listening to others and not God, not believing in ourselves, and not seeing ourselves as God sees us.

I praise you because I am fearfully and wonderfully made; your works are wonderful, I know this full well. Psalm 139:14NIV

Who are we to doubt God's creation? Your Greatness is right there inside you; it's always been there. You've had the power all along, my friend! Just remember to forget what they told you!

About Dawn Lieck

Dawn Lieck is a world-class business professional with remarkable expertise in the areas of business and multidimensional coaching.

A *mirrored portrait* of what it means to be a *"Renaissance Woman,"* Dawn's abilities have earned her professional respect amongst generational influencers.

Setting the standard in her field, Dawn is an International Speaker, best-selling author, and the CEO of both Finally Free,

LLC and Dawn Lieck Enterprise. Affectionately known as the "Transformation Life Coach," Dawn helps successful professionals harness their true potential by putting them in touch with themselves on an intrinsic level. Having an unyielding passion for personal development, Dawn motivates clients to renew their perspective, conquer fear, and create life balance using a system of pragmatic strategies.

Dawn's mantra is simple; "DO IT SCARED."

The result has been phenomenal, as Dawn has enjoyed wide-ranging success and is in high demand from both domestic and international audiences. Dawn has held a three-year consecutive election as one of the Top 100 Women to Know on the Gulf Coast, where she was also featured as a Woman of Achievement Entrepreneur Finalist.

Though her talents lead her reputation, her heart for service leads her path, as Dawn is involved in many organizations on the Gulf Coast, including the Gulfport Chamber of Commerce Board, Back Bay Mission Advisory Council, Leadership Gulf Coast Graduate, VP Membership Chair for Lighthouse Business and Professional Women, Chair for Success Women's Conference and a team lead for women at Habitat for Humanity.

Email; Dawn@dawnlieckenterprise.com
Facebook; Dawn Lieck

From Near Death to Hollywood
By Sam Humphrey

My life has consisted of extreme highs and lows, a nonstop roller coaster, and a journey of living and dying. In my first six weeks of being alive, I was challenged with survival. Since then, I've been in and out of the hospital more times than I can count. I shouldn't even be alive today!

There were many complications prior to my birth. In the last month of pregnancy, my parents and doctors discovered that I was not growing. Upon delivery, I was placed into an incubator. The doctors expressed their concerns about my life expectancy. One doctor had said to my mum, "I don't know what the future holds for your baby." My parents were stunned. They didn't know how to accept the news; to my mum, it sounded as though I was going to die at any moment. And I was.

Despite my circumstances, I prevailed. At the age of 3, I was diagnosed with a very rare genetic condition called 'acrodyplasia,' which can also be referred to as 'skeletal dysplasia.' To put it into layman's terms, it simply means my bones don't develop to that of a "normal" person my age, and I am, and always will be, smaller than most. As a kid, I didn't understand any of this. All I knew was that I was very different. As I got older, I still didn't really understand why I was so different. I felt unattractive and ugly. My teeth were so badly deformed due to my condition, and I hated my smile. Everyone would tell me I was unique and special, but I didn't care.

I didn't want to be special or unique; I just wanted to fit in. I didn't understand why I couldn't be normal. I often asked myself how I could be accepted and loved by others, being the way that I am.

I grew up in a Christian home and spent the bulk of my time at church. I was taught that God never makes mistakes and that he is perfect, but at the time, I couldn't understand why he would create me to be and look so different. If he was so loving and just, why was I burdened with these challenges? I thought that I was a mistake. I have a loving family who supported me and treated me the same as any other member of the family (for the most part). At home, I felt safe and comfortable. To my family, I was simply short, though it wasn't always easy to pretend that life was normal. I can remember moments when I felt so alone; no one could understand me or the emotional pain I buried inside. There were moments at home when, as an adult, I still felt very different and small; like when people came around to the house that didn't know me and started talking down to me or using language that you would use to speak to a 5-year-old. Because of this, I never wanted to meet new people, which made me a very reserved kid; I was tired of not being treated or accepted for who I was.

Growing up with my condition was tough. My family did their best to create a normal environment at home, which for them, they didn't really know any different; there were obvious adjustments that were made around the house to make life easier for me. For example, the kitchen was arranged so that I had plates, bowls, cups, and other everyday things accessible to me.

Acting was a natural fit for me. My first love of acting came when I was just five years old; my family friends' kids (Olivia and Ben), my older brother/sister (Josiah and Esther), and I were putting on these mini productions for our parents. I also wanted to join the army during that time. I pretended to train for the physical and was excited to be a soldier. At that age, the possibilities of what I could be were limitless; anything was possible.

At age 8, I saw Hugh Jackman for the first time, acting in X-MEN™ on the big screen and at home on the TV. I made fake claws from cardboard and wanted to be Wolverine. I ran around my house pretending to fight like him. Running around yelling, stabbing, and slashing at the pretend enemies. From that day, he became my role model and inspired me to pursue acting and follow in his footsteps as an actor, producer, and philanthropist, though it would take me a long time to actually do that.

I was a very shy kid though that was the least of my problems. I was always sick, and this affected my education. My family and doctors were confused by many of my physical and mental developmental issues because although acrodyplasia does affect my entire physiology and overall health, it couldn't explain all of the symptoms I was having. Around the age of 15, the doctors in Australia finally gave me a diagnosis for why I was so ill all the time: Crohn's disease, yet another incurable mutation. I was already dealing with so much, and on top of all this, I now had an additional and very serious health issue that would present further challenges for me to live with.

Then came high school and my challenges were only about to multiply. It's like someone flipped a switch and the intensity of being a teenager increased. I was already different and was dealing with challenges like coming to terms with my own mortality or feeling attractive to the opposite sex. I felt anxious, unworthy, depressed, not accepted, and suicidal. I was so caught up in who did and didn't like or love me that it felt like a matter of life and death. I didn't feel like I belonged in the world.

High school was a very emotional period, both physically and mentally. I was not a "normal" teenager. Anyone who knew me in high school would say that I was a very happy, friendly, down-to-earth, confident, and easygoing kid. On the surface, that was my disguise. Because I was an actor, being able to hide my realness and vulnerability came naturally. No one knew that I was unhappy. No one knew that I thought of suicide. They never knew the pain behind the smile or the sadness and depression underneath the laughter. While I was smiling, confident, and full of joy at school, on the inside, I was filled with fear and self-doubt. Having missed so much school because of my Acrodysplasia and desperate not to be left behind, my feelings were amplified times ten.

My siblings were both academically bright, and that only added more pressure on me to succeed. With all that my family had to do to support me, I felt like a burden. I still sometimes feel like that today.

One of the symptoms of my diagnosis was delayed maturation, so I looked and sounded years younger than my teenage classmates. No one wanted to date me; I was 16 but sounded and looked like I was eight years old. No girl wants to feel like they're dating a kid, let alone deal with the judgmental stares/opinions that society would perceive about the relationship. My voice sounded like a chipmunk, and I was less than three feet tall. I was the cheery best friend to girls but never the one they dated.

    I struggled to accept myself, the way I looked and felt about my image. I couldn't look in the mirror without wanting to change everything about myself. I would smile in the mirror, at friends in school, and in photos for social media, but it was a fake smile, and I didn't love the smile I saw smiling back at me. Behind that smile was a lot of pain. I couldn't accept myself, and it was reinforced by strangers' comments, stares, and whispers; I was my own worst enemy. Not receiving the love that I wanted and feeding lies to myself that I wasn't good enough...didn't have anything to offer...couldn't measure up to others (especially my siblings)...no one would love me...or want to have a family with me...led me to a very dark place during my teen years. I tried several times to commit suicide. I couldn't see a reason to continue on. My life seemed to have run its course. If what the doctors said were true, I didn't want to keep being a burden on my family or pointlessly existing, only to die a few years later. If I was going to die, I wanted to end it on my terms.

    When my family discovered how many times I had tried to end my life, they were shocked. They knew I was struggling but didn't know my desperation. They had this perception of who I was, and I didn't want to destroy that. When you're struggling, and in a vulnerable position, no one wants to show that. Everyone wants to seem like they have it all together. Everyone kept telling me that I was such a strong person, being able to deal with this. I didn't want to ruin that. I was just trying to get through one moment, one day, one emotional crisis after the other, hoping eventually I would get to the end of the tunnel and it would all be okay. The only way for me to feel like there was going to be a light at the end of it all was to fake it until I made it.

    After graduating high school at 18, I seemed to be thriving. I simply kept looking forward to being grateful and having an attitude of extreme gratitude for both the big things and especially the little things. I worked several jobs, including admin, cleaning, retail, sales, education, and finally, hospitality at a casino in Melbourne, Australia, but while they paid the bills, none of these satisfied or stimulated my creative mind.

Growing up in the shadow of my older brother was tough. I was always known as "Josiah's brother." He ran a very successful tech development company called "Appster." Over the years, we would have many one-to-one deep talks, where he would give advice and share his experiences to inspire and push me. He never sugarcoated or pulled his punches during these talks. He said you've got to take risks and give it everything you have. Similarly, my youth pastor would say, "The only way to know if you're going to be an actor is to give it a real shot." While I dabbled at acting, I let my fear of failure hold me back. If I didn't try that hard, then I couldn't really fail.

One day, my brother and I were sitting in my dad's car outside my brother's office building in Melbourne. It was late afternoon, and we were waiting for Dad so we could go out for dinner. I was in the front passenger seat, and my brother was in the back. He was living in the city then, and we didn't see each other that often, so we were just chatting and catching up when Josiah suddenly asked me, *"If you had all the money and time in the world... What would you do?"*

He already knew the answer before he even asked the question, but I had never allowed myself to admit it.

The answer came automatically: "I would be an actor."

He knew this already, and after sharing it with him yet again, he started laying it on heavy: what was I doing? I wasn't taking risks. What had I really done to make it happen? I knew I should be doing certain things, but I wasn't doing them because I didn't want to fail. He was driving home what I already knew, and I started to get emotional. His probing questions made me realize I wasn't really trying. It finally clicked inside my head: *I was born to be an actor.*

I began to change my mindset. I admitted to myself that acting was my true passion, my biggest ambition, and what I had dreamed about since childhood *was* a possibility for me. Since I was born, doctors had told my parents that my future was very uncertain and it was unlikely that I would live past my 18th

birthday; if I did, they said, "*We are unsure of the quality of life he will have.*"

I was determined to make a career in acting, and I wanted to live my life with no regrets. At 22 years old, I outlived what the doctors had expected: being alive. This was the year where it all changed. After quitting my job in hospitality, I refocused my vision and ambitions. I wasn't gonna waste any more time on things that weren't propelling me forward. I remember standing in my bedroom looking out the window, and I had this intuitive feeling. I told myself: "*I will work with Hugh Jackman and walk the red carpet one day.*" I didn't have a clue how I was going to make that happen, no idea where or when, but I just knew I was going to do it.

In pursuit of my dream, I invested every dollar I had (about $3,000) into shooting a showreel called *Ricochet*. I believed without a doubt that this was the right move. Shortly afterward, a very close friend, Olivia Shvias, chose me as a young person to follow in a documentary as part of her not-for-profit organization, *Attitude Live*. The organization documented my life as an individual with a rare-ability pursuing my ambition to be an actor. They filmed behind the scenes while I shot my showreel and lined up a mock audition for the famous TV series *Neighbours* in Australia. At that audition, I impressed the casting director so much that they decided to create a role specifically for me: "James Udagawa," a young finance whiz kid.

I believed in my skills and talent, and everyone called me a natural; however, this was my first professional audition with a casting director. Up till then, most of my experience was from studying drama during high school and attending a few minor certificate-level courses and workshops. I had no major formal training with drama-theatrical schools. The audition for *Neighbours* validated my talent because I was now a *professional working actor*. That validation was the confirmation I was hoping for; that I had a lot to offer with my unique gift for acting, film production, and my authentic, charismatic personality. I started to believe in the possibilities that could become available to me, helping me to accept myself for who I am.

I began auditioning for more parts and roles, aspiring for bigger films and projects. Within a few weeks of being cast in the role on *Neighbours*, I was at home watching TV. I heard a "ping" and glanced at my phone. It was an email notification saying, "*We just heard back that Sam has been approved by the studio for the role of Charles Stratton/Tom Thumb! Sam is going to get an offer.*" I had just landed my first major role in a Hollywood feature film, Hugh Jackman's *The Greatest Showman*. I was completely stunned; my mind began racing a million miles an hour. So many thoughts were running through my brain, trying to process the news and holding back waves of constant nervousness; such a surreal feeling. I could hardly believe it as I told my family. It was my dream coming true! Being cast as Tom Thumb, *aka* Charles Stratton, next to Hugh Jackman surpassed my wildest expectations. This was my time to shine, my big break. I was off to Hollywood.

For seven months, I acted alongside some of the best people in the industry. I was living full-out. It was mind-blowing to be working with them as one of their co-stars and colleagues! It goes to show that determination, commitment, and belief can make anything possible.

The next thing that I made possible was getting my "MILLION DOLLAR" smile. After *The Greatest Showman*, I had earned enough money to pay for my teeth to be fixed. I felt truly confident in not just the external way I looked but internally. I could feel the shift in my mindset. I could look in the mirror with a newfound sense of love for myself; I loved my body and my smile even more. I remember having a conversation with my sister on the phone, telling her that my new smile endowed me with the confidence to embrace whatever possibilities this world could throw at me.

I am now a positive, confident, strong, and resilient person. I have fought my way through all those character-building challenges — all the impossibilities that I thought were my destiny — to not only survive but to thrive. I now see unlimited possibilities for my life going forward. What I thought was once impossible for someone dealing with such overwhelming odds to simply live was now a reality, and many more possibilities lay on the horizon; my story really is climbing from near death to Hollywood.

You can experience the most unforgettable moments and live life without regrets. Nothing can stop you. If this world wasn't designed for you, change it. Redesign it. Any little dream is possible. As PT Barnum says, "We *can* live in a world that *we* design."

Ignite Action Steps

It takes a lot of self-confidence, determination, and hard work to be ready to embrace the opportunities that present themselves to you. Every day, I try to live by these five rules for mental health to keep my confidence and determination high.
- Express extreme gratitude every single day.
- Spread love to both self and others.
- Be positive with your attitude and outlook.
- Self-care is vital. It's not selfish to take care of yourself.
- Speak positive affirmations. Words have power.

About Sam Humphrey

In a world where equitable representation is the main topic of conversation, in film/television, there are many individuals that seek to understand and speak on what diversity, inclusion, and disability empowerment representation means. Though very few can understand or match the authenticity, wisdom, and life experience on the same level as Sam Humphrey.

Sam's personal intention is to inspire people by demonstrating that no matter what your challenges or obstacles are in life, nothing is impossible. All you need is self-confidence, determination, a lot of hard work, and a single opportunity. Sam's hope is that he can empower you to achieve anything your heart or mind conceives. You can experience the most unforgettable moments and live life without regrets. Nothing can stop you.

Sam Humphrey is an Actor-Producer, RARE Advocate, and Motivational Speaker with his combined experience spanning more than ten years. Sam is famously known for playing the role of Tom Thumb in the feature film, The Greatest Showman. In 2020 he began working as a freelance development producer and now has a number of developed independent feature film/television projects in his portfolio. Since his breakout role in "The Greatest Showman," Sam has been frequently invited to speak about his accomplishments, time on-set, and advocacy work, focusing on mental health & disability awareness; while overcoming his own struggles and challenges to achieve success.

He began his career studying theatrical arts in high school, appearing in many on-stage productions (Midsummers Night's Dream as "Puck," Alice in the Wonderland as "Dormouse" and several others) and further studies at the "Australian College of Dramatic Arts." The Greatest Showman (Sam being a part of this film) won a Golden Globe for "Best Original Song" – THIS IS ME and was also Oscar-nominated for "Best-Picture" feature film. Sam has been mentioned in various media outlets, such as Vogue Magazine, Vanity Fair, and press interviews with major international news/media networks.

Currently based in Los Angeles, working as an actor-producer, RARE Advocate, and public speaker, Sam enjoys keeping a healthy focus to artistically create a legacy that helps to change the world and leave it kinder, positive, safer, and full of love.

"Failure isn't the end of the road; it's really the beginning."

Sam Humphrey ~ New Zealand & USA,
Actor I Producer I Motivational Speaker I Author I Rare Advocate
Instagram: @thesamhumphrey I Facebook: Sam Humphrey

Adornami
By Andrea Edwards Adams

"**L**ove *encompasses a range of strong and positive emotional and mental states, from the most sublime virtue or good habit, the deepest interpersonal affection, to the simplest pleasure. An example of this range of meanings is that the love of a mother differs from the love of a spouse, which differs from the love for food. Most commonly, love refers to a feeling of a strong attraction and emotional attachment."* – Wikipedia

Many forms and varieties of love have been distinguished like:

- Eros – romantic love.
- Philia – brotherly love, platonic.
- Storge – friendly love.
- Ludus – playful love.
- Philautia – self-love.
- Pragma – committed love, not romantic.
- Mania – obsessive love.
- Agape – universal love, such as love for strangers, nature, or God.

In accordance to Wikipedia, **philuatia or self-*love* is** *defined as "love of self" or "regard for one's own happiness or advantage" and has been conceptualized both as a basic human necessity and as a moral flaw, akin to vanity and selfishness, synonymous with amour-propre, conceitedness, egotism, narcissism, et al. However, throughout the centuries self-love has adopted a more positive connotation through pride parades, Self-Respect Movement, self-love protests, the hippie era, the modern feminist movement (3rd & 4th wave), as well as the increase in mental health awareness that promotes self-love as intrinsic to self-help* *and support groups working to prevent substance abuse and suicide."*

Our deepest fear is not that we are inadequate. Our deepest fear is that we are powerful beyond measure. It is our light, not our darkness, that most frightens us.
– Marianne Williamson

This chapter is for the girl in the mirror. Fix your crown. You are a powerhouse. Love yourself fully, and stand firm in the truth that you are inherently worthy of love. Love doesn't have to be earned by proving yourself or proving your worthiness. Instead, the best way to earn love is to love yourself unconditionally first. Be always reminded that the love that you are seeking is already seeking you, too. That love is within. Adornami. Adorn yourself.

Your journey was not easy, and facing your fears took and continues to take courage, but without taking risks, there can be no gain!

Reflect on the time when there was a lack of love found within, and you constantly needed external validation and developed the habit of hiding behind a facade. You can now see that many of your choices had been to please others or because you felt justified in doing so. In the absence of love and approval, who were you?

You lost everything you knew and understood that the only way was to go back and heal your inner wounds.

The two most important days in your life are the day you are born and the day you find out why.
– Mark Twain

The Day You Were Born
You queried, "Will you tell me about the day I was born?" You were told of the Nissan Blue Bird that raced through the streets of Georgetown Guyana, heading towards the public hospital. Smiling parents, grands, and family members were excited to welcome the firstborn of the next generation for both sides of the family. Vague memories of laughter, dancing, and

abundance in your early childhood were replaced by borderline poverty, sexual abuse, bullying, and a broken home.

You were ripped away from the life you knew. Parents were gone, and you and your siblings were separated and sent to live with family members. The white picket fence was gone.

Statistics show that one in four girls and one in six boys have been sexually abused by the age of eighteen. As you reflect, you wonder why me, why did I have to be the one? Also, over sixty percent of children live with both parents, but why did you have to live without yours? Almost one out of every five children is bullied in school. Why did you have to be the one?

As a teenager, you felt abandoned, unprotected, afraid, and unloved. That led to feelings of inadequacy, lack of self-esteem, and self-confidence. Yet you managed through high school and managed to live like many others hiding your pain - placing a coat of paint whenever unresolved issues surfaced. You threaded the waters and managed to smile your way through your internal pain and insecurities. Your family tried, but nothing could have replaced the absence of both parents.

You sure were not able to choose where you were born, but you sure can choose where you go.

The Day You Found Out Why You Were Born

Adornami is an Italian word that translates to "I adorn me." As you stand in front of your mirror, you whisper Adornami. You remind yourself daily of your journey. Some persons have their 'aha' moment; for others, like you, you had an 'aha' season. A season where you stopped and reflected, discovered, and fell in love for the first time with yourself.

That didn't come easy. Like many young girls, you always believed the many stories you read. Your prince charming was going to show up and rescue you from yourself, your past, and your circumstances. You would then ride off into the sunset and live happily ever after.

You always craved the love that was missing, especially in your teenage years when you were becoming conscious of yourself. Now two marriages later, you have come to the realization that there is no prince charming. No one will rescue you. Only you alone are responsible for how the fairy tale ends.

It's your narrative; it's your story. You are the main star and leading character in your own life story. You simply must write your own love story, and you can only do so when you love yourself first.

You were told, "You are beautiful for a black girl." That statement heightened your insecurities and reminded you of those days you played with your dolls and secretly wished that you had long hair like Barbie. You were too young and naïve to see your own beauty and uniqueness, which you were never taught to appreciate. Yet many still dare to question the value of self-love and, furthermore, the value of building a solid foundation for our sons and daughters by teaching them to love and value themselves as they are.

You continue to reminisce about the time you were told, "I am better than you." You smile as you remember the pain of that moment and your audacity for believing, even for a moment, that hideous lie. How dare you? As you continue to reflect on your memories, many negative comments come to mind, such as, "You look amazing but imagine if your tummy was flatter, or your skin was lighter, or your hair was longer, and your eyes were lighter." "If only you were taller or spoke a second language." It gets more ridiculous because as you age, a natural process every living being experiences, you are now faced with comments like, "You are not getting younger," or "If only you were younger."

You stand strong and confident now, ready to hold your crown up and empower other women. You know you may sometimes be faced with opinions of others who feel entitled to voice their reasons why you didn't meet their requirements. However, you now understand that someone else's opinion of you is none of your business. It doesn't matter what someone's opinion of you is. What matters is how you see yourself. You understand that you will never be perfect for anyone because perfection is a myth; it is nonexistent.

Your aha season fell upon you when the world stopped. You were forced to slow down. Self-development began. You were forced to ask, "Who am I?"

Who are *you*? Not your title, nor accolades, or possessions. With everything stripped away. Reflect, be true to yourself.

You bravely hold many titles: sister, friend, mother, aunty, wife. And your true power is in being all of those at the same time – never just one. You are not your titles.

Who are *you*? Since your journey from that place of being unable to speak up, unable to create healthy boundaries, you now understand that how you allow others treat you is a reflection of how you value yourself. You hold the key to your own happiness. Happiness lies in your own hands. As you transitioned from a child to a woman, you were always seeking outside validation. You did what others wanted instead of following your own desires. You never knew who you were nor your true purpose or value.

You no longer must question your value to others because you understand that if you have to, then it's time to reevaluate that relationship. You learned that there are many kinds of relationships, some of them your heart and mind choose, and others were chosen for you. They all have one thing in common - you. You can define them by what you choose to accept. You can change the course at any time.

Now reflecting, you understand that love is a choice. You must choose to love and respect yourself. With self-love and self-respect comes an open window for reciprocation. Others around you will be forced to love and respect you since they are only allowed to treat you the way you allow them to.

You write yourself a love letter, it reads:

I am unique and outstanding
I am beautiful beyond description
My eyes are the window of my soul
They are the color of love
My hair embellishes me
And my captivating smile is contagious; my lips are as soft as a rose petal
I illuminate every room, and my energy is uplifting
I am a work of art
I am a work of art

I don't wear my heart on my sleeve

THE GREATNESS IN YOU

I choose not to wait on someone to love me because I love myself first
I am love eternal
I am love
I fall in love with me
You are, I am Adornami
You are, I am Adornami

I am beautiful beyond description
I act with love and kindness toward myself
I forgive myself.
I forgive others.
I fall in love with myself.
I believe in me
I am powerful.
There is greatness in me
There is greatness in you.
I see the greatness in me.

You are, I am Adornami.

ANDREA EDWARDS ADAMS

About Andrea Adams

She dives into life fully through the exploration of new experiences with adventures fueled by curiosity and love. Skydiving, scuba diving, horseback riding, coasters, motorbikes, tranquil foods, big city lights picture taking, nature views and high heel shoes are a few of her favorite things. Also, a lover of books, this avid reader is the co-founder of "KEG Book Club", "KEG Kids Book Club" and "KEG Tweens Book Club;" and book podcast called "B.A.B.B.L.E With Me." This speaker, coach, mentor, radio, and television host "Power Voice" was unleashed after receiving mentorship from Les Brown. Andrea was also mentored to "Think Into Results" by Jon Talarico and uses this experience through role modeling and self-expression, to empower youths to develop public speaking skills, access their inner self-talk, change their mindset, and transform their lives by improving their relationship with themselves and others. She is the founder of "Adornami Llc", "Adornami Learning Institute," "Global Kids Speak Oratory Club" and "Caribbean Things by Adornami" Connect: www.linktr.ee/adornami

Growing Into Your Voice
By Jodie Solberg

*"It took me quite a long time to develop a voice, and now that I have it,
I am not going to be silent."*
-Madeleine Albright

You have a voice, even if you haven't discovered it yet. It is as powerfully unique and individual as you are. You were born with the ability to step into your greatness by using that voice. It is inside you, perhaps hidden deep within, waiting for you to develop it, to grow and strengthen it. Finding and growing your voice will impact not only every area of your own life, but it will impact the lives of countless others, creating a ripple effect, the magnitude of which you can only imagine. I know this to be true because I have been on this journey myself, and growing into my voice changed my life in remarkable ways, so I know it can change yours as well.

Today, I am proud to say I am an international speaker and author. But I didn't always see myself that way or even imagine that one day I would say those words. In fact, I spent most of my early life terrified of speaking in front of groups and being recorded on video. I am an introvert, and growing up, I was quiet, shy, and reserved. It wasn't that I didn't have anything to say, as I was very independent and had a strong mind of my own. It also wasn't that I didn't like people because I loved connecting with people and had a lot of friends. I was also highly empathic, knowing from a young age that I wanted to become a therapist to help people heal. But I was more comfortable one-on-one, not in front of a classroom or in other large groups. I had strong inner convictions, but I was lacking in knowing how to project outward confidence. In school, people would often comment that I put my head down whenever I walked into a room. I didn't want to be noticed, let alone to be the center of attention.

As I got older, however, small hints of my natural leadership abilities began to show through. Known as responsible with great empathy and patience with others, I was asked to take on leadership roles. First as a student teacher and peer counselor, and then at one of my first jobs in high school working in retail, when I was promoted to assistant manager and given the responsibility to close the store on my own. The adults in my life saw glimmers of greatness in me before I saw it in myself. But the real tests started when I was doing my internships to become a therapist. My fear of public speaking and video cameras was still very prevalent, but in order to pursue a career I was so incredibly passionate about, I had to face those fears and do it anyway. Suddenly in my early 20s, I was facilitating parenting training classes, guiding children and teens through therapy exercises, supervising court-ordered visitation in severe abuse cases, and giving recommendations about custody outcomes. So many people were looking at me to lead them. To do this, I had to step into my confidence, release the fear of what other people would think, and realize that I had something to say that others could relate to and benefit from.

The true test came when I started graduate school for clinical psychology. Working in a mental health clinic, all our client therapy sessions were video recorded, and then we would sit around a conference table and watch the videos for feedback. In my first year of grad school, I was also dating my now husband of over 20 years, and he was deployed overseas in the Navy. This was just after 9/11, and a big box electronics store had offered for loved ones of deployed troops to have a professionally recorded video message sent on our behalf as Christmas gifts. This was such an incredible opportunity, as we had been separated for many months, only able to email basic messages and speak by phone for 10 minutes every few weeks. So, very aware of my fears but also caring even more about sending this very special message, I subjected myself to the video. With my voice shaking and visibly fighting back the tears, I managed to make my way through, saying all I wanted to express. That was a pivotal time in my life, as I learned how to harness my voice, growing my confidence bit by bit, one opportunity at a time. I realized the importance of having passion and purpose and that I could do anything using those as my motivators. When I understood why it was worth it to me to push through my fears and take action, I was able to face those fears and do it anyway, gaining more and more confidence with each experience. In the process of becoming a therapist, I was learning emotional management and assertiveness skills that guided me in presenting myself with greater outward confidence to match my inner strength and resolve.

That focus on learning and growth also propelled me forward in starting my own business as a consultant and coach for other female entrepreneurs. I had always worked in high school and college, but graduate school presented new challenges in terms of lack of time and the accumulation of debt. This new business venture led me to step into the role of leader, and I continued to build my confidence in using my voice incrementally. First with one-on-one appointments, then leading small groups, then larger groups through networking, which led me to guest teaching at a college business class on professional interviewing and presenting yourself with confidence. I truly was coming full circle, the student now becoming the teacher. I began stepping up more and more to be a leader both in my community and in my career. Eventually, I started showing up online and wanted to start my own private practice. The thought of working virtually from home after so many years of working with non-profit organizations and court-appointed clients intrigued me, and I wanted to learn all that I could about social media. This was a whole new world, outside my comfort zone once again. But I also knew how much I wanted that lifestyle, and the ability to reach more people by working virtually meant I could help clients from all around the world, not just in my immediate area. I started taking action, learning from mentors, and growing my own audience. Showing up online began to open doors for opportunities to be a guest speaker for other people's audiences, be on podcasts and join speaking tours, reaching thousands of people in an international audience. From those speaking opportunities, even more doors opened, including invitations to become an author and reach more people than ever before. It is truly nothing that I could have ever imagined for myself, back when I was that shy, quiet girl who looked down when she walked into a room. But to quote William James, philosopher, and father of American psychology, "The greatest use of a life is to spend it on something that will outlast it." I know that the effects of using my voice to help people in their healing journey will echo through the lives of generations to come and thus will live on long after me.

Today, in my private mental wellness practice, I help others find their own unique identity and voice and grow both their inner and outer confidence. Just as my own personal growth in finding my voice and stepping into my greatness has been a lifelong journey, it truly is a process, not something that happens overnight. There isn't a destination or some point where you will have arrived. But in that journey of growth, there are very tangible steps that you can take to identify, define and begin to grow your own voice. First, be intentional about looking at each new experience as being a step toward that growth and looking for the lessons you can learn from it. It can feel scary to step outside your comfort zone, but a zone of growth and learning lives between where you are comfortable now and what seems scary. Focus on expanding your comfort zone one small step at a time rather than trying to make giant leaps all at once, which can cause overwhelm and anxiety and shut you down. Confidence is built by taking consistent action, and those small gradual steps you take will accumulate as you make progress in stretching your belief in what you can achieve. Keep in mind that it's not about the absence of fear but how you respond to it. As actress and writer Carrie Fisher said, "Stay afraid but do it anyway. What's important is the action. You don't have to wait to be confident. Just do it, and eventually, the confidence will follow." Consistency both in cultivating a growth mindset and taking action is key to building confidence. Create new positive affirmations telling yourself that you are learning, growing, and becoming stronger in finding your voice and sharing it with others, and take small actions toward that goal daily.

Another important step toward growing into your voice is to be aware that your voice is unique, unlike anyone else's. This means that finding your voice is not at all about being someone you aren't or imitating anyone else. It's about becoming the best version of you and tapping into who you were created to be! I mistakenly thought that I wasn't cut out to be a speaker because I didn't have a loud voice. Now I'm often told that one of my greatest strengths is having a voice that is calming and soothing. You don't have to be loud to be powerful; being assertive is not the same as being aggressive. But perhaps your voice is naturally louder, and you have been shushed and told you needed to tone it down and be quieter all your life. If that's the case, unleash your enthusiasm and let the true you shine through! Many of us were taught growing up that we needed to play small, to fit in, and that standing out was a bad thing. In stepping into your greatness and using your voice, the opposite is true. It's about becoming more of the true you without worrying about what others will think because the right people, your audience, will be magnetized to you when you let go of that past programming and show up as authentically yourself. Stepping into your greatness is stepping into being your own remarkable self and sharing that with the world.

Once you have adopted a growth mindset and recognized that you have a voice that is all your own, it's key to become clear about what message you want to share and why. What are you most passionate about, and how can you take that passion and use your unique voice to fulfill your purpose? Take time to get to know yourself and create a vision for not just your life but how you will affect the lives of others by growing stronger in using your voice. Make the decision each day to take a step forward in your journey. As psychologist Abraham Maslow said, "One can choose to go back toward safety or forward toward growth. Growth must be chosen again and again; fear must be overcome again and again." Stepping into our power and greatness allows us to reach countless people, affect generations, and attract who we were meant to help. You serve no one by NOT stepping into your power. Growing into my voice has helped me to build a rewarding life and career of purpose and fulfillment, and I know that growing into your voice will help you do the same!

About Jodie Solberg

    Jodie Solberg is a Mental Wellness and Success Coach, Certified Master Hypnotherapist, Transformational Speaker, International Best-Selling Author, and the founder of Psyched Up Success. Jodie loves working with purpose-driven professionals who are on a mission to live in alignment with their passion and values to create real and lasting change in their lives and the world around them. She helps them tap into the power of their subconscious mind to gain the clarity and confidence they need to up-level and achieve both their personal and professional goals.

    Jodie has been working therapeutically for more than 20 years, with degrees in both Psychology and Sociology. She started her entrepreneurial journey as a consultant and coach for female entrepreneurs while still in graduate school studying Clinical Psychology, which is where she first began practicing as a Hypnotherapist as well. Jodie's experience working with diverse populations such as adults and children suffering from the effects of abuse, teens in after-school programs and group homes, parenting coaching programs, people dealing with chronic illnesses and addiction, and burned-out caregivers gives her a unique perspective to help her clients overcome their limiting beliefs, break through blocks to progress, and heal past hurts so they can be free from anxiety and fear, beat burnout, and have more inner peace and joy, and create work-life harmony.

Alongside her therapeutic career, Jodie is also known for her work as a consultant and coach for women in business. Her transformative coaching programs build self-esteem and confidence and increase focus, strength, resilience, and emotional intelligence in her clients. Jodie teaches about the importance of prioritizing self-care so they can go out and give back to their families and communities to create positive changes in the world and serve others as their best selves.

Jodie founded Psyched Up Success in 2019, fulfilling her long-standing dream of having her own private mental wellness practice, working virtually with clients worldwide from her dream home in the foothills of the mountains in the Pacific Northwest. Always a believer in creating work-life harmony, Jodie enjoys spending time outdoors and traveling with her family in search of great food, music, and culture. Jodie is also a great contributor to her community, with a long history of volunteerism. In addition to her own personal fulfillment, Jodie's greatest joy and purpose is in helping others to find their voice, become their best selves, create a life they love, and pass those lessons on to the next generation.

To connect with Jodie, please email her directly at jodie@psychedupsuccess.com or visit her website at www.psychedupsuccess.com. You may also follow her on social media on Instagram at @psyched_up_success or Facebook at @psychedupsuccess

THE GREATNESS IN YOU

1983
By Carmen Cadena

We all have greatness in us, but unfortunately, we waste so much time admiring and wanting the greatness of others.

I discovered this truth about myself in my 30s after trying to be like everybody else. I was spending money I did not have and buying clothes I could not afford. I tried hard to keep up with society. I worked three jobs at some point to be able to afford what I thought was supposed to be life. I slept very little in order to fulfill my commitments at work. Bills were piling up, and I felt as empty as my bank account. This behavior of fitting in did not happen overnight, and having no awareness of it made it difficult to change. A decade or so went by, and I was sitting in a jail cell. I wondered what it would take for me to stop my obsession with fitting in. Who was I trying to prove anything to!? And why? Or for what? I embarked on a long journey trying to forget that I was me. Just another undocumented Latino in the USA trying to thrive but was merely surviving. I wanted to hide my past out of fear of rejection. I was trying to prove that I belonged just like everybody else. What I went through in Mexico changed me, and so did every experience or the lack thereof.

Looking back at my life, I felt like I lived under a curse or a spell. My story is remarkably familiar, nothing special nor unique: born in the hood, from a teenage mother, no dad, raised by grandparents, humble beginnings, sexual abuse, domestic violence, drugs, and violence on the streets; maybe it resonates.

Grandma said I should have been born a boy since I acted like one. Do you know the kid who always gets in trouble in the classroom for talking back or, even worse, getting into a fight with other boys? Well, that was me. I did not fit in with the girls, and the boys were bullies, and I was the girl not to back down. As a result, I ended up at the principal's office for either causing a fight, getting into a fight, or stabbing a boy with a pencil to defend myself. I still question if my behavior was the result of some of the traumatic events I had experienced.

The man who molested me had awoken a rush of emotions —one of them was excitement. My subconscious mind sought after the excitement in every situation. I was addicted to the adrenaline rush I felt in extreme scenarios, but I was not aware of it. That is what made me feel different. I was a risk-taker, and the girls in my classroom were not. I did not think like them, nor did I act like them.

Feeling different came with its challenges. It made me act differently, and it would get me in trouble most of the time. Though I was a great student with some of the highest grades in the whole school, I still felt like I did not belong. I guess the feeling started at home after I realized that the people I called "mom" or "dad" were my grandparents, or the ones I knew as "sisters" were my aunts. I certainly could not fit in. I did not look like them, and I did not even have the same last name. My grandpa's daughter from a previous marriage constantly reminded me that the one I called "dad" was not related to me.

Story time at bedtime was my favorite. Grandma was full of stories that happened to her growing up. She shared her brave moments and the sad ones too. For instance, when she lost her dad. She also shared how much she loved him and how much it hurt when he died. I didn't understand pain the way I do now. Now I understand the tears in her eyes when she shared those stories with me. Some nights she would share stories about my mom when she was young. She would say that I reminded her sometimes of her.

The monthly mail was my favorite occasion. The mailman would deliver my mom's letter from Los Angeles. When the letter arrived, I could see how meaningful it was for grandma to hear from my mom again. My mom had moved to Los Angeles to get a fresh start in life. My dad had taken away from her the privilege of being a normal teenager. He got my mom pregnant when she was 17, and then he fled. My mom then moved to The City of Angels – I used to imagine the angels living up in the sky, like the angels Grandma talked about at night. I had imagined my mom living somewhere in the sky, perhaps in a cloud. Grandma reinforced the belief by agreeing with me every time I said it. Oh, the little knowledge I had of the world. I often looked up, hoping to see her wave at me someday. Each time an airplane flew by, I ran outside, thinking mom was in one of them. I don't recall questioning it at all. It was a fantasy I believed in. My earliest memory of my mom was when grandma showed me a photo of my mom holding some flowers and wearing a lavender color. The closest thing I had to her were those letters, the smell of her perfume sprayed on the envelope, and the red kiss print she used to say goodbye on the second page.

Children are resilient, brave, and intelligent. We all have our own God-given superpower. Mine was strength. I cannot recall a day when life was peaceful. I guess the time I felt the most peaceful was when grandma was not mad at us for not cleaning up.
Our crumbling humid house looked old and dirty, but it was only from the humidity the walls soaked up from the neighbors' trees.

It terrified me to hear her call my name because it meant that I was in trouble. I wrote letters to express my dislike of being in trouble. Having no one to talk to and no one to understand me was frustrating. The pen and paper were my best friends, and writing had become my favorite form of self-expression. Other times I wrote poetry, and other times I drew. My aunts avoided trouble by following the rules. I, on the other hand, had my own made-up rules. I dreamed of the day that I was old enough to move far away, away from grandma, away from school, and away from all the violence on the streets. I was scared. Especially after I saw how some gang members stabbed a man right outside my house, everyone thought he was dead until the man stood up soaked in his own blood. Experiences like that shaped who I was to become someday.

Only God knows why children go through hardships. For many years I could not look at pictures of my childhood. Let alone pictures of me. I was such a happy little girl. One day things were scary, and the following day I was back to being the playful child that I was. Unlike adults who find any excuse to complain, I found every reason to play and be happy.

As I was holding a picture of myself as a grown woman, I couldn't help it, and I cried. I held the picture close to my heart, and for once, I was able to have a heart-to-heart with that little girl again. I couldn't help but wonder how much she must have needed a mom like the mom I have become—wishing that I could have been there to comfort her and to love her the way she deserved. I wanted to reassure her how loved she was and how deserving she was of all that love. I wanted to tell her that though mom and dad were not in her life, and even though grandpa only had one leg, those were only small bumps on the road to her best self. Unfortunately, it's not possible to go back and save her from the addiction or domestic violence. I wouldn't be able to save her from the sexual abuse. I wouldn't save her from all the rejection that was to come her way. The paradox is that if I could have had the power to go back, maybe I wouldn't have been the woman that I am today. In the end, that little girl saved me: her strength, her beautiful heart, and her determination to keep going saved my life.

    I don't know what you're going through as you read this, but I know one thing: we all have greatness within us, whether you believe it or not. Life is not fair, it never was, and it never will be. Our stories feel so personal to us because they are happening to us. I wished that my dad had been there. I wished that my mom would've never left. But never forget the God we serve.

    My God took me through the storm holding my hand, and it didn't feel that way in the beginning, but I am alive for a reason. My job is not finished. If you feel like you don't fit in, congratulations. You are different. You stand out from the crowd and belong at the top. When I was in the jail cell, I knew that I didn't go through all that pain to take it to the grave. I didn't know what I was good at aside from creating chaos and trouble, just like everyone around me said. Not fitting in is part of my story, and that's OK. Because I fit in my daughter's heart, I fit in with what the Bible says about my life, and I fit in with myself.

> Life is never fair.
> Life is never just.
> Life is simply life.
> And to that, we must adjust.
>
> Life is as you see it
> Be it black or be it blue
> Based on your understanding

THE GREATNESS IN YOU

Of your story and your truth

Miracles always happen
Every second of each day
But it is in the eyes of the beholder
What you see and what you say

Life owes me nothing
Not a penny, nor excuse
If you play the game of life
You can win, and you can lose

Life is never fair
Life is never just
Life is simply life
And to that, we must adjust.

Written by: Carmen Cadena

CARMEN CADENA

About Carmen Cadena

Carmen Cadena is an Experiential and Clarity Coach. A Best-selling author, poet, storyteller, vlogger, teacher, and mentor. She has genuinely shared with many her in-depth ideas, processes, and know-how to prepare those who seek clarity in their life.

She is a certified Health and Life coach and a Success Advisor who is currently working on establishing her own business in the coaching industry. She has also connected herself to many personalities that molded her into a POWERFUL and UNBREAKABLE woman.

Carmen's upbringing was not easy, and the challenges she faced in the early years of her life made her feel that she was not an ordinary girl, "[She] was different" –as she would say. Her ambition for success and personal development helped her overcome obstacles that could have discouraged many.

What is so amazing about Carmen is that she knows exactly what she wants in life. She is living her purpose, and there is no stopping her. She will always be unapologetic about how others may see her as she courageously fights for her place in this world.

As you dive into her way of thinking, you will realize that hardships happen for us, not to us. Carmen's energy will make you feel UNBREAKABLE when you are in her presence. Her desire is to be healthy, to be heard, felt, and seen, and she wants the same for you.

"To be HUMAN, you can't be just who you are; you need to grow from the hardships of life. Becoming a BETTER VERSION of yourself means being in touch with your own greatness!" -Carmen Cadena

Connect with me:
IG: @coachcarmencadena
FB: Carmen Cadena
Web and Blog: carmenspeaks.com
For questions or bookings, please email:
carmenspeakstoday@gmail.com
Write Me: 21781 Ventura Blvd #470
Woodland Hills, CA 91364

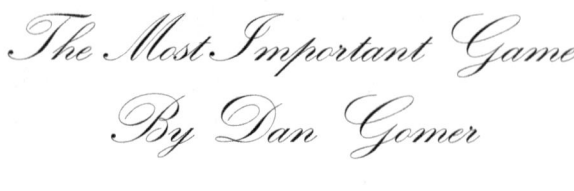

The Most Important Game
By Dan Gomer

L ife is a game, and just like any game, there are wins, losses, victories, and heartbreaks. Just like any game, there are moments where the impossible becomes possible and when dreams crumble, and just like any game, we get to choose how we play. Some of us play to win, hoping that hoisting the trophy will guarantee happiness. Some of us play for the fans in hopes that adoration will fill our cup. Some of us are perfectly content sitting on the sidelines in hopes that everything will simply work out.

And so goes the game of life. We have a choice of how we play. However, not only do we get to choose how we play, but we also get to choose what we play. In other words, we get to define the game that matters to us most—our most important game (MIG).

Once we bring awareness to what we value most and why that's important, we get to play a game where we can't lose. We step onto a playing field where we make the rules and determine the outcome. It's unlike any other game in the world, but it is a game we all have the opportunity to play. We simply have to make a conscious choice to define and then play our most important game.

So, what's your MIG? WHAT do you truly want to create in your life, and WHY is that important to you? Define those questions, and you can start playing your most important game.

I spent the majority of my life secretly struggling with depression and overwhelming feelings of unworthiness. It's no surprise then that one afternoon in 2015, I found myself alone in my bedroom, on the brink of self-destruction. Just like all of us, I had been playing a game my entire life. I just didn't know it yet. Up to that point, I had no idea what I really wanted, and so I was destined to play someone else's game at the cost of my own fulfillment.

THE GREATNESS IN YOU

My game had given me permission to play small and blame others. It was a game where I competed against myself as I undermined my own success. It was a game that nearly took my life. However, on that day in 2015, as I stood alone in my room, I finally realized that I wanted to play a new game. It was time to play that game of "success."

At this time in my life, I was tired of feeling like a failure, so I set out to prove to myself and the world that I could create the kind of success that was obvious to everyone around me. Looking back, I know this was the path I had to travel, but in hindsight, I've realized that when I was defining this new game, I failed to ask myself a simple question that could have saved me a lot of time and energy.

WHY did I want to play this new game?

From childhood, many of us are taught that we should only strive to be the top dog. If we're not first, we're last. Go big or go home! It is perfectly acceptable in our society, if not preached, to strive for the biggest house, the fanciest vacations, and the most elite positions. So, we grind it out, we go to bed later, we wake up earlier, we work through lunch, we skip our breaks, we work to keep pace, we pile on responsibilities, and we do the best we can to convince ourselves that this is the game we are supposed to play.

However, it seems all too common for people to reach their "dreams," achieve greatness and acquire the riches they worked their entire lives for, only to realize that many of the spoils are actually relics of happiness unfulfilled.

In a similar fashion, my journey followed this same path. I put my head down, got after it, and set out to achieve victory. And it paid off! 2020 marked the most productive year of my decade-long career in real estate. I'd nearly doubled my production from the year before. I'd reached a pinnacle that I believed was impossible for someone like me. I had finally succeeded. However, as I stood on the deck of my dream home, gazing at an unobstructed view of the Rocky Mountains, I couldn't help but wonder, "Is this all there is?"

We live in a 10x kind of society. It's as if the phrase "I'm so busy right now" is worn like a badge of honor. Almost as if we're not over-committed, we're lazy. So, we run the gauntlet for two-thirds of our life with the hope that one day we will finally see the opportunity to slow down, retire, and smile once again. Let life begin!

What game are you playing in your life right now? Is it the game you truly want to play? The fact is, we can all improve, so it's not bad to want to play something new. It simply indicates that we want more in our life. So then, what if there was a different game you could be playing? One that isn't about wins and losses, trophies, accolades, or success in the traditional sense. What if there was a game where the act of playing is the ultimate reward?

Perhaps it's time for us to stop asking what do we want to capture from life and start asking who do we want to be? How do we want to show up? How do we want to feel? Think about what might be possible for your life and the lives of the people you serve if you could embody the answers to those questions every day. Don't wait for outside circumstances to gift you with the life you desire. You already have everything you need right within you.

The most important game is played internally, and it is only experienced in the here and now. It's not a destination or something that can be acquired. Therefore, it can't be tallied on a scoreboard or displayed in the hall of fame. The MIG is found in the competition itself. The game within the game. Striving after the spoils of victory is an ever-elusive target with no chance of capturing the deepest form of success.

To be clear, just because we are playing a game for the joy of playing, it doesn't mean that we are not competing at our highest level. I am not talking about giving blue participation ribbons; we all win, pie-in-the-sky shenanigans. No, I am talking about competing at 100% and creating the life you TRULY desire from a place of conscious awareness. I'm talking about a healthy competition where the end game is not just a W but rather something much more fulfilling. A win may be one of the prizes, but not the ultimate prize. Heck, maybe a loss is actually more valuable sometimes. After all, we're talking about your MIG here.

There's magic in competition! Those moments when we know we have to bring our A-game and the pressure is on. Those are the moments that create opportunities for us to find out what we're made of, discover our blind spots, and reinforce our assets. Without competition, how do we learn and grow? Competition is a beautiful thing, and it may be our best teacher, but only if we know what we are competing for (our end game) and, more importantly, WHY we are competing in the first place.

The most important game shows itself when we get curious and seek to understand ourselves on the deepest level. By asking two simple questions: "What do I truly want?" And, "Why do I want that?" over and over again, our MIG begins to reveal itself. The solution to understanding our MIG is very simple yet difficult at the same time. The questions are simple, but answering those questions requires an open mind and a commitment to self-discovery.

Playing our MIG requires courage and vulnerability because we have to call ourselves out and go against the status quo, and sometimes we even have to be willing to miss the game-winning shot when everything is on the line.

This world is our playground if we choose to see it that way, but remember, the joy of a playground is not found in the domination of it but rather in the act of playing on it. We get to create our own reality. Through awareness, you get to choose your game, you get to make up the objectives, and you can change the rules anytime you want. After all, this is your MIG, and you have the power to create whatever you desire.

The more clarity you bring to what you truly want and why that's important to you, the more clearly you understand your MIG. The awareness and willingness to play and grow will ultimately allow you to enjoy the ride as you compete at 100% and create the life you've always dreamed of.

That afternoon in 2015, as I stood in my room, I created a new game for my life, complete with a whole new set of rules and objectives. I called it the game of success. At the time, I thought this new game would make me happy, and while it probably saved my life, it was created in the act of desperation, which is why it didn't bring me the happiness I hoped for. The game of success may not have been my MIG, but that's ok because it was a new game that ultimately moved me forward and fertilized the soil for my own personal growth.

I played the success game for years until that day when I found myself looking out over the Rocky Mountains, wondering why I still wasn't happy. At that moment, a new game emerged, which I play to this day. I have no idea if the game I'm playing right now is right or wrong, but there is one thing I do know. I'm trying, and I believe that's all that really matters in the end.

So, here's my challenge to you. Be willing to play a new game if you want. Even if you're not sure, it's your MIG. Your game doesn't have to be perfect. The important thing is that you are consciously moving forward towards the highest version of yourself. The more you play and explore, the closer you get.

It's ok to play with all sorts of ideas while we grow. It's ok to make mistakes and fail forward. The key is simply knowing that every time we make a conscious choice to grow, we move one step closer to the highest version of ourselves. None of us are ever done playing, refining, or growing. And that is what makes the game of life so much fun.

This chapter is meant to create an opportunity for you to reflect on your most important game, because once we start playing our MIG, the world becomes our playground, and our true nature begins to shine.

What game are you playing right now? Is that the game you want to play, or is there something more fulfilling that lights you up?

What is your MIG?

You have to power to play any game you want. The world is your playground, and the choice to play is yours.

Here's to your journey in our world, my friend. May you find the game you were born to play!

About Dan Gomer

In order to cultivate aspiration in a culture ignited by fleeting successes and social media influences, a sense of unfeigned leadership with a propensity for ethics, personal growth, and credible synergy must be readily available to make an organic impression on the masses. Meeting today's generation with that exact quality; is the effervescent professional, Dan Gomer.

DAN GOMER

Dan Gomer is an educator, coach, Realtor, and serial entrepreneur with a distinguished ability to invoke lasting and profitable change in the lives of others. Having spent many years merging an innate gift for business with note-worthy careers in education and real estate, Dan is known for his ability to build relationships and help clients align with their purpose, shift perspectives, and attain the fulfillment that comes with a purpose-driven lifestyle.

His mantra is simple: He helps people clarify what they truly want so that they can embody the highest vision for their lives.

Avoiding the mundane, Dan Gomer combines his tenacity for life with sincere regard for education, achievement, and community involvement. Dan holds a Bachelor of Arts, in General Earth Science, with an emphasis in Elementary Education, along with certifications in MCNE (Master Certified Negotiation Expert) and CDRE (Certified Divorce Real Estate Expert). His intrinsic leadership has been proven boundless; as his commitment to both personal and professional excellence has yielded diverse achievements and elite membership acquisitions, such as Platinum Club member status with his brokerage for his attainment of 275k in GCI, in 2019 and Vice President Club member status, with his attainment of 386k in GCI, in 2020. Having innate respect for community, Dan served several years as a basketball coach to diverse youth groups.

Whether it is in reality, education, authorship, or world-class coaching, Dan Gomer distinguishes himself as one who is driven to witness the evolution of humanity towards a happier and healthier existence. When he is not out changing the world, he is an asset to his local community and loves spending time with his friends, wife, and two kids in Highlands Ranch, Colorado.

Dan Gomer. Leader. Inculcator. Energizer.
Contact Dan:
www.dangomer.com
facebook: dangomer
danielgomer1@gmail.com

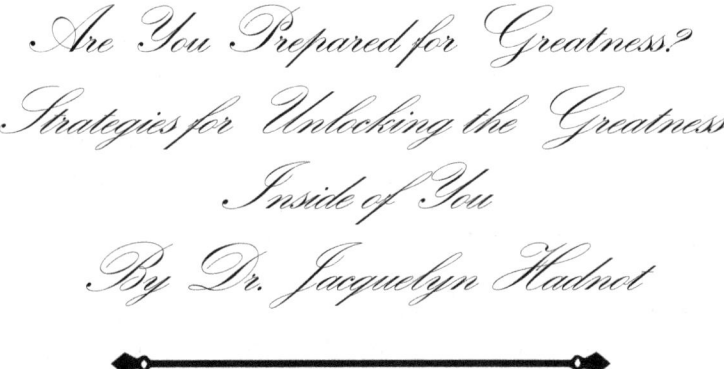

Are You Prepared for Greatness? Strategies for Unlocking the Greatness Inside of You

By Dr. Jacquelyn Hadnot

The word *greatness* has become the latest catchphrase. Greatness has been attributed to many areas and individuals, especially with the popularity of social media. We use acronyms like G.O.A.T. (greatest of all time) to describe high-profile figures who have excelled in areas like sports, music, and acting. Many of the people who have been considered great will tell you that they don't feel great; in fact, they believe the opposite. In their respective fields, they have excelled and made many contributions, but they believe there is always more to life and their contribution to it. They also understand the hard work and responsibility that goes along with being considered great or greatest of all time.

I hope that our journey into the subject of being prepared for greatness will enlighten you on the subject as you prepare to walk in greatness in your life.

What greatness is NOT? First of all, greatness is NOT something handed to you on a silver platter. Greatness is earned. Second, just because you have a large bank account does NOT make you great. Being a social media influencer or celebrity does NOT make you great. Driving an expensive car or living a lavish lifestyle does NOT make you great. Often it simply means that you perform well or have a level of status or position, but it does NOT make you great. Again, greatness is earned.

What is greatness? Merriam-Webster defines greatness as ***the quality or state of being great (as in size, skill, achievement, or power).*** How do you define greatness? Sherman G. Finesilver said about greatness, "*Do not confuse notoriety and* *fame with greatness. Many of the titled in today's world obtained their fame and fortune outside their own merit. On the other hand, I have met great people in the most obscure roles. Greatness is a measure of one's spirit, not a result of one's rank in human affairs. Nobody, least of all mere human beings, confers greatness upon another, for it is not a prize but an achievement. Greatness can crown the head of a janitor just as readily as it can come to someone of high rank."* -Sherman G. Finesilver

Helen Keller explained greatness this way, *"I long to accomplish great and noble tasks, but it is my chief duty to accomplish humble tasks as though they were great and noble. The world is moved along, not only by the mighty shoves of its heroes, but also by the aggregate of the tiny pushes of each honest worker.* -Helen Keller

What does the Word of God have to say about greatness? *"And I will make of thee a great nation, and I will bless thee, and make thy name great; and thou shalt be a blessing."* Genesis 12:2 Many people chase fame and fortune, but are you pursuing greatness? Chasing fame and fortune can be exhausting and disappointing because the road to fame is often paved with failure and setbacks. People who chase fame, fortune, and clout often find that the pursuit is an exercise that leaves many empty holes in them. The sacrifices made are just not worth all the effort. I believe that greatness will find you when you position your life for greatness.

What is true greatness? *"Whoever wants to be great must become a servant."* -Mark 10:43 (MSG). Many great leaders were servants first and embraced the role of servanthood, knowing that it would help to produce character, integrity, and compassion.

Where is greatness found? Greatness can be found in every one of us. We just have to access it. Greatness is not going to knock on your door; you must press into it. We were created by the Divine Greatness of God to be great. He did not intend to make us famous; He said He would make our name great. That was a covenant promise that He would never break, but it is up to us to walk in the greatness that is rightfully ours.

If greatness is rightfully ours, then how do we get to it? How do we embrace the journey to greatness? How do we avoid the pitfalls and excuses that come with failure? Understand that greatness does not run away from failure; greatness will embrace failure and use it as a tool for growth. Your inheritance of greatness is not defined by the expectations of others. When you allow others to define you and your destiny, you will always fall short, get discouraged, and give up.

Again, greatness is rightfully yours, and here are some strategies to prepare yourself for greatness. Do you possess the following attributes that lead you to the place of greatness?

DO YOU POSSESS THE FOLLOWING?

- **Sense of purpose and vision**. Is your sense of purpose clear and concise? You must have a strong sense of purpose and vision in order to move in the direction of greatness.
- **Strong set of core values**. Without a strong sense of core values such as character and integrity, you may get on the road to greatness, but without character and integrity, you will fall by the roadside.
- **Unwavering belief**. Your beliefs develop the foundational rules of how you travel the road to success. You cannot be tossed and driven by your belief system because you will get swept away when adversity arises.
- **Enjoyment of the process**. Greatness is not about the goal as much as it is about the process of getting there. Don't despise the process of growing in greatness.
- **Efficient decision-making**. Greatness is a decision; you must decide that you want to be great. It doesn't matter what you are going through as long as you decide to be great.
- **Daily goals and work habits**. In order to be successful, you must have discipline. Behind every success story is the discipline of creating daily goals backed by work habits that result in huge rewards.
- **Confident self-identification**. Your success and ability to achieve your goals essentially means seeing and identifying yourself as one the most formidable influences on your future.

If you don't possess any of the seven core disciplines, it's time to develop the habits so that you can begin to walk in the greatness that is legitimately yours. When you discover the habits of successful people and integrate them into your life, you will see a mindset reset that will enable you to walk in passion, purpose, and greatness.

I teach on the mindset of greatness, and through my classes, I empower my students with twenty-one strategies that will reset the mindset to tap into the greatness locked inside of them. If you are unprepared for greatness, now is the time to grab these strategies and posture yourself for greatness. Are you prepared for greatness?

Strategies for Preparing Yourself for Greatness

- **Greatness Strategy #1: Create a vision and develop a plan.** Develop a clear picture of what a successful life looks like to you and put together a well-defined set of goals to get you to that life.

- **Greatness Strategy #2: Turn adversity into advantage.** If you are given lemons, learn to make lemonade. Turn your mess into a message of hope, healing, and growth.

- **Greatness Strategy #3: Embrace dissatisfaction.** Discontentment is one of the first steps on the path to greatness. When you become content or complacent, your growth will stop. All leaders are unhappy with something.

- **Greatness Strategy #4: Confess frustration to yourself and to others you trust.** Don't allow pride to keep you muted. Find a confidant to express your feelings of frustration.

- **Greatness Strategy #5: Face discontent with optimism.** If you sink into despair, you're done. Millions of reasons say you can't. Find one reason you can and hang on. One good reason changes you.

- **Greatness Strategy #6: Set realistic goals**. The dream you set for tomorrow will change your today. Does your dream inspire you? If not, it's below you.

- **Greatness Strategy #7: Press through fear**. On the other side of fear is greatness. When you walk in fear, it will keep you average. Let go of average so you can reach higher. Philippians 2:5

- **Greatness Strategy #8: Cultivate a champion's mindset**. Philippians 2:5: *Let this mind be in you, which was also in Christ Jesus.*

- **Greatness Strategy #9: Master your body**. Practice habits of self-care through rest, good eating habits, exercise, and living stress-free.

- **Greatness Strategy #10: Practice positive habits**. Change your habits, and you will change your life. Good habits will yield great results. Develop good habits that will carry over into your vision and dreams.

- **Greatness Strategy #11: Prepare for the unexpected**. Plan for the unexpected so that you will not be shaken when adversity arises.

- **Greatness Strategy #12: Build a winning team**. Surround yourself with success. Read, research, explore, and ask questions.

- **Greatness Strategy #13: Live a life of service**. Serve others by helping others reach their goals. Serve others so they can serve others. Exponential influence begins with multiplication, not individual performance.

- **Greatness Strategy #14: Develop a lifestyle of prayer**. Stay intimate with God so that He can birth greatness

through you. When you are intimate with the Lord, He will impregnate you.
- *Luke 18:1: And he spake a parable unto them to this end, that men ought always to pray, and not to faint.*
- *Ephesians 6:18: Praying always with all prayer and supplication in the Spirit and watching thereunto with all perseverance and supplication for all saints*

- **Greatness Strategy: #15: Don't ride on the coat tail of others**. You will never walk into your destiny when you are riding the coat tail of others. Your purpose is the grand design of God, and He is giving it to you to fulfill.

- **Greatness Strategy #16: Whenever the grasshopper mentality arises, shut it down immediately**. Never compare yourself to others because you will always come up short because we have the tendency to minimize our accomplishments.

- **Greatness Strategy #17: Prioritize your goals**: Manage your time wisely so that you don't become overwhelmed.

- **Greatness Strategy #18: Turn your goals into actions**. Once you have defined and prioritized your goals, turn those goals into actions.

- **Greatness Strategy #19: Master the art of saying "NO."** The word NO is not a cuss word. Don't allow others to keep you so busy with their lives, problems, or visions that you forget about the greatness inside of you.

- **Greatness Strategy #20: Learn from your mistakes**: It is vital to your growth that you learn from your mistakes. It's in learning that you will grow. Learn to accept responsibility for your mistakes and watch your life change.

- **Greatness Strategy #21: Learn from the experts**: Successful people follow successful people. The best way to understand success is to follow successful people.

In closing, success takes hard well-organized, and determined work. It is a step-by-step process, and you cannot afford to skip a step; you must walk it out. Success is within reach if you are willing to put in the work. But in order to do the right work, you must first learn how to be successful. Don't despise the process that you encounter on the road to success. True success will not fall into your lap, and it won't come knocking on your door. You have to do whatever it takes to demolish what's holding you back from reaching your full potential. You are the **only** person who can give yourself permission for greatness. Today is the last day that success will elude you; today is the day to discover the greatness that is inside of you. Are you prepared for greatness? It's time to prepare to unlock the greatness inside of you!

DR. JACQUELYN HADNOT

About Dr. Jaquie Hadnot

Genuine leadership is found amongst those audacious enough to signal the importance of others, to the rest of the world. Trailblazing a path where philanthropy meets world class ingenuity; is the compassionate professional; Dr. Jacquie Hadnot.

Dr. Jacquie Hadnot is an 8x international best-selling author, cleric, entrepreneurial enthusiast, and CEO and Founder of both, **Mallie Boushaye Essentials** and **Purpose Life**

Coaching, LLC. No stranger to establishing anomalous conglomerates, Dr. Hadnot has enjoyed the *flex* of sustaining a six-figure manufacturing and retail business, without compromising the mandate of her life's core intendment; the will to inspire, empower, and implore, people. Reputed for her uncanny ability to shift perspectives, enthuse purpose, and invoke change in diverse clientele, Dr. Jacquie Hadnot remains a highly sought after proponent in the world of business, ministry, and social purlieus.

Her mantra is simple: Dr. Jacquie is led by a conclusive resolve to help individuals attain the strategies they need to succeed in life, because therein lies assured greatness, and that greatness lives in all of humanity.

Dr. Jacquie Hadnot combines unyielding excellence with a sincere regard for education, achievement, and community involvement. She holds a PhD in Pastoral Theology, a MA in Leadership and Education, a BA in Theology, and a degree in Accounting and Business Finance. In accommodation to her propensity for educational acumen, Dr. Jacquie has also attained certifications in life, business, and cancer care coaching. Her contributions in vocation, workshop facilitation, and ministerial advancements are awe-inspiring; as she has not only managed to lead in sales and ethics, but also in creating quintessential forms of humanitarianism, including support groups and multi-dimensional outreach programs. Dr. Jacquie's serviceability has proven highly prolific, as she was the **2022 recipient of the Joe Biden Presidential Lifetime Achievement Award**; easily yielding her one of the most effective leaders of our time.

Whether she is coaching the masses, empowering entrepreneurs, or overseeing her own television network, Dr. Jacquie Hadnot displays no corroboration in slowing down. When she is not out leaving a lasting impression on the world, she is an asset to her local communal body, and a loving member of her family and friendship circles.

Dr. Jacquie Hadnot. Leader. Organizer. Philanthropist.

Expect Great Things in Your Life
By Carolyn Brooks-Collins

"You must learn a new way to think before you can master a new way to be."
– Marianne Williamson

Has there ever been a time when you've had a song playing in your head, and you couldn't stop thinking about it all day? Well, for me, that song is "I'm living my best life…." I know there's more to it, but I always ruin the rest of it and make up my own lyrics, so I won't go any further. However, the song's hook keeps repeatedly playing in my mind. I would say that's my mantra and exactly how I feel – At the age of 68, I am finally beginning to live my best life and continue to grow and learn so that my life gets better and better. I am living my life abundantly and expecting great things, including taking the best care of myself.

When was the last time you expected great things in your life? Was it today, last week, or last year? Maybe it was when you were a child, on your birthday or even Christmas? Perhaps, it was so long ago that you have forgotten. Whenever it was, the question becomes, why aren't you expecting great things every day now? More importantly, what has changed your perspective? We expect small, unimportant things to occur daily, but many have stopped believing and expecting the big things in life. These big things are the dreams we have hidden away, even forgotten, or at the least have not shared. We all have the power to take control of our lives, find our purpose, live on our terms, and live life to the fullest. Doing so can alter our life by rejecting anything contrary to our desires and goals. When we control our lives, we learn to live from the inside out, singularly focusing on our goals and blocking out all the extraneous external noise. Living from the inside out means we stop being the thermometer in our lives, reacting to everything external to us, and we set our internal compass or thermostat towards our vision and goals. My message is to start living expectantly, knowing you can achieve and have anything and everything you want in life. You can accomplish great things regardless of what you've been through and your current experiences. We need to know that the life God has planned for us is bigger than the one we live.

I'm sure you're wondering how this is even possible, that perhaps I don't know your story, and if I did, I wouldn't say dare say this. I realize life is complex, and we all have our stories, some more heartbreaking than others. However, we have the power to create and achieve whatever we can imagine. Your greatness is your mind – yes, your wonderful and powerful mind! Whatever you can visualize and imagine, you can attain. The mind is a powerful tool and controls everything we do. Our conscious and subconscious minds work together to move us to our results. We first have thoughts, feelings, actions, and ultimately our results. Simply put, we change our results when we change our thoughts, our mindset, or our beliefs that shape how we view the world. These beliefs also influence how we think, feel, and behave.

So, what do you envision for yourself? Do you have big dreams? Perhaps you are like I was and have stopped dreaming. I didn't even realize it, for it was not a conscious thought. A few years ago, when asked what my big dreams were, the question stopped me in my tracks, and I had to admit I had stopped dreaming. I was in my late 60's and had been in survival mode for a very long time, taking care of my family, focusing on maintaining a roof over my head and keeping a job, conforming to the rules of society, and doing what was expected of me on my job and focusing on not rocking the boat too much, so much so that I had forgotten how to dream. I was playing it safe and planning for "retirement," a time in my mind that meant we stop working hard and rest. At work, though there were times when I challenged the comments that my personality was too big, too strong, or "too something else," for the most part, I played it safe, thinking I needed to hold on to the job for in a few years and then retire. I was not surrounded by people who encouraged me to succeed, perhaps because no one had encouraged them. However, that changed when I encircled myself with people who thought you are never too old to start dreaming, which meant you never stop dreaming! As C.S. Lewis said, "You are never too old to set another goal or dream a new dream." Thus began this new phase of my life.

However, the question remains, why do we stop dreaming? Why don't we recognize the greatness that is within us? As Les Brown says, "You can't see the picture when you are in the frame," meaning we don't have the same perspective when we are in the middle of a situation, or we can't evaluate our skills because we are accustomed to seeing our shortcomings and our faults. Yes, we can be our worst enemy and chief critic! Sometimes it's the company we keep – people who have stopped dreaming and therefore don't want us to dream. At other times it is our fears that hold us back - fears of failing, fears of being ridiculed for trying something different, or even fear of success. Staying where we are is more comfortable because we know what to expect versus traveling that unnavigated path. Other times we have a dream but feel we aren't ready, taking one course after another. But we need to face our fears and take the leap! Bob Proctor of the Proctor Gallagher Institute was known for saying, "Faith and fear both require a belief in something we cannot see, so why not choose faith." Sometimes we need to step out on faith, but not blind faith. We choose faith, and then we work to achieve our dreams. As the Bible says, faith without works is dead. It takes more than just wanting to reach a target. It requires work – hard, consistent work, steady work toward a dream to attain a goal.

As we begin to live expectantly, this means all aspects of our lives – <u>professionally</u>, <u>personally</u>, and <u>financially</u>. Included in the "personal" category is the need to take care of our health, both our mental and physical health. Often as we age and enter our 50s, 60's, and 70's, we begin to feel we have less control over our lives, especially the physical part. We start to believe that we have to accept that our bodies will begin to break down as a fact of life. We stop doing the things we can maintain our health naturally and start taking more medicine. It is not uncommon to see a group of seasoned citizens sitting around discussing their aches, pains, and drugs. If we are not careful, we could adopt the mindset that this is a normal process and there's nothing we can do about it!

You have more power and control than you think. Half the battle is believing we can change our circumstances. Part of the battle also is changing our behaviors to match those beliefs we espouse; in other words, our actions and words must be aligned. We need to elevate the quality of our lives and raise the expectations of what we can achieve and how we can live. Attitude is the key to any success we have. Earl Nightingale stated, "We become what we think about." Sometimes that also means changing the dynamics of our (genes, characteristics, inherited properties, etc.)

Friends and family have always "accused" me of walking through life with rose-colored glasses or looking at life optimistically. While others may find it problematic, I have never seen anything negative about this and used this approach regarding my health. My mom, who I resemble increasingly as I get older, had severe osteoarthritis and, at the time of her death in 1995 at the age of 74, had already had three hip replacements, one side twice. She was also a candidate for knee and shoulder replacements, and her doctors discussed which should be done next. Prescription and OTC medicines in the early/mid-1990s, not being what they are today, left my mom in excruciating pain during the last 10-15 years of her life as most of her major joints were at a point of bone-on-bone. It's a fair statement to say I have been running from her genes for a long time. However, as the phrase goes, "You can run, but you can't hide!" For me, this means my mom's problems with her joints. As much as I wanted to avoid it, I, too, needed knee replacement surgery. After years of other therapies, including chiropractors, physical therapy, knee injections with hyaluronic gels, and steroids, my knees became bone on bone without cartilage. People told me not to have surgery, to continue with the shots, but as my legs became more bowed and deformed, I relented and decided to have surgery in 2016 at 62.

Though I had not been introduced to mindset thinking formally, I believed in the power of prayer and mind over matter. We can take positive actions and improve our health by maintaining a positive attitude. Well, that applied to my surgery as well. I worked hard before and after my surgery to ensure it would go well. I prepared my body by working with a trainer to strengthen my knees and legs and started taking extra vitamins and eating better to improve my nutrition. Afterward, I followed the physical therapist's instructions and exercised every day. Most importantly, I visualized myself back to my routine, walking and exercising without pain. Within six weeks, I was back at work and walking without a cane. I took the same approach later that year when I had rotator cuff surgery and two years later when I had another total knee replacement. (Yes, I am rather bionic now!) I found the best doctor, prepared my body, and then had the calmness of mind that all would go well. The mind is so powerful. We can tell our subconscious mind anything, and it will be impressed upon it. I know many other people who are apprehensive about having surgery and put it off, preferring to deal with the pain or not being able to walk because they expect it not to go well. Maintaining a positive attitude and embracing the idea that "we are who we think we are" will help determine our quality of life!

Know that you have the power to live your dreams by staying focused, motivated, and disciplined. Wherever you are now, know that you are on the right path to bringing your dreams to life. So, start taking control of your life, living it to the fullest, living it expectantly and abundantly. Then you will know the greatness that is in you and start living your best life!

About Carolyn Brooks-Collins

Lives are often changed when ignited by esteemed voices, enthused to share the message of empowerment, inspiration, and hope, with the world. Emboldened with this exact synergy; is the compassionate professional, Carolyn Brooks-Collins.

Carolyn Brooks-Collins is a #1 best-selling international author, organizational proponent, and CEO and Founder of M. Carolyn Brooks-Collins, LLC; a multi-dimensional coaching and consulting specialty fashioned to develop and educate professionals on how to eliminate personal and financial profligacy to experience persistent victory, in their own lives.

Her mantra is simple: Carolyn is passionate about empowering women to transform their lives, step into their purpose, and become financially independent.

No stranger to personal excellence, Carolyn couples her proficiency with sincere regard for education, achievement, and communal involvement. She holds a B.A. in Accounting, an MBA in Project Management, and is a certified CPA (Certified Public Accountant), CFE (Certified Fraud Examiner), and CGMA (Chartered Global Management Accountant).

Yielding an undeniable propensity for leadership, Carolyn holds memberships with several organizations, including the Black Speakers Network, Innovation Women, and the Association of Certified Fraud Examiners, along with the GA Chapter of the ACFE.

Displaying an uncanny ability for the stage, Carolyn Brooks-Collins is a Certified Speaker and has successfully completed programs with world-renowned influencers, such as The Power Voice with Les Brown and Lead the Field with Jon Talarico; along with her current enrollment in the Global Speakers University, with Dr. Cheryl Wood. Trailblazing a path for others, she developed her own program (women of purpose network) in hopes that women would find their own voice and begin their personal journey toward becoming the best version of themselves.

Significantly inspired by empowered individuals dedicated to breaking barriers and reconstructing societal norms, Carolyn is committed to the call of drawing out this same excellence in others. In that spirit, she vows to remain a reputable resource to personal and corporate environments, teaching the world the importance of freedom in all areas of life.

When Carolyn is not out showing the world how to win, she is an asset to her local community and a loving member of her family and friendship circles.

Carolyn Brooks-Collins. Leader. Organizer. Innovator.

Connect with Carolyn Brooks
www.carolynbrookscollins.com
Facebook: www.facebook.com/MCarolynBrooksCollins

Embrace The Wilderness
By Angela Bennett

I am dying...but I look great!
A friend called to congratulate me and said, *"You look so good. You're doing so well; look at you, you're killing it..."*

Not knowing...it was killing me.

"Thank you," I said. Receiving was all I could do. The interaction was short, effervescent even, and wholly devastating.

No one in the world could see what was inside. The glamour shone, the put-together look so perfectly put together. Matching outfits and red-soled shoes coloured everything for them when the real picture painted a far cry – a rawer, wilder, darker scream from within that no outsider could have guessed at.

I was drowning.

Killing myself was the solution.

Not just an out for the pain, but a relief for all those I touched in my wake...my living wake. It felt like time for another kind of wake, and I felt reconciled to an ending of my choosing.

The bottom of the bottle. Literally - looking into it and myself, from the outside in.

An outsider hovering over her on the bathroom floor as she went to end it all...bottles strewn, pills upended, water streaming, tears too, intention bound...

But who was the real outsider?

Those looking in from a distance? Or me? Disconnected me, who knew the truth.

There was no greatness within me; there was just sorrow. She, who knew exactly what lipstick and heels were redirecting everyone's attention away from.

The disconnect was palpable, inescapable.

The emptiness ran deep. Roots had spread into every fibre of my being and taken hold... active rot, everywhere threads of hollowness and quiet desolation, and still, no one could tell.

That no one even suspected was the bigger tragedy.

The charade of my life was only foolproof for so long. The outside projection of having arrived. Somewhere.

My lipstick smile is megawatt. I know it is. I relied upon it.

But it hid years of shame as a prostitute for a profession. My secret life - hidden behind toned arms and high-end heels. Arms that have been bruised and beaten and heels that have been discarded down back-alley stairs as I ran for my life.

Make-up can only do so much to make up for all I have done and lived through - put my children through. No concealer was ever enough to mask the ugliness from myself.

The quiet irony of having spent so many years and so many dollars to portray myself so civilised was not lost on me while in full judgement mode, primal and unhinged as I spoke to myself in ways that would ruin a small child for life.

I no longer recalled the joy my inner child once danced in the rain with, the fearlessness she roamed the playground with, or the laughter she knew was contagious because it came from the depths of her belly.

My mind had plunged to new depths. Had shifted gears into survival mode, my nervous system was in flight mode, and my internal esteem - feral mode. A wilderness surrounded me that I could see no way out of and no way clear of. There were too many tempests and storms for me to ever be given a season of calm again, let alone forgiveness, let alone peace.

Destruction felt obvious. Clean almost. It had already claimed me anyway, except that still, no one knew.

With this one act, they would.

The outsider in me watched on until she had finally had enough. Enough of all the triaging to stay covered over but not enough to watch me end it all. It felt like the outsider in me fought hardest in those desperate moments, to rally...to see the person within, to catch an ember that was still worth something, still someone worth fighting for.

My core was damaged, sure, but still kind somehow. Kicked in, yes, but still held compassion for others. Destroyed maybe, but not dead.

Yet...

It felt like an incineration of my old self. How fire can ravage a landscape and yet Mother Nature, in her tenacity, can still grow back in another season. Thrive even. My outsider was not defining me by the fire, the flood, or any other catastrophic mash-up I had put myself in the middle of. My outsider had witnessed it all and still had the capacity to pull me from death and embrace me.

The wilderness started to feel welcome, just for a moment, but a moment was enough.

From the shower floor, naked and done, I called for help and went into rehab.

Now there's a piece of information for the outside world to pick over.

And yet I didn't care.

A memory returned of a mentor telling me once that a plea for help is not weakness but a show of how we can remain strong.

My underbrush of self was gnarly in its persistence. A wily faith accompanied it. God could see there was still something worth watering within me, worth tending and pouring sunlight upon.

This is why I write and share my story - for the outsiders.

For the ones living lives in the shadows that no one can really see. For those who have lost faith and cast out their own selves to feel or stay alive. For those living in the wilderness of uncertainty, shame or blame, guilt or garden-variety unworthiness.

This life will rape and pillage our character in some form or another, and yet all of us deserve to see ourselves from a vantage point of hope and compassion, to know that our inner nature can still grow and evolve beyond the choices of who we once were. To a place of being forgiven and redeemed, loved even, importantly and especially, by ourselves.

I write this not only for women either, but for the men who read my story too. It is not the oldest profession in the world for no reason.

It is not even an original story, but it is mine. My secret life was the life of an outsider with a rarefied view.

An outsider with a glimpse into marriages and careers, into wealth and reputations. Into people whose external lives you might even envy.

Or worse, aspire to. And yet...

And yet...

So many are lost in a wilderness our society would have us believe is no longer present. Society would have us believe we have left it behind for greener pastures of concrete towers and office buildings and social status and ladders and bonuses and trimmings...Trappings, for many.

I have been privy to the underbelly, though.

Where the landscape is stripped bare.

The desire is for a simple conversation, a caress. A search for things that should come free but are somehow commodities in a world of mortgages and possessions, promotions and obsessions.

They pay in cash, but the true currency is secrecy, and it is held by me.

The outsider. The one they would deny over and over.

And over again.

The one who knows that no matter how finely the suit is tailored, our actions can still corrupt us inside. Something, once stirred, that may fill a void but will create a hole.

Needs are real, though. Everyone has them but what this outsider knows is an even more primal truth, that the ask is not always for sex. It can be for touch or femininity or to be heard, listened to, or witnessed.

This outsider has seen it all.

Now, she sees things from a different viewing platform - a fully clothed and sober one.

A grateful one even - that a good woman can do all manner of things to survive and feed her children and good men touched her life, too - ones seeking something she could give and giving something she needed. Just like any other transaction going on outside, in the world of insiders.

Nightmares still haunt me, but time and perspective have had their way with me. It softened me enough to release the hard-earned judgements of myself and others. Not every interaction was hostile, and being the insider in my old profession, as well as an outsider, taught me the great benefit of suspending judgement. To not judge that book...

For we are all walking wounded in a wilderness, we must carve our own path through.

Maybe the outsider we all feel we are is really our own savage insider. Who trades on all our flaws but, if spoken to kindly enough, can turn around and use them as leverage to build afresh and start anew.

This story is for the outsider in us all.

The one that feels we least deserve loving and yet needs it the most - the ones who have cloaked their wounds in armour and now wish to discard everything in favour of their truth, to risk living free and being seen. Who recognises other outsiders, can see their spark of greatness before they do, and who gives them permission to mess up, foul up but still show up.

I am all of you.

I am the outsider who can see your beauty within, who is cheering for you to reveal it, embrace it, and roam free with it. Cheering for you to speak kindly to that self within, allow yourself grace and compassion to go easy enough on yourself for long enough to see what might be possible...when you become GRATEFUL for who you are, APPRECIATE all the aspects of yourself, darkness and light and ACKNOWLEDGE yourself for all you have withstood and been through.

ALLOWING yourself to feel worthy is the only way through the wilderness into a life GREATER than you could ever have imagined.

Dignity restored.

I have allowed you to be an insider in reading my story. I hope and pray it inspires you to start looking within for the wild and precious things of value and beauty just waiting to be recognised and explored.

Start where you are.

Most people have no idea what anyone else has been through, but if we start viewing each other through this lens, we will ignite compassion for others, as well as our own inner selves.

Take it from me. YOUR GREATNESS is an inside job.

Bottom Of The Bottle

The bottom of the bottle was where I found her
A fragment of the woman I once knew
The woman I was striving towards... Gone
She was fractured
Broken
Lonely and sad
Sad and empty
Empty and lost

Desperate in her depths of despair
Grief and sorrow suffocating her, a smothering blanket
Paralysed and motionless
Tired of the fight, the tyranny of life

Her inner beauty, desperate to remain radiant and afloat
In a losing battle
Drowning instead
Despondent and devastated

Wanting so much more for her life
Struggling to find its meaning
Desperate to make it
Straining to fake it

Longing to be loved
By herself
By her King
By her God

How could anyone possibly love her like this?

The chewed up, spat out, broken version of what was left
Left to wither and die on the vine

Til the Breakdown
Gifted her the Breakthrough

ANGELA BENNETT

So sad, so beautiful
So quietly spoken
In the restoration
of Dignity
The rebuild
of Strength
All the while,
Gracefully broken…

About Angela Bennet

The transformative power of personal restoration, self-actualization, and radical change; is often fueled by anomalous individuals, who've mastered their own personal storms to act as a reliable anchor in the lives of others. Proving this ethic undoubtedly; is the effervescent world-changer, Angela Bennett.

ANGELA BENNETT

Angela Bennett is a speaker, 4 x best seller and international bestselling author, coach, and CEO and founder of **Angie B Transformation's**; a multi-dimensional coaching specialty, centered on the complete revitalization of the lives of despondent women. Seamlessly infusing personal style assessment and recreation, coupled with the facilitation of transformative life coaching, Angela offers clients an authentic depiction of what life looks like, when changed by the power of spiritual, physical, and mental edification.

Her mantra is simple: As one reshaped from the ashes of an unfortunate past, Angela exists to help women know and understand that one's past does not define them, it refines them. She pledges to reach out to those who are at their personal breaking points; lifting them out of the pits they find themselves in, as she has done, for herself.

Proving her skill sets uniquely quintessential, Angela Bennett displays a sincere regard for professional accretion, education, and personal achievement. She is certified in a myriad of vocations, including personal styling, Clean Health 1&2, Transformational Coaching Mastery, and much more. Polarizing audiences with her transparent and energetic orations, Angela is the proud mentee of both World-Renowned speaker and coach, Les Brown and Jon Talarico, and has completed and facilitated several public speaking workshops and intensives, under his tutelage.

Inspired by the will to see lives transformed, Angela remains as one driven by the diligence of ethics, life composition, and the essence of personal renewal, in the lives of other women.

When Angela is not out changing the world for the better, she is an asset to her local communal body, and a loving member of her family and friendship circles.

Angela Bennett. Leader. Motivator. Advocate.

Angela (Angie B) Bennett is contactable on https://linktr.ee/angieb_transformations

THE GREATNESS IN YOU

Transform Your Mind, Believe, And Receive What You Ask For
By Carrie Watson

It is said, "When you transform your mind, everything you experience is transformed," Yongey Mingyur Rinpoche. I am a witness to this quote as I was once at a critical point in my life. I had a choice - to either succeed by my own efforts or fall completely.

On a beautiful Sunday morning in August of 1976, it was my first time leaving home to attend one of the most prestigious HBCU colleges in the United States, Talladega College. I was so excited to begin my new journey and endeavors. The only thing, I didn't really know what I wanted to major in, so I chose music. My awesome mother was a minister of music and exposed my sister and me to as much as she could, including piano lessons, sewing lessons, beauty pageants, and anything she felt would give us exposure and inspire us. It just didn't seem like enough once my feet stood on the grounds of that institution. To my surprise, most of the music majors were so well learned. They were scholars of their craft, for they all were from larger cities and states in the United States, Chicago, New York, Atlanta, California, and other places. They were exposed to the best when it came to the fine arts. Many were singing operas and playing classical music; I only really knew the very basics of piano and gospel music. I felt so unqualified and inexperienced. I began to feel like a failure from the start; discouraged, I began to wonder what I had gotten myself into.

I didn't know what else to major in that I even related with. The opportunity to major in the different fields just didn't exist at that time as they do now. I only knew about music, which I was most familiar with. I felt I couldn't accomplish the requirements to complete this so-called music degree. On top of that, it was stated to me by others that the music program there was one of the hardest majors to complete; many did not even complete the program. So, what was I to do? Many freshmen music majors started out with me on the journey, but by our senior year, it had dwindled to less than a handful. They couldn't handle the pressure, and the professors were not letting up on their expectations and requirements. My fellow colleagues ended up leaving the music department or withdrawing from the institution altogether. Here I was left with not even a handful of my classmates that I came in with, nor did I have the musical skills to get me through.

Should I change my major? Should I change to a major I had no knowledge of at all? I was only a daughter to a mother who played gospel music at the church, and I only knew the piano basics. Classical music was not in my repertoire.

Fast forward, I chose to stay in the program. My senior year came up so quickly. But I wasn't ready. The prior piano professor seemed more interested in the maestros at hand; therefore, I didn't rise to any expectations because there were none. Eventually, he left, and another adjunct piano professor replaced him. He began to work with me. He showed an interest and made me feel I could learn what was needed. It was my senior year, and I was still stuck. I was still at a basic level with my piano skills. I knew I had to do something.

Just before the Christmas holidays, I chose my recital pieces, and my professor approved the selections. I didn't know how to play any of the pieces - not one note. As I glanced over the musical pieces, the task at hand looked insurmountable, unreal. It would take a miracle for me even to figure this all out. Beethoven, Chopin, Schumann, and Mozart pieces would be my centerpiece for my Christmas break.

So, I became determined; I made up my mind that I was going to give it all I could. I asked God to please do the rest because it would take a miracle, a true miracle, for me to be ready to present my recital to the music professors in the spring for approval of a concert by May of that year.

Over the Christmas break, instead of going out and socializing with friends, I made up my mind that I would study and practice day and night on the selected pieces of music materials. Realizing responsibility for your destiny is only yours. I started practicing for hours throughout the day. I stopped for lunch, started back up, stopped for dinner, and sometimes I skipped meals, and I would fast instead.

Beginning to develop the hunger to accomplish your goal is a magnificent pursuit. I became hungry. During those times, I cleansed inwardly, spiritually, and physically. I would read God's word, and I also stopped eating meat and began only to eat vegetables. I would practice all day, take my breaks, and start back up. When my mind would say, "You can't do this, you can't learn this difficult music," I had to train myself to imagine the inevitable. I transformed my mind, pushed through, and told myself, "Yes, I can, I can do this."

When I got sleepy, I would sleep. I would get up and start practicing all over again at two and three in the morning into the early morning. I would break and come back to it. As I practiced repetitiously, I began to see that the dexterity of my fingers was improving, I began to retain, and I began to sound just like the actual music on the cassette tape of the classical pieces. I also began to memorize the materials. I was in awe. This boosted my morale; it was my motivation. I kept practicing and believing. I continued to progress from each musical piece to the next.

By the time I returned to Talladega within the four weeks we were out for the holidays, I had learned all my pieces, all of them mostly from memory. My piano professor was astounded. He began working with me on some needed skills: fingering and expression. I stayed in the music hall day and night, polishing and finishing up my assignment. "You don't have to be great to get started, but you have to get started to be great" are the words of Les Brown. This girl from a small town in Alabama gave all of the music professors what they weren't anticipating and expecting. On the day of my hearing, I had to play the whole recital from memory, which would either be approved or not; I nailed it.

The professors were stunned. But God! Yes, God! He stood me up on a solid rock to ensure I wouldn't slip. I didn't slip. That was the day I realized I had greatness in me. I had told God I would do my part if He would do the rest. I asked Him for a miracle, and that's what I received, a miracle. I am now a retired teacher that has taught thousands to harness the greatness in believing whatever they put their minds to and work toward, and they can achieve it. If you ask, you shall receive, that's what I did, and I believe anyone can. Speak what you want. Truly believe you can have what you want. You can do all things through Christ who strengthens you. I found that I had greatness, but I had to go through the journey, the process to realize the abilities and giftings that were lying dormant inside of me. Lewis Howes says, "You have a gift inside of you, something unique to offer the world. No one else will be you." You must take that first step towards your greatness. I had to get myself out of the way and began to believe that I could ridiculously accomplish what I set out to do. If the odds are against you, you still pursue your goals and dreams even when there seems to be no hope. Become ridiculously focused and transform your mind into believing you have already accomplished what you have set out to do. If you can see it, then it is within your reach.

No, it's not always a piece of cake, you're going to have to be diligent, persistent, and faithful to the cause, but you will reach your goal/s. Stay the course. I left out of my hearing as a maestro concert pianist. You see, you must know it doesn't matter what you've been through in life, where you are now, or what skills you do or don't have. It does not matter what you've failed at in the past or accomplished; have radical confidence in yourself.

Below is a list of five ways you can begin your journey to start working towards completing your goals.

- Ask yourself these questions - How bad do you want this? Will it make a difference in my life? Will it change my circumstance? Will it make a difference for my family?

- Plan - What do you need to do to begin to work towards your goal? Start. If it takes rearranging your schedule and sacrificing extra time to help you progress toward your goal, start there. You will begin to enjoy seeing yourself moving towards your dreams and goals.

- Take it upon yourself to become more disciplined. Turn off the television, come off your phone, whatever it takes to get you closer to your goal. Make an effort to put those things that are most familiar to you to the side and do the work.

- Take time to work on yourself spiritually, mentally, and physically. In these times, many do not have many hours to do everything that is needed, but wherever you can get the time in, give yourself time to replenish and rejuvenate.

- Really speak into your life. Speak affirmations. Tell yourself I can do this. You must believe in yourself that you can accomplish whatever you set your mind to do. Stick to it even if you are the only one that believes in you.

Believe you have everything you need already inside of you to succeed. You are a conqueror. You are a winner. You have power! There is greatness in you.

CARRIE WATSON

About Carrie Watson

Inspiring, energized, and creative; known for her enthusiasm in shaping the next generation of accomplished vocal performers. Stewarding these traits with a heartbeat of a servant role to others is the educational professional Carrie Watson.

Carrie Watson is a retired choral teacher. An expert in her field and respected as a highly influential instructor, she was awarded the "Be" the Difference Award. Carrie is an inspirational piano worship instrumentalist and Zumar Studio of Arts owner.

Carrie's heart is for women to conquer and subdue.

Carrie's mantra is simple: her goal is to equip women in understanding God's true love, knowing they are captivating, unique, and enough to thrive.

She holds a Bachelor of Arts degree in Music Education, M.Ed in Education Administration, and a Bachelor's Degree from North Carolina College of Theology.

Hosting other professional skill sets ranging from a certified personal trainer, Zumba instructor, and certified lifestyle coach, Carrie is intentionally designed to focus on empowering women to cultivate the benefits of self-esteem and their well-being.

Carrie Watson resides in Gadsden, Alabama. She is the loving wife to Tony Watson Sr., a mother of two beautiful children and an ideal grandmother.

If you would like to hear the covers that I play, go to my Facebook page Carrie Watson.

Influential. Motivator.

Carriewatson92@yahoo.com
Facebook: Carrie Watson
Instagram: Carrie Watson

DONATO PERRICCI

Playing the Cards You're Dealt
By Donato Perricci

I may have grown up just like you in some ways. My parents divorced when I was just nine years old, and unlike most people, I stayed with my dad as my mom was the one to leave. I grew up in the country living in a farmhouse, and then we moved to one of the roughest cities in all of America, Gary, Indiana. Kids my age were packing guns in school. My first high school was nicknamed "Murder High" as three girls killed a teacher the year before I started there. Talk about a culture shock. This moving around happened multiple times in my youth throughout the Midwest, starting in Wisconsin, then Gary, then Chicago, and then ending in the Minneapolis/St. Paul area. Going from school to school, having to reacclimate, find new friends, learn new things, and so on. Oh, and I forgot to mention that my sisters and brother were taken away when we were all very little. I was the only one allowed to stay with my parents because I was the oldest, but I was only about five years old, so not that old. Things like this in life can be challenging when you are a kid but heartbreaking as you lose things like family and friends while moving from place to place, being uprooted from everything you know.

So, what can be done when all these things happen to you in your life? How do you play the cards that you are dealt in life and come out ahead? There are things that happen to all of us that, to some degree, we can't do anything about it, like my siblings being taken away when we were all but children. This is what we can do! We can decide how those things are going to shape our lives. The good news is that you can change that hand you were dealt and be a winner after all. Meaning that you do not have to accept those cards, and you can make changes to what you do in life to come out ahead. Now, this may not be an easy process and will take some time and possibly some help from others, but I am here today to tell you that you can get through it. You can make something out of your life. Those things that happened may have been some of what has shaped you into the person that you are like they did for me. But, you are the one that defines what you are and what you will become. Your life can be much more than what it is if you want it to be!

What are those things that make you who you are? It is what you choose to let in and run your life. It has a lot to do with our mindset. Our mindset is both our conscious and our subconscious mind. I have also heard it called our "stinking thinking!" We often do the thing that we do not want to do. We may even put off things because we lack the motivation to get off the couch and do something. You can easily change things by changing some of the habits that run your life. How do you change them? You start by creating good new habits that replace the bad ones. Start with simple things like getting up early and filling your mind with uplifting messages that motivate you to become the person that you want to be. We are a three-part being, body, soul, and spirit. You must feed each of the parts to be completely full and well balanced in your life.

One of the things that I suggest is what I like to call the power hour. Now, if you have heard that term before, know that it may not be the same thing as what you are used to. To have balance in your life, you must work on all three areas of who you are and give each area at least 20 minutes every day. For example, let's start with our bodies. Working out your body for 20 minutes a day and doing exercise, even if it is light, is key to your physical well-being. Studies have shown that if you do this first thing in the morning, you will sleep better at night and be well rested when you awake. Next is our soul, which is our mind, will, and emotions. This is where listening to a positive and uplifting message comes into play. If you do this when you first wake up also, it helps to set the flow for the day. I tell people that they should have multiple mentors. This helps you to be well-rounded and opens yourself up to thinking differently about things in life. Having both men and women mentors as well as people from different cultures will help you and will be able to challenge you to grow. Ray Kroc said, "When you are green, you're growing, and when you ripe, you rot." So, challenge yourself and grow! Think about it. You can listen to something for just 20 minutes a day, and if you do that for around four years, it will be like going to college.

You will get almost the same amount of knowledge over this timeframe. You can learn a language. Study your favorite topic. Learn something completely new and even become an expert at it! The sky is really the limit with the amount of information that is out there nowadays. Just think, if you gave it more time than that, what you could accomplish. Lastly, our spirit. This is often overlooked. We need to feed our spirits positive things. For example, if you are a Christian, you can read your Bible and pray. Listen to spiritual music. Some people may meditate, while others may find peace some other way. The point, here again, is to feed all three parts of our being so that we can be the best versions of ourselves. You can change your life by feeding these three areas for 20 minutes a day. You could also multitask while you work out and listen to something. Make better and more productive use of your time.

Goal setting is another key to improving your life and becoming who you want to be. It is important to have goals, write them down and even make vision boards to keep the goals before you. There are several ways to go about this, and I am sure that we have all heard of some of them. The question is, though, have you done it? We think about it, and we mean to do it, but we never seem to get around to it. This includes more than writing down our goals if we are being honest with ourselves. Let me ask you something, though. Are you happy with the results that you have been getting up until now? In what direction is your life heading? What direction do you want it to head? Where do you want to be a year from now? What about five years from now? It is all in your hands. You are the only one that can do it. You must set aside the time to do things like the power hour I mentioned and other things that will challenge you to grow. You are the only one that can put pen to paper on your own goals and dreams. So, write them down and get started today. It doesn't matter if they are pie-in-the-sky dreams and you have no idea how to accomplish them. That is what Bob Proctor would call a C-type goal. It is the best kind to have because you have no clue how to do it. But if you reach for the stars, you may just catch the moon.

The Bible talks some about your goals, dreams, and visions in Habakkuk 2:2.

"Write the vision
And make it plain on tablets,
That he may run, who reads it."

Do you still need some help to figure out your goals in life? Grab a notebook and start to write them all down. I don't care if there are a hundred different things. There will be all sorts of things that will come to mind. Write them all down. After that, look through them. There will be different categories like personal, business, travel, etc. Now also, while you look through them, prioritize them. What do you really want to do? What is going to take some effort and/or money? Now take the first few in each category and make a vision board. Make a few different vision boards for each category if you need to. Cut out pictures of whatever, perhaps the type of house you want or the fit body you're trying to get. Put that vision board where you will see it every day, so as you run back and forth, you will see it and remember what you are trying to accomplish. Take a picture of it and keep it on your phone so you can also look at it when you are away. Write it down on a small card and keep it with you.

I am here to tell you that you can win in life; you just have to make that choice. You can be anything that you want to be. Do not let the cemetery have your treasures. Many people have gone to their graves with their dreams, goals, and visions, never to see the light of day. Books that were not written, stories that were not told, things that were never invented. Don't let that happen to you. Do something today that will change your life today, and who knows; you may just change the world while you are at it!

Acknowledgments

I would first like to thank both Les Brown and Jon Talarico for their contribution to this book and the effort that it takes to get all of the authors together to come up with such a great testimonial to the greatness in all of us. Both Les and Jon are my mentors and coaches and have helped me in ways that words cannot describe. I thank you both for speaking to the world about your stories and encouraging us to reach our goals and dreams. A special thank you to Dr. Pamela Henkel. I am so fortunate to have you be a part of my life in so many ways. Your encouragement has always been helpful when I have needed that boost in my life and other times when I have needed to be talked off the fence and guided on the correct path. Though there are many others that I could thank, and I do not mean to miss any of you, as you are all important to me, I just don't have enough room here to really thank everyone properly, so if that is you, thanks for your help and support on my journey in life. Lastly, my wife, I cannot begin to tell you how much you mean to me and to many others. Your love and support mean the world to me. I truly could not do any of this without you. My life would not be the same without you in it.

About Donato Perricci

Donato Perricci is a Pastor, Coach, Speaker, Author, Businessman, and so much more. Donato has been involved in many areas of ministry over the past 30 years and currently serves as the Senior Pastor of Victory Celebration Family Church in the Twin Cities Metro area of Minnesota. Donato's desire is to not only impact people's lives with the Gospel but also with everything that he teaches. Donato's goal is to inspire, encourage and build a person up to accomplish all their goals and dreams, and visions, so they can be all that God created for them to become.

Donato has been a leader in Corporate America for over 25 years. Donato has served in many different roles, most of which have to do with Technology. Donato has worked for many of the top fortune 500 companies handling many multi-million-dollar projects and the people involved in those projects. All these projects have many challenges, so Donato knows the stress of life that we all go through.

Donato grew up all around the Midwest, but he and his wife Nichol call Minnesota their home. They are parents and grandparents and love every minute of it. They own and operate a few businesses where they provide help to people that need websites, social media support, and much more.

Contact Donato:
Website: https:\\donatomotivates.com
Email: Donato@donatomotivates.com

THE GREATNESS IN YOU

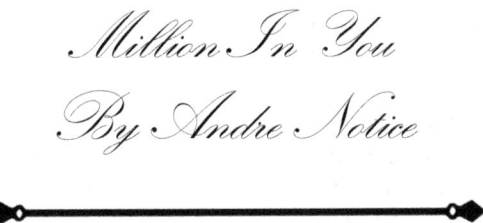

Million In You
By Andre Notice

How do you see life? Do you see it as a game? Is it a test? I personally like to think of it as both. I think it's a game that few people know how to play - they don't understand the rules in order to really WIN. At the same time, I think it's a test - one big test, consisting of a lot of little small tests. Multiple choice, essays, endurance, audio, verbal, and pop quizzes are all tests that can take place at any time, without notice. But taking tests in life is very different from taking tests in school. In school, other than just a few exceptions, almost every test you take is in isolation, you take it by yourself, and you can only pass by yourself. In life, you have those personal tests, but you also have tests where you can utilize others to fill in the gaps in the areas you aren't proficient, ensuring your success in passing.

The beauty in utilizing others is that you can learn from them, and sometimes, you can share the risk of not passing so that it's not all on you. Sharing this risk means sharing the detriment of failing. There are many areas where we can learn from others proficient in that arena. For finances, a financial advisor. For spiritual growth, a pastor. For health/fitness, a personal trainer. Although hiring the help comes at a cost, it's more costly not to hire them, take these tests solo and learn from experience the hard way.

Each new challenge (test) you experience, and you pass, you learn, and as you learn, you grow. Life is about growth and progression. Could you imagine if you went through life and just stopped growing? I believe that is why life is filled with so many ups, downs, trials, and tribulations. It's for us to learn and grow from the experience. But growth is a choice. Just because you're getting older doesn't mean you're growing. It's possible to go through life and its experiences (tests) and not get the lesson (grow). That is unfortunate because I believe to the degree to which you don't pass the test, you're doomed to repeat it. For example, the person that keeps dating the "same person" in a different body. They keep placing themselves in the same toxic relationship because they haven't yet learned the lesson of how to identify the characteristics of that individual; therefore, they shall repeat the experience. Looking back in your personal life, what most recent areas do you feel you may have been tested? Did you pass the test? Did you learn from it?

In my personal life, I can remember one of the hardest tests I've had to take. I would label it an "endurance test" because it lasted for years. Sometimes these tests can go on for a season and this season for me was a long, stressful financial drought.

Almost a decade ago, I made the decision to quit my job and chase after my dream of being a full-time entrepreneur, beginning with real estate. I put in my notice, drained my 401k, and began to work as a full-time realtor. After running into a friend and seeing what he was making selling cars online, I started working with him doing the same. Instantly, I had two businesses: one selling cars and the other houses. Unfortunately, my friend was involved in a tragic motorcycle accident and died. I immediately lost that stream of income. Simultaneously, my roommate at the time told me he would be moving out within two weeks. In less than a month, all my bills doubled, and I just lost half my income, all while trying to learn the real estate business as a new agent. It got HARD! I eventually was evicted from that apartment and found myself living in a hotel. I went from that hotel to a friend's house. From that friend's apartment to another's couch. I left that friend and went to another friend's apartment. I ended up staying in this apartment for almost two years with five adults and a child with only ONE car between us. When my time was up there, I moved back in with my father at 29 and slept on his couch. A week after my 30th birthday, he told me I had to be out. I packed up all my belongings, placed them in my car, and slept night after night in my car for three months, selling homes when I had no home of my own. Waking up to take showers at the gym, brushing my teeth in public bathrooms, and carrying on with friends, church, and life activities like nothing was wrong was completely humbling. But even during these times, I never allowed my dream of entrepreneurship to die.

In order for me to make it out of this situation and to the other side of it, I had to make a change in who I was. I had to learn from my situation and mistakes and make a conscious decision to grow. I couldn't blame anyone else. Remember I stated earlier that growth is a choice? Well, to make any real change, there should be a system in place and a plan to follow through for a successful course of action. In short, there's a formula and recipe for growth and change. Here are the five steps I took that anyone can apply for real, lasting change. I call them Andre's 5 A's to bigger, better, brighter days.

AWARENESS

I believe awareness is the very first step to real change. How can you change something you aren't even aware of? You can't. So what do you need to become aware of? One is your circumstance. Whether it's your financial situation, mental state, emotional health, relationship status, or anything else, you need to be aware of what you're going through. It's possible to be depressed and not even know it, especially if you've been there for so long that it has become your "new normal." Two is becoming aware that a change is needed. I remember speaking with a friend after going through a divorce. She didn't realize that her situation was toxic because it was all she knew. It wasn't until she saw the interaction of another married couple that she became *aware* that her situation wasn't normal and that she *could* experience something different - something she'd prefer. *Awareness* is the first step.

ACCEPTANCE

Another term that could be used here is accountability. Once you become aware of your situation, you have the choice to accept it or deny it. Many people never reach their desired success because they have not taken accountability and accepted the fact that they are where they are because of the choices that they made. If you're constantly blaming things, and people and pointing the finger elsewhere, wherever you point has the power. You can't change a situation that you don't own. Ouch! This is a hard truth, but you must first accept that YOU got you here. You are where you are right now because of your past thoughts, feelings, emotions, and actions. If you cannot accept that, you are not yet ready or qualified for change and growth.

ACTION PLAN
Myles Munroe is one of my favorite teachers of all time. He would say, "Plan your work, work your plan. Those that fail to plan, plan to fail." Coaches draw up plays, businesses draw up business plans, and an architect draws up a blueprint before any digging or building begins. All success begins on paper with a plan and blueprint as to how it's going to look upon completion. Your life should be no different. Have you ever sat and drawn up your life and how it's supposed to look in detail on paper? If you haven't, today is a great day to start.

ACT
Nothing happens with execution. Once you become aware of your situation and accept the fact that you control your outcome, you've mapped out a plan to take; none of it matters if you don't act. It's true you may not know all the steps to take, but taking the first step is key. When driving at night, you can't see your destination in plain sight, but as you drive, you can see just enough to keep moving forward. Take action in your action plan in the same regard.

ASSOCIATION
This is the step that brings everything else together. If you complete all the other steps and accumulate the success you desire, or if you start to progress in that direction, those around you can possibly pull you forward or hold you back. I have a saying, "I treat relationships like math - if you're not in my life to add or multiply, then I have to *do the math* and divide and subtract." Keep no one around that doesn't create a win/win relationship. Make sure those around you are trustworthy, honest, and high in integrity. Your circle should want you to win, and you shouldn't have to ask because those that want you to win will help you do just that.

      This 5 step process is just one of the systems I teach, explain, and elaborate with my clients to propel them from where they are to where they want to be. So many people are living life in cycles, going through the same and similar situations repeatedly. They feel stuck, and as a result, they're often unfulfilled, unhappy, and unsatisfied about life. My passion and purpose are to help them find their purpose and coach them to a place where they can profit from their purpose. If you feel stuck and ready for a real change, if you are working a job but ready to transition to being an entrepreneur, or if you already have a business but are not sure how to take it to the next level, you are a perfect candidate for coaching. The highest income earnest *still* have a coach. These 5 steps are a good place to start, but I'm excited to also have a program to go a little deeper, so you can unlock your greatness and reach your full potential. If this blessed you, or you'd like me to work with you, or learn more, send me an email or direct message.

    I look forward to seeing you at the top. Let's go together and grow together!

About Andre Notice

With serial entrepreneurship on an impending rise, experts must rely on the intangible qualities found in relatability, integrity, and ingenuity. Encompassing these traits innately is the effervescent professional Andre Notice. Andre is a meritorious realtor, orator, poet, and certified life coach, bringing a sui generis experience to the world of business. Having more than 18 years as a licensed real estate agent and over a decade in reputable, full-time entrepreneurship, Andre helps clients to master their highest potential through the power of exhortation, enlightenment, and empowerment. This "Rhyming Realtor" couples an undeniable talent with a sincere regard for education, achievement, and character development. He holds certifications in real estate management, life coaching and has been awarded and recognized by various platforms for his efforts. Enthused by life's infinite possibilities, Andre is inspired most by the personal growth of others. His success came only after being homeless for three years, including sleeping in his car for three months while in pursuit of his entrepreneurship dream. Now, he is able to introduce a benevolent approach in public speaking and coaching, leaving an undeniable impression on the lives he touches daily. Andre lives to give.

Andre Notice. Leader. Motivator. Encourager.
Contact Andre:
@uwillnoticeme
www.AndreNotice.com
Purpose@MyCoachAndre.com

DR. CHRIS LEININGER

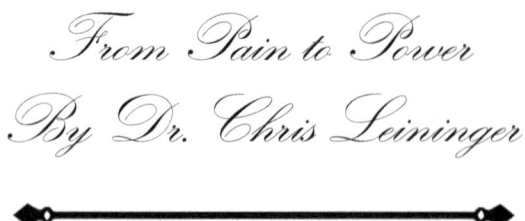

From Pain to Power
By Dr. Chris Leininger

As I waited in anticipation, the nurses surrounded the doctor. He then turned to me, looked into my eyes, and spoke the words, "It's a Boy!"

Then suddenly, a flash of painful childhood memories went through my mind. Struggling with dyslexia, not having a father during my formative years, and not fitting in with the popular crowds in high school; the pain of being bullied; the pain of always being the last one chosen for every sports activity; the pain of knowing I would never receive an academic award or be popular enough to be voted the prom king. The pain was so deep that I chose to drop out of high school at the age of 16.

All these things created a perception that I wasn't smart enough, strong enough, or popular enough. I know now that all these were perceptions or limiting beliefs, but their pain was real, and even at this moment, I can still feel it deep in my soul.

As I held my son in my arms, I knew it was a defining moment in my life. The thought of my son ever experiencing these types of things was even more painful for me than the pain I had experienced. Never again would I let my perceptions and limiting beliefs interfere with my goals and dreams.

I could feel the pain fueling my courage and my commitment. And I knew at that moment I could use the pain as leverage, and I knew the outcome I wanted was to write a new story both for him and for me. My goals were to be a present father and provide abundant provision and opportunity. Most importantly, I wanted my son to have self-confidence and faith in God.

The piercing truth is that until now, I have allowed my whole life to be defined by other people, their labels, and my own perceptions. But now, I recognize them for what they are, and I use them to turn my pain into power. Along the way, I learned that until the pain of staying the same is greater than the pain of change, you will never change.

> *Until the pain of staying the same is greater than the*
> *pain of change,*
> *you will never change.*
> Tony Robbins

My son being born was a positive defining moment. I was able to use all my negative circumstances as leverage to turn them into something positive for him. But then, through the process, what I did not realize at the time was that it was changing me. It developed new character in me, giving me the skills I needed to go forward.
Little did I know that there were obstacles ahead that would challenge these goals.

A few years later, unable to work, a handicap placard hung from the rear-view mirror of my car. I found myself waiting in anticipation as the doctor turned to me and said, "I don't know what causes it, but there is no cure. The best advice I can give you is to learn to live with the pain and train for a new vocation."

Her words traveled through my body like the aftershock of an explosion and threatened all I had hoped to be and do for my son.

It took three months to get an appointment with the infectious disease doctor, who then passed me to the rheumatologist. It took two months to get in to see her, but only five minutes to devastate me with her advice.

Another five months of my life had passed, and the "specialists" had given me no help and no hope. They had only filled my mind with limiting beliefs.

I was left feeling hopeless and defeated. How do I tell my family? What do I tell my family?

As I processed the doctor's words on the way home, I thought, "You have got to be kidding me!" No doctor in this situation would take their own advice. Besides, how can the doctor say there was no cure when she didn't know what caused it? I want to be mobile. I want to be able to provide for my family. I'm not done working. I'm not done walking. I'm not done living a life free from pain. And I'm definitely not done being present for my son.

I went from being a commercial aircraft mechanic to not even being able to wash dishes or take out the trash. It's that thing about giving up control. The journey back begins with surrender and requires a death, burial, and resurrection. I had to surrender to the fact that I was no longer capable of climbing in and out of airplanes. I couldn't run around and teach my son how to play sports or even how to ride a bike. I had to die to the old man so I could be buried and resurrected into something new. I had to have a different perspective of what it looks like to be a husband and father.

I knew it was a defining moment, and life had taught me when a defining moment comes along, you can do one of two things: define the moment or let the moment define you.

At that moment, it occurred to me that if I hired the doctor, I could also fire the doctor.

When a defining moment comes along, you can do one of two things:
define the moment or let the moment define you.
-Kevin Costner

So, I chose to turn my pain into power by using it as leverage to motivate me to pursue a new journey where I discovered my own path to wellness.

I began to ask myself empowering questions: Are there other options? Are there other forms of medicine better equipped to address chronic debilitating diseases? Are there other ways I can provide for my wife and son and be a present father?

I knew that in life, sometimes you can't change your circumstances, but you can change their meaning. And because I have struggled my whole life with dyslexia, I thought one of the things I could do was teach my son how to be the best possible reader during this time when I was struggling physically. And I did that. I took that upon myself to work with him every day. And he was so encouraged and so enthusiastic about reading. He asked me one day, "Can I read before you get up or when you're not feeling well?" I thought to myself, "YES!" and I immediately got him a Kindle account, and it turns out, I taught my son to read so proficiently that when we received the bill for Kindle, while I wasn't working, I realized, wow, I've got to slow this kid down!

At that moment, I knew I had found a way to be a provider and a present father in spite of a debilitating disease. The very thing that would have given me confidence as a child, being able to read, I was able to gift to my son at a very early age so that he would begin the journey from child to adult without having any struggles or inhibitions. My son would have self-confidence, have a present father, and be a proficient reader.

Defining moments helped me go to the next level by giving me leverage and a strong enough why to pursue an outcome of recovery. Recovery from illness, recovery from a disease that had no cure. Recovery from "learn to live with the pain." They were uncomfortable, but they challenged me to grow and what was on the other side was a beautiful thing. Sometimes a setback is a setup for a comeback.

> *Sometimes a Setback is a Setup for a Comeback.*
> *-Willie Jolley*

As I waited in anticipation for the doctor to call my name, I looked across the room and saw my mother, who has always been there for me, my one faithful childhood friend, and my son.

The doctor gestured for me to come forward, looked me in the eyes, and handed me the scroll as she uttered the words, "Introducing, Dr. Chris Leininger." It was a defining moment. I had leveraged the pain of all my limiting beliefs. I knew my outcome, and I had accomplished it. I no longer doubted that there was greatness in me.

I don't believe for a minute that God made me sick, but He certainly used my illness, and I now refer to it as the best worst thing that ever happened to me.

Another thing I learned along the way is the value of the full spectrum of human experiences and emotions. It's moments of sadness that make moments of happiness so great. It's moments of fear that make moments of courage so spectacular. It's moments of scarcity that make moments of abundance so gratifying. One contrasts the other and really brings things to life. The struggle always makes the moments sweeter.

As I look back on my life, I can now see a theme that helped ensure I would achieve my goals and dreams.

Recognize defining moments when they come along

Leverage defining moments by using their pain or pleasure as a driving force

Know your outcome and accept no substitute

The knowledge I had obtained helped me to overcome my illness. I took the power back and am writing a new story for my life. I now live a life dedicated to healing others, both of their ailments and their limiting beliefs.

No patient under my care will ever be told, "I don't know what causes it, but there is no cure. The best advice I can give you is to learn to live with the pain and train for a new vocation." Nor will they leave my office with no help and no hope. I will do everything I can to help guide them from pain to power.

About Dr. Chris Leininger

During a time when patients are often left without answers or solutions, Dr. Chris Leininger offers a unique perspective that adds a third dimension to any problem. He includes solutions to medical mysteries and helps both patients and doctors overcome limiting beliefs.

He is a doctor of acupuncture and Chinese medicine, a published author, and an educational speaker with over 17 years of clinical experience. He is now sharing that knowledge by speaking at prestigious colleges of medicine, nursing, massage, and engineering.

Dr. Leininger achieved the status of double Diplomate, NCCAOM board certified in two forms of Chinese medicine. He has been featured on WTHI TV, CBS/Fox news affiliate, regarding Acupuncture and the Opioid Epidemic. In addition, his work related to the treatment of dry eye syndrome has been published in the esteemed Sjogren's Foundation Newsletter.

Having overcome many challenges in his own life, including a learning disability and a chronic debilitating disease, he has now turned that pain into power by using what he has learned to educate and heal others.

Contact Information
Instagram: @Dr.ChrisLeininger
Website: PureHealthAcupuncture.com

Live a Life You Love and Find Greatness Within You
By Dominika Schwarc

The pandemic was a starting point for my quantum leap. It has been five years that I have been consumed by financial freedom. I remember my first entrepreneurial experience like it was yesterday. I was a woman on maternity leave who did not want to go back to a 9-to-5 job. I wanted to stay present with my family. I was open to any opportunity, and it did not take long before it came along.

I was so excited talking to my husband and asked him to please support my vision for one year. Selling my vision to him, I dreamed for him to go for early retirement, for us to stay together as a family while not stressing out about the money. I wanted to support him in finding what he loves and set up a business for him. In my mind, it was a win-win, and I could follow my ambitions—sweet, sweet dreams. Yes, I am a big dreamer, and this is one of my positive attributes. And honestly, without it, I would not be here writing this chapter.

Time passed so fast. One year turned quickly to five years, and the time in between I barely remember. You can imagine how focused I was. I am the kind of person that when I do something, I am all in. During this period, I finished one maternity leave and went for another one. I was so proud of myself for managing my two kids with clients, especially running a business with a little baby. Mums, you can imagine me in action running the business with a six weeks old baby. It took me so much energy and time to have a client meeting. Let me take you through my usual day back then.

To organize a meeting with the client in a different town, I needed a minimum of 3 hours prior to the meeting to not prepare only myself for a meeting but also for myself to look professional and pack my little one. Possible or impossible? Now when I look back on my story, I think I must have been out of my mind.

Both of my kids did not sleep well at night, so often, wake-ups were on our daily schedule. The older one went to nursery, and I stayed at home with the little one together with my business. I remember it like it was yesterday. I thought that being a successful entrepreneur meant always to be preparing and planning. My business back then was done only at the offline meetings, for which I was preparing during the night. But, where most babies sleep, I was running up and down from my computer all night.

When we managed the meeting date, time, and place, I needed to think of a baby-friendly place where they have a baby feeding zone, a changing corner, etc., so my arrangements needed to be planned for an hour upfront the original meeting. For a meeting, I had a bag prepared with everything, and I mean everything. I had a Jeep Grand Cherokee that was packed with everything from nappies, a bottle of water, toys, and a few sets of clothes for both of us. As each mama knows, incidents happen!

Let's say we were packed as we went for a little holiday. Of course, I needed to pack 4x into a car trunk and have a stroller on the way to a meeting, at the meeting, from the meeting, and back home. The greatest times I remember were in the winters when we had several layers of clothes, and as with the stroller, we put them up and down. I developed strong biceps and, thank goodness for a baby sling because, without it, I would not have managed.

So many times, when we were all done at the door, ready to leave, he did it; poop was born in perfect timing, and it would happen in a way where we could not leave without a shower. Sooooo ready for another round? I think I do not need to say that I was so sweaty after this that I needed to change as well.

Mums are the best planners in the world. Sometimes it feels like what mummy is planning - the baby is changing. As a mum, you learn great flexibility and adaptability. Eventually, I managed time for the baby to sleep in the car during our travel for a meeting. Not every time he did sleep, we needed to make a few stops before the destination.

I must say that although it looked so crazy, my baby was so connected with me, and when I was OK, he was a calm baby, the connection between the two of us was the best. He was so cute. While I was handling the meeting, he was always in the baby sling on me, he liked to be close to me, and I could concentrate on my work.

I was a lion to other mums because I was active, eager, and like Les Brown says, HUNGRY to achieve more. I was not taking my insomnia as an excuse. Instead, I studied and moved my business while managing nappies, teeth, etc.

It was this way for five years. I had become a workaholic, pursuing my dream of financial freedom, thinking that it would bring my family happiness. Yes, many people do not think about the sacrifices or the price one must pay while pursuing their dreams and goals.

Five years later, I came to a turning point in my life. STOP. It came all with the pandemic, where my offline financial business was about to be transferred to an online space. My country went to lock down, and like most of the world, I stayed home with my kids.

I felt the push that this was the opportunity I had been waiting for. On the other side, I had a home with little kids that were taking all my attention. They would say, "Mum please come play with us, muuuum we are hungry, mumm, muuum, muuum, muuum...." They were taking attention and doing plenty of silly things just because their mum was not present with them. They were feeling the same as I did, frustrated and helpless, and I was not there for them. The phone was ringing all the time, and I needed to make calls to find out about various situations for clients with banks, insurances, etc.

This all was my last call before the psychological collapse would surely happen. I needed to step out of everything and take care of myself. It was at this moment that I asked the crucial question! "Dominika, where are you NOW?" Not in terms of your goal, but in terms of your LIFE, your LOVE?

My husband was saying to me, "Dominika, enough, YOU are a mother, YOU are a wife. I have not married an entrepreneur! I married you. I do not need the money. I want our family." Every time he approached me with his disappointment, I got more power inside of me to work even harder to achieve what I had promised earlier. I so did not want to fail.

Nobody but you understands the journey you are on. Others cannot imagine, what you are going through, what faith you need to build, what pain you are going through, and how much you fail. Even though they all will benefit from it, they do not understand what it costs you. I was so frustrated that I was saying loudly, "You do not see what I do. I do it all for you from the bottom of my heart."

Then it came - my BREAKTHROUGH moment. I discovered that I was chasing a future that would never come! Financial freedom will not make us happy! We need to manage our happiness first! I was ready to do anything, and I mean anything, that would help me.

Create a quantum jump. I did not want to wait longer, another five years not being the mother that I wished to be, not being the wife that I wished to be. I felt I needed to change the community. I no longer want to be harsh on myself or my family. I needed to connect with people with a different mindset, with millionaires, because there were my dreams.

While people were scared that there would be no food available and were worried about what would happen in the world due to the global pandemic, I did what everyone around me seemed to be the silliest thing you can imagine, considering I had five years of experience in the financial industry. I took all our savings, investments, and kids' savings. I invested a sum that made me scared me and made me feel sick. I even sold our Jeep Grand Cherokee, which gave me a sense of self-confidence, and I invested all of it in myself.

With that, I have realized that I can not do anymore in the financial business; I am here to do more. But yet, I did not know what it was. So I could not do any more the financial business. You know I said world finance, and my thoughts just locked. I was stopped. I could not any longer sell this kind of certainty.

With the investment of everything I had, I still had no idea what I was going to do, with no brand, no followers, no website, really nothing; I had no other choice but to go and try. There was one salary in the house, but it was not enough.

I'll tell you one thing. When you want a quantum leap, put yourself in situations where you have no other option. You will find the greatness within you, and you will see what you never thought you would be capable of.

I started from scratch. I mean it. Before, I used my car, even for just 3-minute distances. Now, I picked up my kids with an old borrowed bicycle. Searching for who I really was, out of the world stated roles, who I was inside, I was looking for what I love - I was so far from myself. I was learning not to be a perfectionist, searching for my authenticity, learning to love myself, trust myself, and believe in myself.

Thanks to my 5-year experience, I know how I do not want my life to look and started to build it the other way around, based on my rules. This is what I teach now, to live the life you love, to create a business you love, and to live your potential.

My motto is:
"If everyone did what they LOVE, we would LIVE in paradise on Earth." -Dominika Schwarc

Let's imagine you do what you love and are paid for it. I think that both of us agree that you might not feel that you are working. Also, the energy which you are serving is love. Love is source energy, love from which all, including us, are made. But most people do what keeps their bills paid, and some don't even know what they love.

Let me ask you a question. If you win a lottery in a way that you would never need to go to a job, what would you do? After taking a holiday and enjoying the very first money moments, the answer is there. This might happen. You actually don't know!

Another question. If you could do anything that makes you heavily successful and fulfilled, what are you doing? Imagine it as guaranteed. If you stay quiet, it is OK for most people. But keep on trying, look for it, find it. And start to build upon it.

We are so disconnected from ourselves. That is a part of the roles that we play in our life, we often don't know who we are, and neither knows what makes us happy. We are trying to fulfill all expectations coming from others' worlds, and we barely think of ourselves. But there is an old saying you cannot pour from an empty cup. You need to take care of yourself first.

This would not have happened if I had not decided that enough was enough. I invested my ALL, so I have no way of escape. Our mind is so so strong. It keeps us safe in our old selves. So do you really want a life out of your greatness?

I bought a few programs, and in one high ticket coaching, I remember that I was kept in my old business idea, finances. You were working in an insurance company, and you were a financial analyst. Now, you are a financial consultant. Logically, you have great experience in the finance field. So there I was, trying hard to think of a way to work it out. I was so frustrated, so angry, and so upset; it just did not work.

I thank you for this lesson because I was so concerned that I did not want to do it anymore anyhow, and there I learned to step into my power and listen to myself! How many times in your life do you listen to your inner self? And how many times have you let others talk you over your inner voice?

Everything you need to meet your purpose and happiness and achieve the complete fulfillment you already have within you. Your heart knows. Listen to it. It will tell you the answer to all your questions. You have greatness within you.

Acknowledgements

    I would like to express my deepest appreciation to my husband, Benedik, who has supported me along the whole journey, who keeps our family together and who challenges me daily. I would like to also extend my deepest gratitude to my kids, who show love towards me every day.

    I am deeply indebted for the opportunity to be part of Greatness in you anthology to Les Brown and Jon Talarico. The completion of this chapter would not have been possible without the support and nurturing of Dr. Pamela Henkel and her team. I am extremely grateful for Les Brown, who led me through, „my impossible to "my possible." Thank you.

DOMINIKA SCHWARC

About Dominika Schwarc

Establishing a sense of inner clarity can prove itself a challenge in a world seemingly immersed in chaos. Aiding many on the halcyon journey back to themselves is the charismatic professional Dominika Schwarc.

Dominika Schwarc is an author, transformation specialist, and coach with a unique enthusiasm for helping women establish the peace and synergy necessary to achieve their purpose in life.

Her mantra is clear: Dominika shares a unique admiration for women committed to their personal evolution. With her assistance, women can look to reignite their love for success and the assuredness that comes with collaborating with a transformation coach.

Leaving her original roots and traveled to the UK at the tender age of 19, Dominika learned the power of transforming her own reality from a professional novice to a trailblazing innovator, helping to develop high-dollar programs for top-tier female clientele. Dominika holds a Master's degree in the management of small and medium enterprises and has enjoyed several years of success in various corporate arenas. Though the amalgamated success of education and standardized work seemed promising, it was an assiduity to the evolution of women that ushered Dominika into the world of creating promising spaces for other women.
Inspired by the resilience, magnetism, and evolution found in other world-renowned coaches and leaders, such as Les Brown and Jon Talarico, Dominika continues to carry a reflection of their ingenuity onto her own clients.

When Dominika is not out teaching women how to own their own shine and achieve internal peace all over the world, she is an asset to her local community and a loving member of her family and friendship circles.

Dominika Schwarc. Leader. Energizer. Influencer.

Dominika Schwarc ~ Contact Information
Facebook: https://www.facebook.com/dominika.wiesingerova
https://www.facebook.com/DomiSchwarc
Direct Facebook Messenger:
https://www.facebook.com/messages/t/723630986
Email: schwarcdominika@hotmail.com

BARRY OVERTON

The Boy Who Never Stopped Dreaming

By Barry Overton

No one has ever achieved greatness without first dreaming. In the day and age that we live in, being called a dreamer carries a negative connotation because so many have stopped dreaming. At certain points in our lives, we have all had dreams, desires, and goals that we wanted to achieve. And along the way, we likely suffered setbacks, doubt in our ability to achieve the dream or ridicule from outside forces that eventually put us in a place where we stopped dreaming. But we should never allow ourselves to get old enough that we cannot give birth to a new dream.

Do you know who the best dreamers on the planet are? Children. You see, children dream without limitation, fear, or doubt in the ability to reach their dreams. So, not only do they dream, but they dream big. Think back to your days as a child. What were your wildest dreams? What were your expectations of who you would become, of how you would live your life?

When I think back on my own life growing up in Austin, Texas, in Section 8 housing, living on food stamps, and just being able to get by, my dreams were the one thing that no one could take away from me. My mother was a single parent and did the very best that she could. Still, as a child, I experienced homelessness, and not in the sense of actually living on the streets, but living in multiple households with family members for a period of about nine months. In second grade, I attended three different elementary schools for that school year because of how often we were moving around. As a seven-year-old kid, I wasn't really phased by this potential disruption. It was later in life that I realized what we were experiencing. Still, through that process, my mother instilled a mindset of stability, even though everything around us was very unstable regarding our living arrangements.

THE GREATNESS IN YOU

I remember my biggest dream as a kid was to be Superman, and I don't mean to play Superman in a movie or on TV. I wanted to be the real-life Superman. You see, at four years old, I was introduced to a TV version of Superman that, in my eyes, was a real person. So, from that day forward, I was Superman in training. I was able to leap tall trash cans with a single bound, dash across the street without getting hit by a car, and scare away the neighborhood cat with my Man of Steel stare. Oh yeah! I was definitely Superman in training. One thing interesting about dreams. The biggest concern that you have to worry about is someone stealing your dreams. That sounds like that may be someone sinister. Someone that is just out to do harm to you, but in most cases, the dream stealer is someone close to you, someone, that feels like they're helping you to not dream. You see, in many cases, the dream stealer gave up on their dreams many years before you. They feel like for you to have dreams is only setting yourself up for failure.

My very first dream stealer was my grandmother. I remember her telling me, "Baby, you're going to have to stop running around the neighborhood with that terry cloth towel wrapped around your neck. People think something's wrong with you. They think you're slow." Well, I didn't want people to think there was something wrong with me. I was just a kid having fun believing in my dream, but it was through that conversation that I gave up on my dream because of someone else's opinion. It was later in life that I learned a very powerful message about opinions. Mr. Les Brown often shared a story of one of his mentors, Mr. Washington, who told him, "Someone else's opinion of you does not have to become your reality." I believe that God put those words and that quote in my spirit as a child because even though I allowed someone to take the dream of being Superman away from me, I did not allow them to take away my ability to continue to dream.

A few years passed from my "Superman" years, and I found another dream manifesting inside of me, coming to a boil. Oh, and this dream was huge. It was grand, but at the same time, it was attainable. I wanted to become an NFL football player, but I didn't just want to play in the NFL. I wanted to go to Super Bowls and win them. I wanted to be the league MVP and eventually be inducted into the Pro Football Hall of Fame. See what I mean? Big dreams. This one was more realistic for me because I had a family member who played in the NFL, and he played for my favorite team. Thomas "Hollywood" Henderson was an NFL linebacker for the Dallas Cowboys. He played with flash and flare, hence the name Hollywood. I wanted to be like my cousin, but only greater. Having his example pushed me to be the very best that I could be every time I got on the football field.

From the time I was seven years old until the time I was 17, I ate, slept, and, yes, dreamt about football. Then during my junior year playing wide receiver in a practice scrimmage, all of that came to a screeching halt. Not for the reasons you might think, but something that could have been even more detrimental to me throughout life. I remember the day vividly. I was a wide receiver, and I was running across the middle. The quarterback sees me open and throws the ball. It's high and to the left, and I reach out with one arm to grab that ball. You see, I was going to do a one-handed catch. I was doing Odell Beckham before there was an Odell Beckham. As the ball touched my hands, so did the crashing linebacker touch my ribs with his helmet, knocking the wind and the dream right out of me at that moment.

I suffered a pinched nerve in my shoulder that set me out for the next few practices, but more importantly, it put me in place for the first time where I quit on my dream. I gave up football. Now it's bad to allow someone to steal your dream, but it's even worse when you give up on your dream. Quitting on that dream that day haunted me for many years to come after that. For a very long time, I was tormented with one question, "What if I didn't quit?" Where would my life have ended up if I didn't quit? Now you recall the name of this chapter is, The Boy Who Never Stopped Dreaming." So even while I'd done one of the worst things you could do by giving up on a dream, I've also done one of the best things that I could do: finding a new dream. Now at 17, going into my senior year and realizing that my dream of becoming an NFL player was now unlikely, my thoughts were, what am I going to do with my life?

Going back to the thoughts of being Superman, what I learned at 17 that I didn't understand at four years old, is that I had a real-life Superman that was also a part of my family. My uncle,

THE GREATNESS IN YOU

Freddie Maxwell. You see, he was the first Black Sergeant, Lieutenant, and Captain of the Austin Police Department, my hometown. It was at that moment that I thought to myself, I have a real-life hero in my life, a true role model. He was the epitome of success in our family, and I wanted to be successful. I realized it wasn't Superman that I was seeking; it was the greatness that was inside of me that was telling me there is something special for you to do in this world. You see, greatness is not something that you go out and achieve. It's something you become. It's something that's already inside of you, and your only duty in life is to bring it to the surface and share it with the world so that you inspire others to do the same.

You see, the image of Superman was an inspiration to me. That was greatness. The image of my cousin Hollywood Henderson was greatness. The success that my uncle had as a police officer was greatness. I was inspired by it, and it motivated me to find it in myself. Now once finding greatness, I've held onto it and never let go. It allowed me to have a 26-year career in law enforcement, be a Sergeant during the Gulf War and lead troops, own multiple successful businesses and be a top-producing real estate agent in Colorado for the last 21 years. Now, as I constantly get into quiet places, I listen to the whisper inside of me telling me service to others inspires the masses. I now focus my attention on inspiring those that are looking for Superman inside of them.

Tony Robbins once said, "If you want to be successful, find someone that has achieved the results that you want, and copy what they do, and you'll achieve the same results." I guess you could say I've made a living being a copycat, but it's okay to be a copycat as long as you copy the right cat. You see, success is duplicatable. Why reinvent the wheel if you can take something that someone else has already done, put your own spin on it, and achieve those same results? Now I spend my life teaching real estate agents and entrepreneurs how to follow some very duplicatable success traits that will put their life on the path to greatness and high achievement. Still, it all starts with the dream and understanding that while the dream may change through the course of your life, the ability to dream is always there as long as you don't let anyone steal it from you and you don't give up on it.

The best advice that I could give to anyone that's looking to take their life to the next level is to find what that burning desire is inside of you, then pursue it like your life depends on it. Because guess what? It does. Then make these three key things part of your lifestyle: belief, planning, and execution. You have to believe in that dream as though it is already a reality. You have to have unwavering faith behind that dream, a faith so strong that nothing can steer you away from it. Planning. Set yourself up with a blueprint to success. That goes back to following the path that others have laid that has proven successful in the past and building a plan around it that helps you to attain your goals and dreams.

As you create your plan, seek mentorship to fine-tune it to ensure that it's a solid plan. Then there comes the execution. Out of the three, this is the most important because you can say that you believe in your dream. You can put all the plans on paper, but if you don't take that first step to execute and take action, the dream remains a dream, and it's just on paper, but it's through this unrelenting belief and an incredible game plan that the execution becomes easier to do. Once you execute consistently and without concern for failure, you will see your dreams transform into your reality. 18th Century Evangelist John Wesley said, "Set yourself on fire, and the world will come see you burn." This book will start a flame in you that the whole world can't help but see. I want you to treat this chapter as the flint. This is the spark that ignites your greatness.

About Barry Overton

Barry Overton worked for 26 years in law enforcement. His experience ranges from a military police officer where he served as a Non-Commissioned Officer during Operation Desert Storm. Barry further spent 21 years with the Denver Police Dept. For 17 of those years, he worked as a Narcotics Detective.

    Through his military and police experiences, Barry learned structure and thinking outside the box to create effective plans that lead to successful outcomes. His ability to make split-second decisions in life-threatening situations has served him well in other aspects of his life.

Mr. Overton has also been an entrepreneur since 1998 and a real estate agent in the Metro Denver Area since 2001. Through mentorship and continuously developing a "Can't Lose" mindset Barry has become one of the top-producing real estate agents in the state of Colorado. Barry has also mentored many other business owners in areas of brand development, vision and execution, to mindset. Barry often says, "In my world, there aren't wins and losses, only wins and lessons. I'm a perpetual student. I receive every lesson and get better from it."

In addition, Mr. Overton has embarked on lucrative entrepreneurial endeavors that have allowed him to show others how to generate significant income in recession-proof industries. One opportunity actually retired him ten years early from a 6 figure income as a police officer. He has produced over $75M in real estate sales during his career, which has allowed him to give back six figures of his income over the last three years.

Through his speaking engagements, Barry delivers fiery yet relatable stories that engage the audience and call for them to stretch their current thinking to find the greatness that lives inside them. Barry's book, Ignite Your Greatness, The Secret to Lighting the Fire Within, helps the reader build belief in their talents and gifts and offers a foolproof system through action steps that allow the reader to light the fire and share their greatness with the world.

Speaking engagement topics for Mr. Overton include entrepreneurship, real estate, the power of a positive mindset, troubled childhoods, overcoming fear to become fearless, community policing, self-belief practices, identifying your gifts, and sharing your greatness with the world.

Contact Barry:
Instagram: @barryloverton
FaceBook: barry.l.overton
LinkedIn: barry-overton-871b892a
www.igniteyourgreatness.com

Enough Is Enough! Empower Yourself to Help (Your) Children and Teenagers Discover Their Greatness!
By Ellen Wulfert

> "Mothers, honor yourself and your children by pursuing your dreams!"
> - Les Brown

Especially as a single mother and educator, Les Brown's quote has resonated with me so much. Everybody who is around children or teenagers a lot or who works with them should honor and empower themselves and pursue their dreams.

Only when we take on the responsibility for ourselves, when we are centered in our own power, feel healthy and fit, have a strong and positive mindset, and do this to build up our confidence and believe in ourselves, pursuing our goals and dreams, when we are happy, full of vibrant energy then we can also fully take care of our children and teenagers and be the role models they need to be able to "dance" through their lives, discovering their greatness and developing their potential to live the lives of their dreams.

I want to start by asking you:

- Have you ever had dreams when you were a child or teenager?

- When you look at your life today, have you fulfilled your

goals and dreams? Or have you procrastinated or even given up on them because you doubted yourself, lacked self-confidence, and grew negative beliefs like, *"I am not good enough?"*

Due to my profession as a teacher and as a coach, I have come across many teenagers who either don't have any goals or dreams or have already given up on them because they already have been infiltered with negative beliefs about themselves.

I remember a girl, about ten years old, hopping and smiling happily on the way home from school. But as soon she comes home, she feels the depressing atmosphere that almost takes her breath away. Entering the door, she already smells the smoke of her mom's cigarettes. Then she sees her mom sitting in a cloud of smoke in the kitchen, pulling on her cigarette, having a big coffeepot next to her, staring into space, and pulling out bundles of her hair, hardly looking up, and if, only with an empty look, not able to smile, when she sees her daughter because she is suffering from severe depression.

Wanting to tell her choleric and unpredictable father enthusiastically all about her school day, he would suddenly freak out. He shouts and insults her for no reason. When she is questioning why he is yelling at her or telling him to leave her mom alone when he is having a go at her again, his huge hand would fly across the girl's face and head, and he would beat her up for no obvious reason. Sometimes, she manages to run down the stairs and lock herself into the little cold restroom one stair down in the stairwell. While he was hammering with his fists on the door, her heart would beat so fast she thought it would explode at any minute. She stays there for hours until she hears him leave, even though there is no heating, and, in the winter, it is freezing cold in there.

When she isn't fast enough, she stands right up to him, rebelling and challenging him, fighting back with words. Then his face would turn pale, his eyes wide open, and he would beat the hell out of her, hitting his daughter in the face and on her head until she screams so loudly to wake him up from his trance of madness.

The neighbors and her grandparents, who live in the same house, must have heard her screaming. But no one ever intervenes. Instead of somebody protecting her from an early age on, she takes on the load of the family drama on her shoulders, fighting for her mother, brother, and her own life.

Experiencing all this drama at home day in, day out, this girl goes to school like any other girl apart from the fact that she feels ashamed and thinks that something is wrong with her because of her mother suffering from bipolar disease, wanting to leave her by even trying to take her life several times and a father who was overwhelmed and didn't comfort his children but reacted with violence instead. Consequently, she grew negative beliefs like she isn't worthy of being loved or good enough for anybody or anything.

Luckily, the girl has a hero by whom she is inspired: Pippi Longstocking. This character, invented by Astrid Lindgren, is a girl who is so strong that she can lift a door with her horse and several men standing on it, and she helps other children and protects them from bullying.

Determined to be as strong and free as Pippi Longstocking, she not only starts to wear two funny pigtails like her hero but most importantly, she decides:

"**Enough is enough!**" and to never give up. She swears to herself – *"One day, I will be able to do 100 pushups, and then I will punch HIM back."*

Consequently, she started exercising even more as she already had been doing. She trains and increases the number of her pushups and sit-ups every single day. She would even compete with the boys in arm-wrestling and turn out to be stronger than many of them. Because of this, she is growing not only her muscles but also her self-confidence.

When she turns 16, she can do 150 pushups at once! She now feels ready to punch her father back after having prepared herself physically and mentally for this moment all these years. With this, she shows him – "**Stop! Enough is enough!**"

"You gain strength, courage, and confidence by every experience in which you really stop looking fear in the face."
- Eleanor Roosevelt -

This girl I am writing about, who was left by both of her parents and fighting for herself all by herself throughout her life, was me.

My Vision and Mission

Because of my personal background story and experiences that my students and clients shared with me, I am today empowering children, teenagers, as well as mothers, parents, and educators on and offline to discover their greatness within themselves, to take their power back and to "dance" through their dreamlives with a healthy and fit body as well as a positive and strong mindset to live a purposeful life in abundance full of joy, love, and happiness pursuing their goals and dreams and be the heroes of their lives that outlive them.

My mission and vision are that children and teenagers live a happy childhood, be elevated, and grow up to be happy, healthy, and strong adults, building loving relationships and later as adults empowering their own kids and creating a better world for our next generations.

Especially as parents and educators, we need to elevate our children and teenagers, give them hope and show them perspectives for their future, to give them a reason and motivation to take over responsibility for their lives.

"Those who win in life take responsibility and create their own destiny."
-Bob Proctor-

If you are working with children or teenagers, please, do not judge them. Maybe you are their only hope, voice, anchor, the only person who listens and says things like, "Everything will be alright", and "I am here for you." Or, like my dear mentor

Mr. Les Brown always says:
"It's not over until you win! You have greatness within you!"

Empower Yourself to Empower Your Children!

The empowerment of children and teenagers begins with empowering ourselves. If we are really stressed out and lose the connection to ourselves, as a consequence, we also lose the connection to our children and teenagers. We then maybe do or say things that influence them negatively, and so they grow negative beliefs like so many of us have done and do not follow through on their goals and dreams.

However, suppose we are in our power, feeling strong, healthy, centered, and full of positive, vibrant energy, pursuing our dreams, being happy and successful, and having the choice of how we live our lives. In this case, we show our children and teenagers that everything is possible. They then are very likely to be motivated to do this like us because they learn by observing us, our deeds, and our actions.

Having worked as an educator for almost 20 years as well as a body and mindset coach, I created the ***EWM-Empowering Winners Method***; a program focused on the mental and physical empowerment of both children and teenagers as well as parents and educators to learn how to use their body as an instrument for their success in combination with a strong and positive mindset to:

-**FIND** out about their goals and dreams
-**FOCUS** on their strengths and develop their potential
-Believe in themselves and have **FAITH**
-**FORGIVE** and "remember without anger" (Les Brown)
-Learn to speak **FOREIGN LANGUAGES** fluently in combination with self-empowerment tools and use their voice to connect with people around the world
-**FOLLOW THROUGH** and fulfill their goals and dreams and even start their own business while they are at school
And through this, to:

"Rob the cemetery from their talents, gifts, and dreams, to live a life that outlives them!"
- Dr. Myles Munroe, Les Brown -

If this chapter is reaching you today, I can help you. I would love to share more important tools, and steps that I have been using which can help you as a parent or educator to empower yourself and help (your) children and teenagers or your students step into their greatness by using the power of your body, mind, and language! Learn how you and your child or teenager can create your own destiny!

ELLEN WULFERT

"You don't have to be great to get started, but you have to get started to become great."
- Les Brown -

Discover the greatness in you, and help your children or teenagers discover the greatness in them!

"Falling will never make you a failure unless you quit!"
- Bob Proctor -

If I can do this, YOU CAN DO THIS!

"Alone we can do so little; together we can do so much."
-Helen Keller -

Always remember what Les Brown says:

"It's not over until you win!"
"You have greatness within you!"
"You are chosen to be here!"
"[…] Honor yourself […] by pursuing your dreams"
To help children and teenagers discover the greatness within them!

Please reach out to me to get your free steps or schedule a free session with me.

My name is **Ellen,**

E - **E**mpower and **E**xercise
L - **L**ove **L**ife
L - **L**earn **L**anguages
E - **E**mbrace
N - **N**ew possibilities!

Acknowledgments

I would like to thank ...

My wonderful teenage son Milan Marek who has been my "why" and the apple of my eye since he was born,

My mother, who is watching us from heaven and gave me all her love while she could,

My father for introducing me to the world of sport,

My brother Jens, who I shared my childhood and youth with.

Furthermore, I am so happy and grateful for ...

My best and long-term friend Antje da Silva Santos, who has always been there for my son and me since our schooltime, "dancing" through the ups and downs of our lives,

Ina, Karsten, Dorothea, Silvia, and their families for all your support and kindness for my son and me throughout the years,

My Karate – trainers and friends Frank and Katrin, who have been showing me how to use my energy and powers,

Frank Siegmund for taking the headshots of me,

My colleague Andy Walessa who has always been reliable, helpful, and loyal to me, as well as a joy to work with.

Moreover, I would like to thank my mentors and coaches, whom I have been allowed to learn so much from and who lent me their belief when there was a time when I couldn't believe in myself.

I am so grateful that the universe has been sending me living "angels" in my ways like my mentor Mr. Les Brown, who has touched my heart and soul with his voice and words and thus has changed my life, my coaches and mentors Mr. Jon Talarico, Dr. Pamela Henkel, Apostel Deborah Allen, and Kelisha Worrell as well as my very first mentor Joao Heep who saw something in me that I could not see in myself then and without whom I wouldn't be here today.

A BIG Thank You to all of you and those who I didn't mention here!

Love, peace, health, and happiness to you all. Be blessed!

To Your Greatness,
Ellen Wulfert.

ELLEN WULFERT

About Ellen Wulfert

Global motivators are born with a sense of universal influence, bridging various gaps between adolescence and maturity, rebellion and grace, body, and mind. Embodying this nature in unyielding measure; is the compassionate professional Ellen Wulfert.

Ellen Wulfert is an international bestselling author, body and mindset coach, multivariate educator, and founder of the EWA - Empowering Winners Academy, helping children and teenagers, as well as mothers and educators, be the heroes of and in their lives.

Also, Ellen is the creator of the EWM-Empowering Winners Method; a program focused on the mental and physical empowerment of both children and teenagers, mothers, and educators. Having spent more than 18 years as a German bi-lingual educator, Ellen's facilitation has helped many to develop and create positive mindsets and gain a deeper sense of self-confidence in combination with learning a new language.

Her mantra is simple: She wills to empower children and teenagers as well as their parents and educators to dance through their lives and to live the life of their dreams by having a healthy and fit body as well as a positive and strong mindset in order to lead and impact our next generation through the power of self-actualization, physical competence, and mental strength.

In congruence with an outstanding commitment to professional excellence, Ellen holds sincere regard for various forms of education, achievement, and community involvement. Alongside her educational acumen in English and Physical Education, she also holds certifications in Dance, Yoga and Mindset instruction, Fitness, Zumba, Karate and more. No stranger to word-class achievement, Ellen has facilitated international workshops for those looking to enhance their propensity for education as well as physical and mental enhancement in Trinidad/Tobago, Germany, America, and more.

Her passion for serving goes beyond humanity, as Ellen spent two summers in Crete, Greece rescuing sea turtles as a youth volunteer.

Displaying proficiency in a myriad of vocations and service-based business led Ellen into a profound relationship with mentorship and personal coaching. Having been taught by professional coaches and mentors like Les Brown, Jon Talarico, Bob Proctor, Tony Robbins, Dr. Pamela Henkel, Apostel Deborah Allen, Tanya Powell, Joao Heep, choreographers and dance instructors like Marvin A. Smith, Milo Levell, and Madonna Grimes, just to name a few, Ellen has acquired quintessential skill sets; yielding her as one of the most impactful influencers of her time. She is a proud international graduate of the world-renowned speaker Les Brown's "The Power Voice Academy," establishing her well-earned appellation as an international speaker, author, and coach.

ELLEN WULFERT

Enthused with a vision to accompany children and teenagers as well as parents and educators on their life-long journey toward wholeness, Ellen is committed to her craft on an intrinsic level. When she is not out training, teaching, and shaping the world for the better, Ellen remains an asset to her local communal body and a loving member of her family and friendship circles.

Ellen Wulfert. Leader. Educator. Humanitarian.

Connect with Ellen:

What's app: (+49) 15 15 48 40 138
Email: teamellenwulfert@gmail.com
Facebook: http://www.facebook.com/ellen.wulfert.39
Instagram: ellen.wulfert

Destiny Unleashed
By Kelisha Worrell

The Story You Tell Yourself

We all have a story we're telling ourselves. If you want to know what it takes to be happy, you have to know what role you play in the story of your life. Some people's story is that they will go to school, get good grades, find a spouse, have children, climb the corporate ladder and achieve great wealth. Many people don't feel worthy if they don't achieve an enormous amount in life, and to avoid feeling like a failure, they lower their standards to feel like they are succeeding. "*Most people fail in life not because they aim too high and miss, but because they aim too low and hit.*" -Les Brown. With this said, if you are unhappy with how your life is going, all you have to do is CHANGE THE STORY you're telling yourself about your life and RAISE YOUR STANDARDS. It's that simple.

There was a woman who survived a traumatic situation. For confidentiality purposes, we will call her Ashley. The story Ashley told herself was that she was unworthy to be in a healthy relationship with someone who loved and appreciated her. She told herself that she could change her partner without first changing herself. We all want others to change, but it's hard to make the necessary changes ourselves. It's because when we are with another person, we feel more vulnerable. We want to protect ourselves from being hurt or rejected by that person, so in response, we hold on to those harmful behaviors to avoid being alone.

Ashley wanted to be in a romantic relationship with a man who would love her for who she was. On the contrary, the man she was with at the time was verbally, mentally, and physically abusive. She created this story in her mind that she wasn't worthy of having a loving, healthy relationship and convinced herself that she was with a man who really loved her. Her constant thought was that if she waited it out long enough, she could change his abusive ways and create a wonderful life together. As time passed, the abuse and controlling actions became worse, and the abuse almost turned deadly. One night her boyfriend got extremely angry, began to aggressively shout at her, and pulled out his gun. Ashley franticly tried to knock it out of his hand, but he turned the gun to Ashley and shot her in the face at point-blank range. Instantly eighty percent of her face was gone. The bullet obliterated her face, her upper jaw, the roof of her mouth, and her eye were all gone. With the help of a team of doctors and over ten major surgeries, they were able to reconstruct Ashley's face, and today she lives with one prosthetic eye. Doctors took a portion of bone from her leg, formed it into a jaw, and replaced the roof of her mouth. Her nose was completely gone and was impossible to reconstruct, so now she wears a prosthetic nose, and a portion of her neck was taken to create lips for her. After eight years of being in this toxic relationship, it ended tragically for Ashley, and her face will never look the same, but thankfully, her life was spared.

Six years after this tragic event, Ashley says, "*I have more courage and belief in myself; I have more confidence and am a stronger woman.*" She goes out into the world encouraging women to live from a place of strength and empowerment; many people have gratefully responded to this as "*their wakeup call.*"

Although Ashley's story is one of the worst cases of a person who survived, many people are suffering from the same mental bondage of feeling unworthy because of the story they are telling themselves. Are the same deceptive thoughts playing in your mind that you aren't worthy of having more? Are you going to wait until things get so bad in your life personally, professionally, financially, or spiritually until you make the right move? Take a step towards a better future for yourself and demand of yourself that you will never stop going after your purpose! I encourage you to make the right move today.

IT'S YOUR TIME!
    It's time you begin to have more, do more, and be further along than ever before!
Ashley's story started out with a very subtle but dangerous thought, the thought of complacency, the thought of feeling

unworthy. These thoughts can destroy your life completely. You don't have to be in a toxic relationship to experience something tragic. Are you getting warning signs in your health, finances, or relationships that you are ignoring? How long are you willing to play it safe and stay in bondage? Maybe you're at a job that isn't treating you right, and that small voice is telling you to go somewhere you will be valued, but you're afraid of the unknown. You may be in a toxic relationship you know you should have left a long time ago, but you're afraid that there's no one out there for you. Your health may be at risk, but you continue to eat unhealthily. You hear that still small voice telling you to change, but you simply ignore it. All of these warning signs are very quiet before the storm hits, so if you want more than what you're experiencing, you have to develop a new vision for your life. Are you seeing your life as difficult and hard to get by, or are you seeing yourself achieving more and taking action steps towards creating the life you deserve? I've heard the question asked, *"Why do we prefer known hells over unknown heavens?" - Les Brown*

The unknown for Ashley would have been leaving that toxic relationship, believing in herself, believing that God has more in front of her than she would be leaving behind. What is that unknown place for you - that place you fear going towards the most?

The truth is, you have GREATNESS within you, and you can achieve success at the highest level.

Answer the following questions below:
- Do you believe you can do, be and have whatever you want?
- Not everyone can go with you to your next level. Who do you need to eliminate out of your life?
- What boundaries do you need to create?
- What is it costing you to stay in a place where you're not creating the life you know you deserve to live?

ACTION STEPS:
Imagine living a fulfilling life, one that you absolutely love!
- Write out the story of your life in exact detail how it would be. Make sure you are specific, how would you

dress, how would things look, and what type of relationships, friendships, finances, health, and wealth would you experience?

Record yourself reading your vision out loud and listen to this daily.

Next time you are feeling overwhelmed by a challenge, remember that you have the strength to overcome it. God is working inside of you. You may not know it, but you have the power to get through anything life throws your way. You are not alone. Reach out to someone you trust, someone who can help lift you up to a higher level within yourself. Sometimes reaching out can feel like the hardest thing to do, but it's honestly one of the most important things you can do. In the past, I've been in situations where I felt as though asking for help would inconvenience other people but what I found was that asking for help is a strength, not a weakness. If you are experiencing challenges in your life, follow the three steps below, and you'll begin seeing yourself progress.

1) Talk to someone: Talking about our struggles can help us to feel more in control and less alone.

2) Create a plan: A plan can help us feel more confident and in control of the situation.

3) Take things one step at a time: It's important to remember that progress is often made one step at a time. We may not be able to solve all our problems overnight, but by taking things one step at a time, we can slowly progress and eventually overcome our challenges.

Break Through and Unleash Your Inner Power

As a man was passing the elephants, he suddenly stopped, confused by the fact that these huge creatures were being held by only a small rope tied to their front leg. No chains, no cages. It was obvious that the elephants could, at any time, break away from their bonds, but for some reason, they did not.

He saw a trainer nearby and asked why these animals just stood there and made no attempt to get away. "Well," the trainer said, "When they are very young and much smaller, we use the same size rope to tie them, and, at that age, it's enough to hold them. As they grow up, they are conditioned to believe they cannot break away. They believe the rope can still hold them, so they never try to break free."

The man was amazed. These animals could break free from their bonds at any time, but because they believed they couldn't, they were stuck right where they were.

Although the elephant is one of the strongest animals on earth, it can easily be bound by a simple rope and a lot of mental conditioning. The adult elephant could, in fact, escape, but she had given up on herself and the idea of breaking the rope a long time ago. At a very young age, the elephant bought into the belief that placed a cap on what is really possible. She gave up on herself before she could see what she was capable of. The rope is a very simple tool, but it is unbreakable in the elephant's mind. It was enough to make her stop believing in herself and her purpose and kept her from reaching her destiny.

Answer the following questions to help unveil the mental limiting beliefs holding you back. Once you've identified them, you can start to work on releasing them.

- What are the mental "ropes" from your childhood you're allowing to hold you back?
- What past experiences are you still holding onto that are preventing you from moving forward?
- Have you forgiven yourself? Have you forgiven the people who have hurt you? If not, can you forgive yourself and/or the ones who hurt you today?
- A lot of time, we give others more grace than we would ever consider giving ourselves. If a friend shared the same limiting beliefs that you previously wrote, what advice would you give this friend?
- What is the next step you can take towards building a better future?

- Who do you know that can hold you accountable to take the necessary action steps?
- What new program or community could you get involved in that would support your goals and dreams?

A strong self-image is essential for living a happy and successful life. When we have a positive image of ourselves, we are more likely to believe in our abilities and take risks that lead to growth. On the other hand, when we have a negative self-image, we are more likely to doubt our abilities and to play it safe.

Fortunately, it is never too late to improve our self-image. Here are some tips:
- Keep your word, do what you say you're going to do, even if it's really hard.
- Stop comparing yourself to others.
- Focus on your strengths and accept your flaws.
- Dream bigger

YOU HAVE GREATNESS IN YOU! It's time for you to unleash your destiny and take the next step toward designing the life you are truly meant to live. You are one decision away from living a phenomenal life; think about how amazing your life could be!

"It's not who you are that holds you back, it's who you think you're not."
- Denis Waitley

About Kelisha Worrell

Kelisha Worrell is a #1Bestselling Author in 8 categories, International Bestselling author in 36 categories, television host of Destiny Unleashed, professional speaker, and Elite Coach. She has topped the charts by landing on the front cover of Woman of Dignity Magazine. She has been personally mentored by Bob Proctor and given the honor of receiving her speaker's certification by none other than the world's most renowned motivational speaker, Les Brown. Through her coaching, Ms. Worrell equips women with the support, tools, and resources to become successful entrepreneurs, creating an amazing life while having ONE mission - to help you COME BACK STRONGER and to share your talents with the world.

Website: Kelishaworrell.com
Social Media: IG & Facebook @Kelisha Worrell

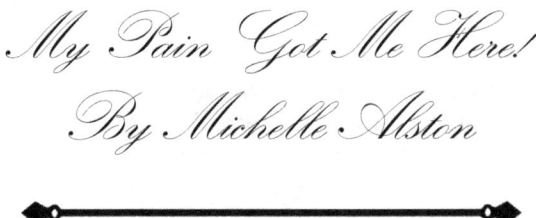

My Pain Got Me Here!
By Michelle Alston

Have you ever been so broken that you could not think straight, walking like a zombie? April 6, 2013, was the worst day of my life. She left me again, and this time, it was forever. My mom was gone, and I didn't say goodbye. I could not pull it together. I walked and cried, drove and called; I even went to work and cried while I was working. I did not understand why God let her leave me again. I was broken because we were never taught how to live without a loved one. My mom abandoned me once and put me out at 17; now, at 35, she was never coming back. God reminded me that He was with me when my parent left me the first time. I survived; depression tried to take me out.

Healing Inside Out

My mom's death took me out mentally. As a child, our parents taught us the alphabet song at home. They taught us the sounds and letters to create words in school. Life taught us some words hurt; life hurt, death hurt, and felt like a dart piercing my heart. Abandoned, broken, cursed, damaged, touched, pulled; fighting, judging, killing, lacking. Making mistakes, being nasty, a people pleaser, a quitter, and violent. I could not get it together. Depression was winning. I wanted to stop crying, but I did not know how. I lost everything.

All that I worked for was gone. I lost my car and my job, and I became homeless. My business was not even up and running anymore. I let the license expire, and now I owed everybody. Death was the pain that got me here. Your pain may be something else or even someone else. You have to look at your life from the eye of a child and then an adult. Don't be ashamed of what you are going through or have been through. Your family can only give you what was given to them; for some, that was nothing. Give them the board game called "life" instead of allowing people to play with your life. Don't keep dragging other people's life problems and issues. You have enough of your own unless you like toting trash. I know you heard the saying hurt people hurt people. I say hurt people get healed to help other people recover. Forgive yourself first and pray for guidance from God that He heals whatever pain got you here.

Reset Is Important

You have to believe you have been created for a time like this. So, you will never even imagine praying, asking, seeking, building, creating, and collaborating with people. You must first know where and who you are.

Generation after generation is crying for help. Is anyone listening? Could you not do it by yourself. Seek help? You have goals and dreams and don't know where to start. You can get a professional life coach or mentor or take some classes. Your life may not be all that you want it to be right now. It is not too late to dream out loud. It's an exceptional talent locked inside you that needs to have its birthday, so push. Somebody needs what you have, so don't isolate yourself. Now that we are here resetting our minds, we must get out of the rearview mirror. Living in the rearview mirror can cause unwanted pain, prolong your healing process and keep you in a pity party state of mind. Do you know what that means? Well, let me tell you. The negative energy will only attract those negative people who keep bringing up old stuff. You begin to complain about everything from a to z. There is so much in you, but you refuse to forgive yourself and break the cycles of generational barriers and pain, so you will miss out on so many opportunities because you refuse to shift. Listen, if we want better, we have to decide to break up that old toxic foundation and rebuild the life we only dream and imagine on a new foundation. They say you can't put new wine in an old bottle. Do you believe there's greatness in you?

Mindset Creates a New Foundation

This is not the time to focus on what they did or said. You have to focus on things above and the Kingdom of God. The Bible says in Jeremiah 29:11 KJV, "For I know the thoughts that I think toward you, saith the LORD, thoughts of peace, and not of evil, to give you an expected end." So, if that is what God sees for us, we cannot spend time worrying about the people who wrong us because those experiences are needed to help us get to the purpose. Not every bad thing that happens in our lives is to take us out. Sometimes, it develops us and builds character. God wants you to be able to handle the things of God and not be so emotional and immature. Think about this - how are you going to be able to make money? When you get caught up in your feelings, you indulge in spending like crazy.

Do you have peace today? Or are you on a search to pay everybody back that hurt you? Get it together and get over it. You must want what God wants for you, so reset and rebuild on purpose. Write the vision and make it plain, Habak. 2:2. If you need to go back to school, go. You are never too old to live your best life. You have to have faith and believe that you can. It's possible. I think you will not let this life pass you by without creating and completing your goals and dreams. I challenge you to write your vision, set some goals to accomplish in your life, fight for them, and don't give up. Although life happens, you must be consistent and build the foundation you never had to become the person you dream of. You are a winner, don't you forget. The pain is a part of your purpose, and you made it here.

Ice Your Purpose
The only way we will see greatness is with a positive attitude and become servant leaders that serve others with quality, results, empathy, and reliability. You were born with greatness. We must believe that no matter what happened to us in the past, we can do all things through Christ. We can't carry all their old baggage in our new foundation. The pain that bought me here taught me how to forgive the people who never showed up. Get your shift together and live life on ice with purpose.

- **Investing** in yourself will be your most excellent asset this season. You may have been burdened with life drama, but now you are ready for life's challenges. Please don't do it alone. Someone is prepared to help you walk in your purpose.

- **Connection** Mr. Les Brown said, "Proximity is power." Preparation with the right people in the right place and time can help you fulfill your wildest dreams. My coach Apostle Allen always says we have to keep moving and don't miss opportunities to show up and be great.
- **Experiences** Don't worry about that pain not coming to break you but to build you. Experiences are going to help you help others come out of pain and walk right into purpose, so don't be afraid to share your story. It's your testimony.

We Can Win
In conclusion, there is no lack in the Kingdom. You are your most significant project. Whatever season of your life you are in, never give up. Look ahead, stay positive and do all you can according to Jim Rohn's four-part ant philosophy. Just because you did not come from a wealthy family doesn't mean you have to stay in poverty. We can manifest the life we want. I often felt like I missed so much, so I used to think. Being around greatness and a positive environment, you will also see the change in your life. I now believe that God allows all the hurt and pain to get me here though I was never in pain; it would help to get me unstuck. My business is no longer falling apart. I now have a support system of friends to turn to for help. I always believed I would be the successful one who changed my family's narrative. Poverty was no longer our potion, but greatness is now.

Eric Worre said there will always be a good reason to quit, and there will always be a good reason to keep going. We must decide what kind of person we will be. Be grateful and show gratitude every day. God will send your tribe from the north, south, east, and west to help you carry out the vision God places in you. Time out for chasing useless things and money. Chase purpose and money will follow. Are you ready? The motivation, the communication, the collaboration, and the celebration will take you as far as your imagination allows you to dream. Greatness is in you.

About Michelle Alston

Michelle Alston is the CEO and Founder of Mtugi Monae LLC, Mtugi Monae was created from a passion for serving the community. Michelle has been in public service for over ten years and now serving as a social service rep in the District of Columbia government. Michelle spent four years as a Career Agent, motivating, facilitating peer groups, and creating workshop topics that will empower the low-income community to find work or finish school. Michelle's lifetime philosophy is to create and develop a solid foundation both professionally and personally. The other one is that everyone needs a plan and purpose in order not to flip flop through life.

Overcoming domestic violence, rejection, abandonment issues, and homelessness, Michelle decided that the victim mindset had to go if she was ever going to Manifest the good things that were already planned for her life. Michelle's desire to encourage family and loved ones to seek help when they have fallen into the difficult barrier in life. Michelle's past has motivated her to motivate others that shifting the mindset can take you far, but you have to be hungry enough to go get what your heart desire.

Michelle has taken the pressure from her past and turned it into her success story. Michelle received her high school diploma from night school. She graduated with her Associate and Bachelor of Science degree from Southeastern University and Master of Arts degree from Strayer University. Michell is a certified life coach, model, first-time two times best-selling author, and international best-selling author of Women ignited to serve. Michelle is also one of the Co-authors of the low-income female entrepreneur project (L.I.F.E. project). Michelle has received multiple community service awards from organizations that serve the urban community. As an inspiring motivational speaker, Michelle desires to lead with excellence, motivate with class, train with integrity, and serve underserved communities.

Follow Me:

Face book -Michelle Alston
Linkin Michelle Ann
Twitter Mickie204
Instagram Mtugimonae2
Tictoc Mtugimonae2
Snapchat Mtugi102
Telegram Michelle Ann
WA app MtugiMonae.
Email mtugimonae@gmail.com

Potential Greatness And Your Participation In It
By Rodney Lucero

MY PERSONAL PATH: THE BOY "MADE TO BUILD AND DESIGN"

Even at the age of three, I was fascinated with how things worked - and why they behaved as they did. I was even interested in the supernatural and how it worked, though I probably couldn't have put it into words at the age of three! I had no father in the home, and my mom needed so much help around the house fixing things. Even as a boy, I was actually wired to analyze, build, and design. I remember how good success felt when it happened! Then my uncle visited when I was seven; I remember him sitting us at the table and putting objects in front of us - making us take them all apart and put them back together again. That was a brilliant strategy to keep us busy! We were poor and had an old TV. At ten years old, I wanted to see programs like Star Trek. Taking the lessons from my uncle, I took apart the television and fixed it. You could say I was motivated! Somehow no hardship stopped me from discovering a part of what I believe I was CREATED to do.

MY BOYHOOD JOY IN DESIGNING

I badly wanted to design a building in a tree - to build something UP IN THE AIR! My mom didn't want me to "waste my time playing." Still, I made time to design a tree house. "*Train up a **child** in the way he should go [and in keeping with his individual gift or bent], and when he is old he will not depart from it.*" (Proverbs 22:6). All these skills led to later careers. Underneath this productivity, however, was an aching question: *why was I created, and for what purpose?* You might not know these questions would be in the mind of a ten-year-old boy who was deconstructing a television; or in the mind of a 16-year-old doing crazy experiments with a chemistry set, obsessed with his microscope.

But my mind quietly searched for more than just the "how-to" of design. I wanted to know about MY DESIGNER. I suppose Mom succeeded in her plan to keep me busy and out of trouble when she got me a job at a naval air station, repairing military aircraft for all three high school summers instead of going to beach parties. But still, the burning question remained: how did my life fit into a larger design? It was not until I understood Intelligent Design - and the Designer behind it - that I finally comprehended why I had been given any gifts at all.

WHAT IS INTELLIGENT DESIGN?

Intelligent design is the understanding that there is a purposeful, conscious, intelligent cause behind our existence, as evidenced in the beauty and order of the created universe (for example, look at the design of nature). Most people would have to be deaf or blind not to give credit to a great composer of music or not give credit to a great architect of a stunning building. Our minds and hearts were meant to recognize the human creators of certain things.

Based on this,
everything in me resonated with this truth:
In the beginning
God created the heavens and the earth.
(Genesis 1:1)

You can imagine how the boy who designed a tree house would be thrilled by this realization: Intelligent Design means there is a *Designer!*

THE BOY WITH THE MICROSCOPE SEES THE BIG PICTURE

I was stunned to realize that not just the Heavens and Earth were beautifully designed: humans also are part of this magnificent design. As I matured, the world of the human heart became fascinating to me, so I turned my gaze on HUMANITY. Why and how had God designed humanity? As my searching mind persisted, I was thrilled when I read these words: *And the LORD God formed man (Adam) of the dust of the ground, and breathed into his nostrils the breath of life; and man became a living soul."* (Genesis 2:7)

MAN: A SPIRIT AS WELL AS A LIVING SOUL
"And man became a living soul" means that when Adam's spirit was put into his newly made body, his new soul was formed (mind, will, emotions). Now, remember, I am the boy who had to know HOW things fit together. Therefore, I loved learning that the soul is the "INTERFACE" between our spirit and the human body. My later research would delve into three areas: the spirit, soul, and body!

YOUR UNIQUE DESIGN AND POTENTIAL
Think for a minute with me: "purposeful design" is even reflected in the heart of the music composer, filmmaker, and inventor. God made sure this bent for intelligent design would be placed in many people. God designed us and in that design is potential greatness. I say "potential" - because this potential can be thwarted. Just as my efforts to build a tree house could have been thwarted if I decided to ignore gravity or certain realities, the fulfillment of our design depends on respect for some underlying principles and truths as well. My scientific mind is constantly marveling at the beauty of Intelligent Design. But please don't confuse this with what some call "The Great Architect" or "A Supreme Being." That falls far short of reality. I was stunned to discover I could have a relationship with my God, who is intimately involved in our creation:

O Lord, you have examined my heart
and know everything about me.
Thank you for making me so wonderfully complex!
Your workmanship is marvelous—how well I know it.
You watched me as I was being formed in utter seclusion,
as I was woven together in the dark of the womb.
You saw me before I was born.
Every day of my life was recorded in your book.
Every moment was laid out
before a single day had passed. (Psalm 139, NLT)

YOU HAVE A "GOD BOOK"
As you can see in this Psalm, there is even a Heavenly Book written for each one of us to fulfill. The biggest part of our destiny includes our relationship with Him. When I honestly opened my entire being to the truth, I also understood that God had sent His Son to enter our timeline and come to Earth; and that this Son of God had come for one reason: to rescue His "us," His creation, from alienation caused by our sin and wrongdoing – by a substitutionary death on our behalf on the Cross, as detailed in chapters of the Bible such as Isaiah 53 and Matthew 26,27, and 28.

PART OF MY CALLING
I've told you my path in resolving my questions on "how things work" on the spiritual level. This has led to one of my favorite areas of study. I focus on the three parts of a person: the spirit, soul, and body. Some of the tools I use are tests for personality, intelligence, and gifts – and evaluation tests for talents; also, research in medical, health, and nutrition knowledge.

OUR RESPONSIBILITY
Every single person is one of a kind. As we unfold different layers built within us, we will learn how to fulfill our design and purpose; but the story will be incomplete until we are in a relationship with Him.

Jesus said to him, "I am the [only] Way [to God] and the [real] Truth and the [real] Life; no one comes to the Father but through Me. (John 14:6 Amplified)

Is it possible
to abandon your highest destiny?
Yes.
I understand the importance of building on the right foundation, which ensures that a design comes into the highest expression intended. In the same way, my deepest destiny requires coming humbly to God and doing things His way, not mine.

FROM TREE HOUSE TO TRUEST PURPOSE
As the boy who built the tree house and the youth who repaired military aircraft, I now continue in my God-given talents with a

sense of purpose. For those who are interested, some of my roles and jobs are below. But for me, the bottom line is that my desire is to hear "well done, good and faithful servant" when I stand before the Lord – as we must all do someday.

I know that at that time,
I will not be rewarded for the gifts He gave me –
but I will be evaluated as to whether I lived in humility and love,
and served Him with those gifts.

There should be no boasting about gifts. If anything, the gifts make me focus on God's mercy, grace, and goodness. Who are we that we receive such goodness from God?

Only a few of the ways God has blessed me to function:
- I've had roles such as researcher, scientist, engineer, inventor, designer, craftsman, builder, businessman, historian, teacher, minister, nutritionist, and alternative medicine designer.
- My careers in the military arena: Military aircraft flight instruments repair; Active and Reserve military service.
- Computer roles: data analysis and diagnostics technician; programmer; and telecommunications.
- Real estate roles: commercial and residential construction; remodeling foreman/project leader, business partner, building maintenance.
- Over the decades, my love of learning has taken me into the realm of medical, health, nutritional, and many types of scientific endeavors.
- One of my passions is researching the supernatural or quantum realm and the Holy Bible Scriptures – and how to apply these to practical concerns in everyday life.

It's not possible to include all of my research here, but please write to me at Rodney@theluceros.com

If you would like to know more about:

- INTELLIGENT DESIGN
- WHO the Most High God is
- Your purpose by design
- How to ask the Most High God into your heart

There is no one who is meant to "go it alone" or be lost and without hope!
Luke 15:10 - *That's the way God responds every time one lost soul repents and turns to HIM. HE says to all HIS angels, 'Let's have a joyous celebration, for the one who was lost, I have found!'"*

About Rodney Lucero

Rodney Lucero has decades of training and study in sciences and relentlessly pursues knowledge of God's wisdom and will.

There is a higher level of knowledge of sciences, supernatural/quantum realm, along with the three created parts of each person: Spirit, Soul, and Body. Rodney has spent a lifetime researching these areas of knowledge. His belief in INTELLIGENT DESIGN and decades of life experiences, education, and training from several different careers contribute to his ability to diagnose matters pertaining to these issues, with practical applications in scientific, spiritual, business, health, and other arenas.

Rodney's passion is to empower others with wisdom and unchangeable truth revealed by God in His Scriptures and the amazing truths he has uncovered in his lifetime of research and experience, resulting in powerful and practical life changes.

Rodney is highly active in his faith community and enjoys his beloved family. He is a business partner - remodeling and maintaining residential and commercial properties. He is a Bible School graduate and has additional college degrees: BA in Economics, Management Information Systems, and Masters of Business Administration. He served a total of 23 years in both active duty and the United States Army Reserves and Air Force National Guard with training in secret military operations. By the grace of God, Rodney is a perpetual learner.

Contact:
RODNEY@THELUCEROS.COM

Position of Power
By Shirley Brown Danzy

"There are powers inside of you which, if you could discover and use, would make of you everything you ever dreamed or imagined you could become."
— **Orison Swett Marden**

They say life is full of challenges and controversy.
Why should mine be any different?
1965 was the beginning of my journey through life. There was so much controversy in the world surrounding human rights at the time.

I was caught in the middle of the transition as we began to evolve as a people. I remember running through the neighborhood, picking plums from the trees in my backyard, and spending the summers in a small town called Crystal Springs, MS, with my grandparents.

I was taught as a child to always be humble, but I had a burning desire for way more than my humble beginnings provided. I dreamed of standing in front of large crowds, and I could see myself standing on a stage speaking to thousands of people.

What did this dream mean?
It was not until many years later that I found out.

The Mystery Woman
While working in a non-traditional role as a Manufacturing Supervisor, a woman walked up to me and asked me if she could tell me something.

I simply replied, "Yes, you may."

She proceeded to tell me that I would not be at the job I was currently working at for long; she said that I would be offered another job within a year and would accept it.

"It will be a good move for you, and before the end of your time, you will be speaking to thousands of people, spreading the Word," she said.

I instantly thought, *"This must be the prophet that my coworker told me worked here."*

A coworker had told me a few days prior that a woman at our workplace was a prophet, and people say that what she had prophesied to others had come true. My friend, Kathy, had been trying to get me to see her, but I had allowed fear to stop me. I believe that what we seek also seeks us. I was afraid to go to her, but she came to me.

I initially had my doubts because I had been working there for over ten years, but I remembered what my coworker said and the dreams I had as a child.

How did this woman just tell me exactly what I had seen in my dreams?

Well, just as the nice older woman had prophesied, I was offered another position within a year, and I took it. In addition, just as she had said, it did turn out to be a blessing for me.

My dreams kept flashing before me, and all I could think about was, *"What about the second part of the prophecy regarding me speaking to thousands of people?"*

Misunderstood
I have always been humble, which made people view me as shy and reserved. The sad truth is, this cost me a lot of great opportunities.

I began to doubt myself. I thought, *How can this be?*
How can I position myself to become a powerful speaker?
What would I speak about?
Who would my message be for?
I had no idea.

I have oftentimes been misunderstood because of my humbleness and quiet demeanor. Some people saw it as a weakness, but those who knew me well knew it was my strength.

At one point, I had a manager who gave me a tremendously hard time. It was as if he could not see the value I had to offer because he judged me by my quietness and calmness.

The Moment of Truth

One day I was asked to speak to a large group of visitors and upper management regarding some improvements made in my area. There were three other supervisors, but we had to talk about our unique issues and improvements.

When it was my turn to speak, I instantaneously started getting nervous. I could feel the fear trying to steal my moment of expression.

The person before me passed me the mic once they were done sharing their story. I took the mic, introduced myself, and proceeded to tell my story.

I could see my manager watching me as I spoke; I continued, and once I finished, I thanked the audience for listening and passed the mic to the next speaker.

As we concluded and the crowd thanked each of us for an excellent presentation, we all smiled and began to disperse. As I walked off, my manager approached me and said, "Wow! You are a silent storm."

This day changed his perception of me. He began to treat me with dignity and respect. It was as though he felt terrible for misjudging me.

I received the opportunity to work in another country to support their workforce. While there, a woman walked over to me and asked if I knew Chad.

"Yes, I do; he was my manager a few years ago," I said.

She said she worked with him for several years on some projects.

"He called me and asked me to make sure you are taken care of while you are here." She added.

I smiled because I knew that speaking that day had a tremendous impact on him and hopefully taught him not to judge people simply because they exemplify a calm spirit. I called and thanked him for taking the time to make sure I was okay and taken care of.

My Voice, My Power

It is amazing how our voice can put us in a position of power[1] – the way we deliver our words, structure our message and draw people into our story by speaking from the heart. From my childhood days until now, I have always struggled to find the power to have an abundant life – a life full of happiness, love, and peace.

My mother and father taught me to pray at an early age, so each night, I prayed to ask God to put the right people in my path who would guide me to my position of power in life.

I wanted to live a life that would serve others and outlive me. However, I just did not know how to do it. This is where I trusted God for direction.

Life has not been easy for me, but I have always kept moving toward my dreams. I often feel and see myself living the life I have dreamed about. I even took the time to place all my dreams on a vision board to keep them in front of me.

Back to my speaking dream, I began listening to the motivational speaker Les Brown. I had to be still when I heard him because he captured my attention. I had to listen to him as he pulled me into his story and motivated and inspired me to look at the good within myself.

His message put me in a position of power to continue going after my dream despite my circumstances. I am reminded of Bill Gates when he said, "*If you're born poor, it's not your fault, but if you die poor, it's your fault.*[2]"

I found myself listening to Les Brown every morning to start my day. One morning, I said to myself just how much I would love him to teach me to speak as he does with power and conviction.

I had started following him on my Instagram business page. One day while on my page, a message popped up indicating that if you wanted to join Les Brown power voice training, type in the chatbox. I became afraid to type the words displayed in the box.

---

[1] Understanding the power of your voice - BALANCE
[2] Bill Gates quote: If you're born poor it's not your fault, but if ... | Quotes of famous people (quotepark.com)

Fear is a powerful thing. People have often said that it has robbed so many of their dreams[3]. I believe it! It stopped me in my tracks, and all kinds of doubt came to mind. Things like, "You know you can't afford Les Brown" and "You have been labeled as shy; you can't learn to speak like Les Brown."

I prayed over it that night and decided to push past my fears and go do what I had asked God about. I asked God to provide me the opportunity to be taught by Les Brown, and there the opportunity was, and I was about to allow fear to destroy my chance to live my dream. I would not let this happen. So I enrolled in the Power Voice program and got the opportunity to be coached by Les Brown.

Your Dreams are Limitless!
I had another dream to write my own book. While in the Les Brown and Jon Talarico Thinking into Results program, I met a book writing coach, Dr. Denise Nicholson, who helped me author my first book entitled, "The Power to Succeed, Unlock your Life, Unlock Your Dreams." All of these just started with a thought.

Bob Proctor said, "Thoughts become things; if you see it in your mind, you can hold it in your hand.[4]"

I have also had dreams of giving back. I wanted to help others who were lost to try and help them figure out how to use their power to succeed in life. I desired to be in a position of power so that I could help others who could not see how to move past their current circumstances. I wanted to show them that if they believe anything is possible and begin to move toward their dreams, they could have the life they imagined.

People and things will start to align with your vision and your dream and lay out the path for you to take and continue your journey. You have the power to do that.

Our minds are powerful. This is why we have to choose thoughts that uplift us over the thoughts that do not serve us on our journey through life.

---

[3] Does Fear Stop you from Achieving your Dreams? - Success Factor
[4] Quote by Bob Proctor: "Thoughts become things. If you see it in your m..." (goodreads.com)

Through my message, I want people to understand that although someone may be quiet, or rather have developed calmness of mind, don't overlook their power to propel you or your business to great heights. They, too, have the power and ability to live the life they have always imagined.

Everyone does not tell you what they are going to do. They show you through their actions. As James Allen would say, "Calmness of mind is one of the beautiful jewels of wisdom. It is the result of long and patient effort in self-control. Its presence is an indication of ripened experience and a more than ordinary knowledge of the laws and operations of thought.[5]"

Finding My Voice
Back to my speaking dream, I have claimed the title of *"motivational speaker."* I am still new in my journey; however, I know I am where I should be. I am on my path to greatness, my position of power, my position of abundance. I am where I suppose to be. I am reminded of Nelson Mandela when he said, "I learned that courage was not the absence of fear, but the triumph over it. The brave man is not he who does not feel afraid, but he who conquers that fear."

Today, I am in control of my destiny, just as you are or can be. I am spreading the word to thousands of people through my books and my message. We all have the potential to place ourselves in a position of power to live out our dreams. Don't stop going after your dreams. Begin by giving yourself permission to shift your mind from average to extraordinary. You will fall during the process, but challenge yourself and keep getting back up, again and again, until you make it. It is worth it!

> *"Your dream was given to you. If someone else can't see it for you, that's fine; it was given to you and not them. It's your dream. Hold it. Nourish it. Cultivate it!*[6]" – **Les Brown**

---

[5] Quote by James Allen: "Calmness of mind is one of the beautiful jewels..." (goodreads.com)

[6] Les Brown Quote: "Your dream was given to you. If someone else can't see it for you, that's fine, it was given to you and not them. It's y..." (quotefancy.com)

About Shirley Brown Danzy

Shirley Brown Danzy was born in the small town of Crystal Springs, Mississippi, and spent most of her formative years there. She spent the remainder of her formative years in Subdivision Number 2, a Westside community in Hinds County. She attended Jackson State University, where she attained bachelor's and master's degrees in Social Work, and she is presently pursuing a Ph.D. in Social Work from the same university.

Shirley is currently a Global Trainer for a Major Corporation and has previously worked with vulnerable children and adults who have suffered from abuse and neglect. But her enduring aim is to succeed, and it was this drive that made her think about how she could help others to do the same.

The answer was to write her first book, **The Power to Succeed**, in which she provides readers with the tools they will need to achieve whatever level of success they are aiming for through a combination of self-belief, developing the right mindset and building resilience, among other positive traits.

In her free time, Shirley loves traveling, spending time with her family, relaxing on her back porch, and enjoying the great outdoors. Above all else, Shirley enjoys helping other people to reach for their personal goals and showing them the ways to achieve them, no matter how big or small they may be.

Shirley is also a member of the National Association of Social Workers (NASW), which offers an array of programs and opportunities that enhance the well-being of individuals, families, and communities through the advancement of social work policy and practice.

In addition, she is a member of The Mary S. Nelums Foundation, which awards scholarships to deserving social work students who display a strong commitment and dedication to excellence in social work practice.

You can contact or connect with Shirley Brown Danzy at:

Facebook: Shirley Brown Danzy | Facebook
Instagram:
https://www.instagram.com/authorshirleybrowndanzy
Email: Shirley@shirleybrowndanzy.com
Website: https://www.shirleybrowndanzy.com

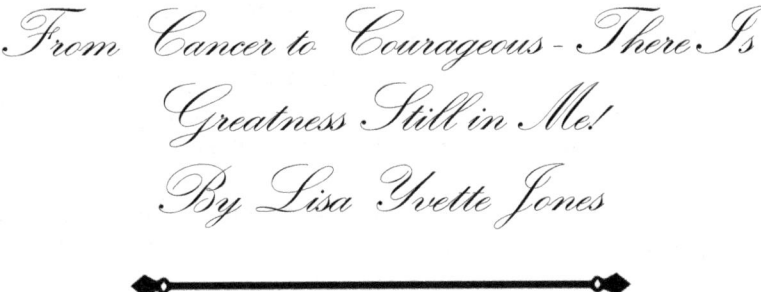

From Cancer to Courageous - There Is Greatness Still in Me!
By Lisa Yvette Jones

April of 2009, my birthday month, I decided to give myself a gift. You know, ladies, that gift that we give ourselves every year, that yearly appointment that we dread, but it is also the appointment that we know that we must keep. Keep all medical appointments. That appointment turned into another appointment, and before I knew it, I was before two gynecologic oncologists.

With empathy and concern, I heard these words, "Ms. Jones, you have been diagnosed with stage three cervical cancer - papillary serous carcinoma of the cervix. It is high grade, and it is quite vicious, so much so that it is eating through your body."

I then had a shock wave go through my body. I could not understand how such destruction was raging so viciously inside of me, and that could potentially kill me. I asked how it was even possible that I could have been diagnosed with cancer, and a vicious one at that! My intelligent brain could not comprehend this news because I had not one symptom or irregularity, and there was no history of cancer in my family. There was no precursor for this diagnosis, but was there a precursor?

At the time of my diagnosis, I was every bit of 362 pounds. I looked good, and I felt good. Yes, I looked good because, listen, if I did not think it and believe it, then nobody else would, right? Well, because I needed more information and a better understanding, I did what any intelligent person would do; I began my research. Studies would reveal that those 362 pounds were my warning, my precursor, my danger for cancer, and for my life.

Studies conducted by the Centers for Disease Control (CDC) reflect that 40% of the cancers in America are related to obesity. Wow! Now please, do not get me wrong. I am not saying that everyone who is obese will have cancer. What I am saying is that the science does reflect that there is a link between cancer and obesity.

In fact, there are thirteen cancers in the United States that have been linked to obesity. A few of them are breast cancer, thyroid cancer, ovarian cancer, and liver cancer.

I advised the doctors that I needed some time. The doctors reminded me that because of the viciousness of the cancer that they diagnosed me with, I did not have time. Notice my language, the cancer that they diagnosed me with. I never took ownership of that diagnosis by staking claim to it by saying, "I have cancer." No! I refused too! It was not that I did not believe that the diagnosis was not true; I was not going to give it life through my words. My Good Book says, "Death and life are in the power of the tongue...!" Proverbs 18:21 I then knew that since I was in a fight for my life, then words of life and faith must come from me.

The doctors advised that if I did not have the surgery within the next few days, but no later than a week, I would certainly die because once the cancer spread to any major organ, they would not open me up. I insisted that I needed time because what I was faced with was a storm.

Wow! I was in serious duress, and I needed to send out my *SOS*, you know, that early signal that they used back in the early 1900s when the ship was in duress, and they sent out that Morse code SOS. I needed to do that immediately because I was in a heavy storm, and the sound waves of this news were catastrophic.

After both doctors gave me two death sentences and declarative statements that I would die, I continued to believe that there was still greatness left in me, and I just could not fathom a premature death.

After leaving the doctor's office and while seated in my car with this dark storm cloud over my life, I called on a few key people who knew the words and the worth of prayer, including my now late ex-husband. He was in immediate shock and disbelief, but he knew I would never tell him anything that was untrue. He was so kind and compassionate, and he said these words, "We will get through this as a family, sweetheart." He immediately stood with me and by me during my entire ordeal. Besides, we both share an amazing son, Anthony Maurice Jones, II, who was only 14 years young at the time of this news about his momma.

As you can surmise from my story, one of the strategies that helped me was knowing my community of support. It is imperative that you know those who will stand in faith with you when you are facing a storm and, in my case, as with many of you, death.

The fight was on! I had to do what I would normally do in any storm. I had to activate more of my *SOS*-*S*helter in Place, *S*hut *O*ut the *S*torm, and *S*hut into God. I had to not only join my faith with those praying with and for me; I had to believe that I was going to come through that storm because I wanted to live and not die! I refused to accept those death sentences proclaimed for my life. My Good Book says in Hebrews, "That it is appointed unto man, once to die...," but I did not plan to keep those two death sentences at that time.

My strategic *S.O.S.* plan was simple. It worked for me, and I know it will work for you.

*S*tay or *S*helter in place and remain in prayer until I knew that the storm had subsided. I knew that any success in the storm was going to come by fasting and praying.

*S*hut *O*ut all those things that would come against your mind and give you all that distorted thinking. If there is anything that is going to distract you from hearing from God, then what you need to do is to get rid of it. I had to remember what my Good Book said in Isaiah 26:3, "Thou will keep you in perfect peace if your mind is stayed on Him."

*S*hut into God! On the third day of my fasting and praying, the storm had subsided, and I heard these words, "It is not unto death. You shall live and not die, and this will never return again!" I knew it! Because there was still greatness left in me! The waves of concern were boisterous, but the fight for my life was greater than the waves attempting to overtake me.

I then gave thanks and praise to my sustainer of life, my Chief Physician, God. I stood up and saw that the coast was clear. I then made the appointment to return to the oncologist. I informed the doctor of what I had heard from my Chief Physician. The doctor then understood Who I was speaking about. I further advised the doctor that although their diagnosis is serious and quite troubling; however, my Chief Physician's prognosis is what I will live by.

I advised the doctor that I would have surgery on June 29, 2009, and I further reminded the doctor that there was no further spreading of the deadly disease. The doctor was not convinced and then told me again that I would die if I waited that long, over one month from my original diagnosis. The disease was too deadly. I then assured the doctor of my faith in God.

The doctor reluctantly said, "Why do I have a feeling that I will see you on June 29?" I said, "Because you will." And he did!

I had the surgery to remove the cancer, and it was undoubtedly a success!

Remember, I was every bit of 362 pounds, but not anymore! I have since released over two hundred pounds and counting! There is greatness still left in me! Our lives are a gift from God and what we do with our life by living out our purpose is our gift to the world that awaits us.

My friend, take a pen and turn all those periods in your life, those declarative negative life-stopping statements, into commas! That is right, do it now because it is not over for you.

Where somebody said it was over, I want you to believe as my Heavenly Father said to me. "This is not unto death, comma, you shall live and not die, comma, you are going to be a speaker at the Power Voice Summit, comma, you will grace the global stage with Dr. Les Brown, comma, you will co-author a book with Dr. Les Brown, comma, you will be one of the most sought-after leadership development coaches, trainers, speakers, teachers, best-selling authors, and an inspiration to millions who hear your story, comma; because there is greatness still left in you!

Therefore, my friend, who has counted you out? Who has told you that you do not measure up? Who has told you that you cannot be all that you can be? Your storm was, is, or shall only be a temporary setback for your setup to your greatest comeback! Do not miss the value in your valley. Get up and live out your purpose on purpose.

In addition to the SOS strategies, here are ten bonus strategies that were the catalyst to my successful journey of courageously navigating the Cancer Storm of Life:

- P.R.A.Y.
    a. **P**raise God.
    b. **R**eflect on all He has already done for you.
    c. **A**dorn Him, His Goodness, His Grace, and His Mercy.
    d. **Y**ield fully to His presence and His purpose for your life.
- Trust God with all your heart. (Proverbs 3: 5-6)
- Since you are a partner in your health care, be relentless about advocating for your own health.
- Know your core circle/community/tribe of supporters and prayer warriors.
- Listen to your body. I began to have an unquenchable desire for berries. My body immediately geared up for attack mode against the cancer.

    According to the National Cancer Institute, antioxidants protect cells from damage caused by harmful molecules and free radicals. Antioxidants are also known to slow the growth of and to prevent further development of cancer (driscolls.com)

- Know what keeps you grounded and centered. My faith is everything to me.
- Never take your health for granted; therefore, schedule and keep all appointments. Remember, I had no symptoms and was already in Stage 3 of a very vicious cancer diagnosis-the eye of the storm.
- Know your numbers and record the date:
    a. How much do you weigh? _____/_____
    b. What is your blood pressure? _____/_____

    c. What is your cholesterol level? _____/_____
    d. What is your A1C/blood sugar level? _____/_____
    e. What is your blood type? _____/_____

- Steal away for self-care/me time. Journal, walk, meditate, pray, swim, bike ride, sail, fly, but do something for yourself and know that self-care is not selfish; it is necessary.
- Celebrate your courageous comeback by having an attitude of gratitude, walking out your purpose on purpose, and no longer seeking permission to live aloud but only giving notice to the world that you are present and accounted for.

The doctors may have given me that *diagnosis* of Stage 3 Cervical Cancer and two death sentences, but my Chief Physician gave the *prognosis* of life! Each June 29, I celebrate another year of victorious navigation of a vicious storm of life. I am still here! The storm may have been a formidable force to manage, but my Anchor was stronger.

    I AM a living, breathing, walking, talking, moving miracle woman of God. The storm of cancer may have been a passing cyclone in my life, not to disrupt it, but to clear the path for the greatness in me that lies ahead! As for me, *cancer* was put on notice and was forever *canceled*!

About Lisa Yvette Jones

Leadership and development are key components of the quintessential journey towards self-actualization. Affording today's culture with the tools necessary for their own expedition; is the compassionate professional, Lisa Yvette Jones.

    Lisa Yvette Jones is a Best-Selling author, orator, success enthusiast, CEO, and Founder of **iC.A.R.E Leadership, LLC**, a multidimensional coaching practice aiding in the production, advancement, and transformation of professional leadership.

LISA YVETTE JONES

Having experienced many years in the fields of business administration and coaching Lisa Yvette Jones has built a meritorious acumen in influencing career professionals to prioritize their health and their love of self and to develop a genuine appreciation for their vocations at large.

Her mantra is simple: She supports leaders on their quest to attain professional success while ensuring their availability to serve others from a place of personal overflow, removed from all exasperation. In short, she reminds clients that a leader's life matters too.

Accomplishing the duality of delivering amicable results with unyielding benevolence, Lisa displays sincere regard for higher education, achievement, and team building. She holds a Bachelor of Arts in Business Administration, a Masters of Arts in Counseling, and is a John Maxwell Certified Coach, trainer, and speaker. Leading by example, Lisa's leadership expertise has yielded remarkable achievements throughout her career; including sharing the global stage with Dr. Les Brown during the Power Voice Summit 2021, appearing as a featured speaker for the United Nations Women's Economic Thumbprint during March 2022 Women's History Month, and awarded recognition throughout her agency, for her devoted leadership sensory, and team success. Not transient to captaincy, Lisa is a member of several reputed organizations, such as the Michigan Association of Female Entrepreneurs, the National Association of Women Business Owners, the American Cancer Society, and many more.

A profound elocutionist, Lisa has been trained by some of the world's most renowned leaders and institutions. She is a Dale Carnegie Leadership Trained Speaker and has completed graduate achievement success from Les Brown Power Voice Academy, Sage Lavine's-Women Rocking Business Entrepreneur Leadership Academy, Jon Talarico's Thinking into Results, and more.

Inspired by the will to see global transformation and humanization of the overall employment experience, head, hands, and heart, Lisa Yvette Jones will stand as one reminding the world that benevolent leadership is necessary.

When Lisa is not out shifting the mindsets of growing professionals, she is an asset to her local community and a loving member of her family and friendship circles.

Lisa Yvette Jones. Leader. Energizer. Influencer.

LisaYvetteJones@gmail.com (email)
LisaYvetteJones.com (website)
(248) 952-8122 (contact number)
https://www.facebook.com/lisa.yvette.jones
https://instagram.com/lisayvettejones2:
LisaYvetteJone1:
https://youtube.com/channel/UCRfcWjiueMYk7nxxXQWPZYQ

SYLVIA TSUI

The Greatness In You
By Sylvia Tsui

It was 6 am on a Tuesday morning. I woke up in a hospital bed with tubes in my veins. My skin was falling apart, my face was swollen, my scalp was peeling, and it was filled with blood and yellow liquid. Food was served. It was breakfast time, but I could barely pull myself up to drink or eat. My family was not with me because the hospital put me in an isolated room. They couldn't figure out what caused my high fever and rashes all over my body. After a couple of days in the hospital, my condition got worse, my face, hands, and body were swollen, and my skin was peeling all over my body. They couldn't put tape on my arms without peeling my skin away when they removed it. My mouth was swelling and bleeding. What could I have done wrong? One moment I was totally healthy; the next moment, I was struggling for life.

Right before the hospital visit, my business was losing money, my children were fighting a lot, and I almost got into a divorce with my husband. I was in a lot of mental pain and couldn't see a way out.

Fast forward to three years later, I have a healthy and amazing body. I am totally healed, with radiant skin, lush, full hair, and lots of positive energy. Our family and I keep moving to bigger homes. I am making ten times more income in the last year without working 10 hours a day. My children get along nicely, and my husband and I love each other more than ever.

I wish I could say it was an easy road, but it wasn't. I kept falling along the way, but I was falling forward, and I learned important lessons that are so powerful. Looking back, being in a hospital was the best thing that had happened to me. I was awakened to the truth of life.

I learned that there are stronger and more powerful forces than we can see and feel. Some Laws run the Universe. If we behave and think in a way that is not aligned with the law, our energy gets stuck or does not flow. Our health, our well-being, and our luck are all affected. And the good news is that the remote control to all greatness and abundance is within us. It lies inside all of us. If we act and behave in a way that aligns with our true essence and the law of the Universe, everything flows beautifully.

You see, at every moment, we have a choice to choose how we think, feel and act, and how we choose will determine what we will experience in the future. However, there are natural laws that cannot be violated. The Universe or nature will run according to the law without fail. We need to hold on to what is true, and we need to work with this law. We all have the ability to heal, have fulfilling love, and prosper. All we need to do is to let go of all the things that do not serve us. Let go of all the beliefs and thoughts that do not serve us.

Here are the lessons I learned that helped me turn everything around. I hope that those of you who are struggling now and seeing no hope at the moment will find inspiration from these lessons I learned. I hope that you will thrive and live the best life of yours.

- **Be grateful.** Change your thoughts to grateful thoughts. When you change the way you look at things, the thing you look at changes. The Buddha calls this the emptiness of all things. Everything in the world has no good or bad of its own. How you look at anything determines what you will manifest in your life. If you see a roadblock as something that will kill you, then you will never have the courage to go over it and see the other side of the rainbow. Find the goodness in everything you see, and your life will be filled with amazing things. Love, health, and wealth are not far away, and it is only a thought away. When you are only looking at the negative aspect of a person or an event, you are collecting misfortune from the person or event because, like vibration attracts each other. You will attract unhappiness, sickness, and disaster. When you look at a person or event as positive, you are collecting good energy and attracting good things to you. Gratitude is training your mind to seek the positive and to appreciate all the good things in life. So be grateful for everything you experience and see. Look for the positive aspect of everything and be grateful. Keeping a gratitude journal is such an amazing exercise you can do every morning that will bring amazing results. One of my clients manifested $12k in a month by simply implementing the morning gratitude practice.

- **Seek growth.** The law of creation says that if you are not creating, you are disintegrating. There is a saying in Chinese that says, "Learning is like sailing in a river against the current. If you are not moving forward, you are pushed backward." It is true that change is inevitable; if you are not seeking change by growing yourself in every area, you are going to be pushed backward. The nature of all life is to grow upward. We can see that in plants where it is always moving toward the sun. Our nature is to seek growth. Always keep learning and growing.

- **The power of the seed.** Every thought and action you have is a seed that plants in your life. If you have negative thoughts about yourself or others, they will manifest themselves. Vice versa, if you plant good thoughts, you will have an amazing life. The seed is the most powerful force in the Universe. Whatever you plant will manifest in your life. If you want wealth, you plant the seed of abundance by giving money to others. If you want love, you plant the seed of love by giving love to others.

- **Learn to protect your energy and thoughts. Energy** is the new currency. The invisible is controlling the visible in this world. Electricity which is invisible is controlling the lights and everything that runs on electricity. Wifi is controlling internet access. Gravity is controlling the way we live in this world. Your thoughts and behavior can either give you energy or drain your energy away. It is important to protect your energy and learn to stop doing things that drain your energy. Everything we see in this world starts with a thought. Guide your every thought. Think in ways that will empower you and others.

- **Live your life from the inside out**. A boat in the sea of uncertainties doesn't sink unless the water gets inside. No matter how big the wave, you see the boat floating on top; however, once the water gets inside, even the Titanic will sink. We do not fail because of what someone said or how unbearable the situation we are in; we fail because we let what's going on outside disturb and affect what's going inside. Will you use the circumstances in your life as an excuse to give up, or will you use them as a reason to bring out the best in you? The choice is yours. You can choose how you think, feel and act, but you do not have the freedom to choose the consequences that result from your thoughts and actions.

- **Live a life that is in harmony with the Law of the Universe.** Learning what the laws are and how they work will help you create the life of your dream effortlessly without many struggles. Therefore, it is important to learn how energy works and how the Universe runs.

We all deserve to live an amazing and abundant life filled with love, joy, and peace. All the solution to our problem lies within us. Let go of all the fog and dust that covered that light in us, and you will find your way to greatness.

About Sylvia Tsui

The road to self-actualization is no one-dimensional fiat; it is rather occupied by individuals equipped with the wisdom, empathy, and internal fortitude needed to guide others through the paths of personal transformation. Embodying these traits with unyielding measures; is the compassionate professional, Sylvia Tsui. Affectionately known as Reya Wan (Sylvia's soul name), Sylvia uses years of her devoted expertise in traditional Chinese literature infused with Feng shui, energy healing, along with coaching to help people transform the way they think about life;

propelling them into their hearts' contentment, by way of visualization.

Sylvia is a certified healer, accountant, and Diamond Life coach, helping many to redesign their lives through the power of energy, mental clarity, and alignment.

Her mantra is clear: She wishes to transform millions of lives, helping people to achieve ultimate tranquility, balance, and overall abundance.

Sylvia combines personal excellence with sincere regard for education, achievement, and influence. She is certified in more than seven elite vocations, including Public Accounting, Diamond Feng Shui Practitioner, MindValley Business Coaching, and more. A bonafide savant in her field, Sylvia translates her practice to current culture seamlessly, as she hosts many on her podcast, Unlimited Manifestation, helping listeners to discover new tools for manifesting their dreams and living their best life daily. Clients have attested that through her program, they were able to relieve financial blocks, find guidance for their personal success, and achieve the empowerment necessary to carry their lives to the highest potential.

Inspired greatly by the coaches who've gone before her; legends such as Les Brown, Jon Talarico, Bob Proctor, Marie Diamond, and many more; Sylvia fashions herself as one positioned to show others the pure light found, in being their highest selves, on purpose.

When Sylvia is not out ushering others into alignment, she is a deliberate asset to her local community and a loving member of her family and friendship circles.

Sylvia Tsui. Healer. Energizer. Visionary.

If you need any guidance and help along your way, please reach out to Sylvia at support@unlimitedmanifestation.com. Her podcast "Unlimited Manifestation" is available on Youtube, Spotify, and iTunes. You can also visit her website www.unlimitedmanifestation.com to read the blogs and listen to the podcasts to find more inspiration.

Take Your Life Back
By Angie Osorio

T his is a story and a framework on how to Take Your Life Back and reinvent your life.

I would like to start this story with these questions: Are you living the life you want? Or are you pretending to live the life you want?

Here I am, in front of my computer on a summer afternoon in Miami, FL writing this. At some point, I am going to be in tears, and it's fine; it is ok to cry and feel sad because of the memories of the past and to move on. What is not ok is to be unhappy for too long, which is what I did. I was miserable for many years because I didn't know better. Life is a miraculous creation, and God designed us all to be happy, healthy, and wealthy. There are infinite possibilities to create whatever we want. "Experiencing our best version is one thought away," and the opportunities to act are limitless.

At a hospital in Colombia, a baby girl was born with a strange lung condition while her mom was declared clinically dead after a c-section procedure. As the story was told, her mother saw a light that many describe as the tunnel. She went through it and started being welcomed by family members and friends that were deceased. She was happy going through the tunnel, but she heard someone shout her name. As she turned around, she realized she had two babies, and she came back; her only memory was lots of pain and several doctors helping her. That mother was full of life; she was always the center of attention wherever she was, remarkably smart, gracious, and fun. But while taking care of her family, husband, and kids, she made the worst mistake anybody can make.

On a Friday evening, she was on the dance floor where she hosted a salsa dance class for family and neighbors, and life was great, music, food & laughs. Because of her, the house was always glowing, pretty, and full of life. She always came up with the most creative ideas, there was always something new and exciting happening around her, and life was full of action. She, one of the smartest people I have known, capable of reading a book in one day, also caused her husband, with all her ideas, to grow exponentially professionally and financially. She could have probably been a brilliant psychologist. I remember how people, family, and neighbors were in her living room asking her for advice. She just knew the answer every time. On the surface, everything looked great, but something terrible was happening. Time was passing by, and she was investing all her talents to only her family and forgot about herself! How is that possible? Wasn't she the smartest person I have known? While others were succeeding, sadly, she left herself last, and that's probably the beginning of the story.

My mom passed away in the summer of 2002 at the age of 54 due to an immune disease that caused a brain-eating bacteria. Yes, a bacteria ate her brain. She died blind, deaf, and with dementia, being fed by a tube in her stomach in her last days. The last time I saw her was at the airport in 1997 when I was leaving my country to live in the United States. I never thought it was going to be "the last" moment. My brother and I have concluded that she got sick as the effect of a deep depression = a multitude of disempowering, unstoppable thoughts and an extreme unfulfillment for her lack of personal realization. Was she living the life she wanted? Well, apparently, no, not at all! The unfulfillment of her life and being at the effect of the political and social occurrences in our country took her to a mental scenario she just couldn't control.

I am not victimizing myself by sharing this. If at the end of these lines you take the decision and the risk of Taking Your Life Back and reinventing who you are, my mission is complete, and this is your call. If you haven't realized it yet, I am the baby with the lung condition. With my mom gone, life was like a boat in the middle of the sea without a lighthouse.

Eighteen years later, there I was, an evening in Miami perusing my entrepreneurial dream in marketing. I was also investing in personal development because I knew something was not quite right! But what was I doing wrong? Everything seems ok. I had a "good" husband who apparently loved me because he didn't cheat on me or hit me, but is that really a good husband? I had two healthy daughters, a roof and food, and the minimal requirements to be grateful in life. But still, a little voice was telling me, "Hey, this is not your life; you are not happy." I started noticing that my husband was serving me wine every evening. There was always a full glass of wine beside my computer, and every evening, I was constantly drinking the wine my husband was pouring me. Until one day, I said, "No, I don't want it today." He then said, "Oh, ok." In a kind of confused/mad tone.

That night was the beginning of the end. That night, I didn't go to sleep late, and since I was not drunk, I didn't have sex with him as he was expecting from me every night. I did not want to have sex with him because it felt like torture for me, and he was mad. That night I didn't watch TV until 3:00 am to fill my emptiness like every other night. That night I went to sleep, and I woke up sober. I started producing results in my business early in the morning instead of dragging myself all day long. I was already getting coaching and support out there in the world; which we should all do. It took me years to ask for help.

One day, I was praying and doing the work of transformation, and I got it! I was living a life I didn't want to live, and I was miserable. I got trapped in this marriage as the effect of my circumstances. My immigration status, the death of my mom, getting pregnant and having no family whatsoever in this country. My father remarried and started a whole new life far from my brother and me. My brother became emotionally unavailable after the traumatic experience of the death of my mother. I had no place to go, no family in the United States, and I had the responsibility of my two kids and the belief that I must have a family on my own and that I had to try harder for everything to succeed. I remember sleepless nights, counting down the years I had left in my jail. I remember thinking, "My oldest daughter is 11, so that means eight more years until she goes to college; I think I can do it eight more years." But since I was not drinking anymore, the blur started disappearing. "Why am I doing this to myself? I am getting fat, I feel tired, ugly, old, unfulfilled, I don't stop working, and I am forcing myself to have sex with a man I don't love, and I haven't loved in years." I was so used to being sad and pretending that everything was ok that it became my habitual way of being.

I was terrified to embrace my greatness! "Now what? Where am I going to go? How is it possible that I have made so many bad choices? What was I thinking? I don't have extra money or a place to go. What am I going to do with my kids?" I tried once, and I failed. I was hiding and avoiding my reality. Living with a person that abuses alcohol and drugs had me living a very unstable life since I left my home. He didn't force me to come to this country; he invited me to live with him with the promise of the American Dream, and I believed. I was 20 years old. It was my choice, my responsibility and I didn't know better, and I got trapped. That was not life, "I didn't kill anyone," I thought. I started to look back on my life to see all the things that happened in those 24 years, how I reinvented myself every time, and how I got to do it again.

The first time, I was full of dreams. I came to Miami to live with my boyfriend and follow all his promises of studying & working. But in just weeks, the dream started falling apart. He didn't have money to pay the rent, and, in a blink, I was sleeping on the floor of his mom's tiny, old apartment. From that moment, scarcity was on the table every day in that relationship. Smoking weed was his everyday thing. The promise of being legal or studying was a fantasy. I was not going to have a status anytime soon. With no English, no work experience, no documents, and no friends or family, the future was uncertain. Then I thought and thought! What can I do? I registered a business under his name to be able to work as a contractor, and I started not because I wanted to but because I needed to, my entrepreneur life. "At least I can generate money now," O thought. But what did I know about business? Not much. I started looking for contractor opportunities in advertising. I remember going to the local library in the morning and taking notes from books to learn the business and how to use the software, and I came back the next day and the next day until I learned by myself and got my first opportunity. I was able to generate money with my career because, by the way, I didn't know how to work.

The second time, I woke up in an intensive care unit bed at a hospital in Denver, CO. Everything was so confusing, but I felt so good. It was probably the calmest I was in years, I had no more pain in my body, no reason to be in a hurry, nothing to escape from, and I didn't have to work or cook. My memory was gone. What happened? I realized that I had the worst pneumonia of my life the night before. I was sent to an investigation center in Denver, CO because my doctors in Miami couldn't figure out why I had recurring pneumonia. They put me on prednisone and antibiotics, and nothing seemed to work. My stressful life impacted my immune system, and my lungs hit rock bottom. I was raising two babies; my husband had lost his job, and he was smoking weed again. I was the main income of my house with my business.

We had recently moved to Texas, and in a span of three years, we had come back to Florida with two babies to solve his employment situation due to the recession. I was exhausted! Pneumonia produces extreme bone and muscle pain. I was diagnosed with Primary Ciliary Dyskinesia, a genetic condition that slows the normal function of the lungs. On the last day at the hospital, the doctor told me that I had to be on antibiotics for the rest of my life and that I was not going to live more than 60 years. I was terrified. I remember crying at the airport traveling back to Miami and telling myself, "Is this the end? This is the end. What is going to happen with my daughters? I know what it is like not to have a mom. This can't be happening. It can't be!"

I asked God for another opportunity! And the "Power of Your Subconscious Mind" by Dr. Murphy came to my hands with "You Can Heal your life" by Louise Hay. I declared to recover my health, did everything in the books, cured myself with no medicine, and pneumonia stopped. I reinvented my life one more time. I left my husband, and I started a new life. However, it didn't happen. Do you remember that I said that I had failed once? We came back because my kids were little, and my business had a crisis. We decided to try again. He promised not to smoke weed again, and a new chapter started.

The third time. That night I went to sleep, and I woke up sober, divorced, and living in peace…

Today people keep telling me that I look ten years younger. Many other reinventions took place in my life that I don't have room to tell at this time, but I will share in the future how I cured my infertility, my diagnosis of a brain tumor after having my first baby, bankruptcy, running a business with two babies, learning English with no resources, closing a business for copyright issues, the death of my father and a broken heart when I thought I found love.

This is my recipe to Take Your Life Back: What do you want? Find a purpose and have it in your mind present 24/7. Pray every day. Mediate. Exercise. Read or listen to the same motivational content every day. Look for other people to hold you accountable in each area. There are amazing communities in the world. Control your sugar & flour and if you really, really want to Take Your Life Back, please stop watching TV and wake up one or two hours earlier every day. It takes something at the beginning, but the result is priceless. If you want quantum results, take quantum risks! I wish no man or woman, to be as profoundly sad as I was for years living a life where I didn't belong for lack of resources and knowledge. Be willing to Take Your Life Back and remember that "The beauty of humanity is having the gift from God to create life over and over." ThinkCheers!

About Angie Osorio

My Name is Angie Osorio, and defeating sadness and reinventing my life over and over in the face of adversity was my calling in life. However, what people don't know is what it took for me to get myself to this point. When I was born, I came with a genetic lung condition, which nearly took my life once; I used to live in the United States illegally without knowing English or having a support system. My husband, to who I was married for 23 years, abused drugs and alcohol. I also lost my mom and dad, and I realized I had no family left. No one was coming. I couldn't help but think life like this was my destiny. While becoming an entrepreneur in marketing and raising my two babies, I was also pretending everything was fine. Yet, I was suffering from insomnia, I was overweight, I had started drinking on a daily basis, and I still felt I needed to sacrifice myself for others and my kids.

The adversities in my life took me to the most beautiful experience anyone can have—investing in oneself and discovering the power of one's mind. In the beginning, it was only to heal my lungs, overcome my sadness, restlessness, and unfulfilled life, and answer my persistent question: "What am I doing wrong?" This has been my most miraculous discovery. It's been about twelve years since I left intensive care in Denver to treat my lung condition, which I triggered by extreme stress. I knew I didn't want to die; my kids were babies, just nine months and two years old. I decided to survive and started reading books. My first: The Power of Your Subconscious Mind by Dr. Joseph Murphy and You Can Heal Your Life by Louise Hay. I healed my lungs with these books. But all of the other areas that mattered to me seemed to never work. My life continued to be miserable, and my never-ending question came back. "What am I doing wrong that's causing this miserable life?" That's when I decided to start vigorously investing in my growth and participated in programs like The Landmark Forum, their "Curriculum for Living," and their "Team Management & Leadership Program," part of Landmark's Communication Curriculum where instead of overcoming my sadness, tiredness, transformation disappeared them. I completed the "Ultimate Edge" and "Build Your Brand Challenge" programs with Tony Robbins. I participated in the "Super Star Business Breakthrough Retreat" of Michelle Villalobos'. I was part of Dean Graziosi's "Inner Circle" and "Thinking into Result Program for Leaders" with Bob Proctor & Sandy Gallagher, with my fabulous coach Jon Talarico. I completed "Winning the Game of Money" with John Assaraf and "Unsinkable Bounce Back System" with Sonia Ricotti, to name a few. I have participated in multiple seminars and meditations to find the source of my happiness. It's been a journey for sure, but I finally started to live a fulfilling and exhilarating life. Some people say that I look ten years younger!

ANGIE OSORIO

Today, I define myself as a Marketing Creator & Mindset Transformation Consultant and one powerful mother. I'm blessed to say this is now how I earn my life—designing marketing pieces, empowering people's commitments through my consulting sessions, and inspiring my two young daughters.

Me, on social media? I was shocked! I was nobody. In 2020, I had my first interview; Voyage Magazine reached out to me to talk about, well, me! I was also awarded by Worldwide Luxe Magazine as Brand Design Consultant. I have been discovering my self-expression and how much I love the spotlight instead of hiding from it. I created my channel @ThinkCheers. Now, I allow myself to be me. I love her.

I will say one thing, and it is this: "The beauty of humanity is having the gift from God to create life over and over. We can always reinvent our lives." Here is my question for you: Are you allowing life to surprise you as an act of faith or surprising life today with tangible actions fulfilling your faith and your dreams?

Connect with Angie:
angieosorio.com | thinkcheers.com |
Follow Angie @ThinkCheers @ThinkAngie

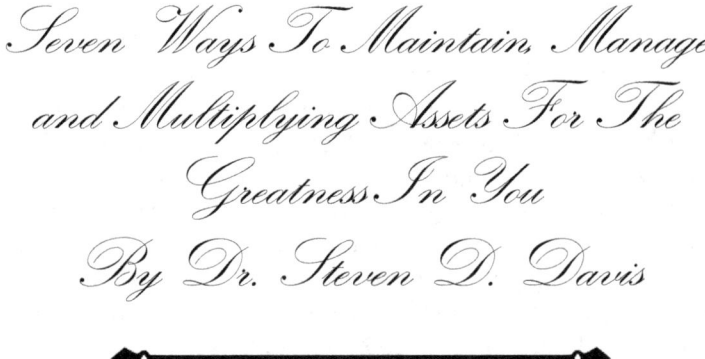

Seven Ways To Maintain, Manage and Multiplying Assets For The Greatness In You
By Dr. Steven D. Davis

A good man leaves an inheritance to his children's children: and the wealth of the sinner is laid up for the just. Proverbs 13:22 KJV!

You have to be disruptive shakeup, change, challenge yourself!

In school they tell you not to copy. But in life you need to copy successful and righteousness people of integrity. Some may be intelligence in business with the savvy business abilities that we need to study and repeat. Most successful people build on one idea or concept and make that a success then go to the next one to development multiple streams of income. It's called priority tasking not multi-tasking. You can only prioritize one thing to be successful. That takes, focus, concentration, and commitment. The moment that you start to try to multi-task you will lose focus, concentration, and commitment on the main thing that you should prioritize.

As an Ordained minister for over forty years and a licensed financial professional I have consistently consulted with thousands of people. It never ceased to amaze me at the number of people that do not know about how to manage, maintain, and multiply their fiancés. I realize that financial literacy is not taught in school. I was very blessed to be raised by parents that understood financial literacy. And taught their children the importance of properly managing, maintaining, and multiplying finances and assets. When I ask people what is an asset? Many think a house, car or jewelry are assets. But the truth of the matter is that an asset put money in your pocket month after month. My chapter will explain seven wealth secrets to managing, maintaining, and Multiplying finances and assets for greatness.

I remember when I had a very successful and prosperous Home Inspection Business for over seven years before the real estate crash in 2007. Later I started my financial services company after the Home Inspection company was a success. I then so focused on building my financial services company that when the time came to grandfather my Home Inspection Business in without being required having the new licensing requirements. I missed Grandfathering my Home Inspection Business in because my focus, commitment and concentration had shifted. Now I am going through the licensing requirements for my Home Inspection Business to be reactivate. My financial services business is successful but when my priority shifted, I missed out on a very important transfer of wealth.

Today I have several streams of income as a retired Chicago Public School Teacher, City of Chicago Operating Engineer, Disabled Military veteran and I am drawing a Social Security pension. My four companies are still producing residual income also. I am sharing seven of the powerful practices that will develop the greatness in you,

Successful people do what unsuccessful people won't do. That is mark the perfect man (woman).
In Christ we copy Christ Jesus!

Please read and study these very powerful verses of scripture, Joshua 1: 1 – 9, Matthew 25: 20-30.

In these verses Jesus tells us that the person that knows how to save what he has given them will prosper. It doesn't matter how small it is just saved something in moral of the above verses. It never ceases to amaze me that the poor never try to save or invest anything. But the above verses in Matthew reveal that those that don't save will lose more and more of what they have. It's just a spiritual law of money.

1). Business Owners consistently do seven things to Manage, maintaining, and multiply their assets:

The wealth pays themselves first through business ownership, proper investments, that produce multiple returns.

Business Owners understand that assets put money in their bank accounts month after month. The efforts of the savvy business owner are finding asset-based investments that will produce income monthly.

In Jesus Christ we copy Christ Jesus and His word here in Matthew 25 you will properly Manage, maintaining and multiply everything of value that God gives you.

Mark the perfect man, and behold the upright: For the end of that man is peace.
Psalm 37:37 KJV

The power of business ownership is also not taught is schools. I have been blessed with several college degrees, but no university really taught me the truth about the power of business ownership. Business ownership has put over 50% of my taxable income back in my pocket. The tax system constantly takes about 40% to 60% of every person in America's income. We have employment Federal, state (over 43 states in America have state income tax), city, county, Social Security, FICA, Estate, Real Estate, and death taxes. Most of the people that I have consulted with do not understand the origin of the 1040 tax system. The word of God says: My people are destroyed for lack of knowledge: because thou hast rejected knowledge, I will also reject thee, that thou shalt be no priest to me: seeing thou hast forgotten the law of thy God, I will also forget thy children. Hosea 4:6 KJV

2) Successful people copied a successful person or successful people that have minimize the tax system. Business Owners are excellent example to copy to learn how to put reduce. It is very important to study a system like the Internal Revenue Services. When I learned of its origin it changed my life significantly. When you look at the reality of taxes about 40 to 60% of the average Americans income is devoured in taxes. They get a paycheck and taxes come out, they go shopping and pay taxes, they eat and pay taxes, buy real estate pay taxes, get a capital gain pay taxes, die pay taxes. It is amazing that most Americans get a Social Security Card before their eighteenth birthday of at birth. will truly get deeper into the IRS in another writing. Business Owners can significantly reduce their tax liability. They showed me how to do the very same thing.

3) They Develop Multiple streams of Income.

Real estate investor, bestselling author, and sales strategist Grant Cardone says, "The really rich never depend on one flow of income but instead create a number of revenue streams. His first business had been generating a seven-figure income for years when he started investing cash in multifamily real estate. Once his real estate and consulting business were churning.
  He went into business development software to help retailers improve the customer experience."
  The average person in the U.S. has one income source, which is usually their job, but the average millionaire in the U.S. has seven streams of income.
  The rich believe in diversifying their income so they're not vulnerable to unexpected events. They have pandemic proof income streams.
  There are 7 types of income that you want to start cultivating when it comes to Managing, Maintaining and Multiplying your finances and assets:

Earning income
Profit income
Interest income
Dividend income
Rental income
Capital gains
Royalty income

Start today by increasing your current types of income and adding more to your pipeline as you develop each one.

Each income type is an added layer of protection against the unexpected and a long-term wealth builder that becomes pandemic proof.

Especially, when you combine it with...

They understand the power of the forth secret:

4) The Miracle of Compound Interest

Albert Einstein called compound interest "the greatest mathematical discovery of all time" and the wealthiest men in history have taken full advantage of it.

The full power of compound interest is realized when you start to earn interest on your interest. This creates a snowball effect where your returns are no longer linear but exponential.

For example, if you invest $10,000 for 10 years, earning a 10% return each year (or $1,000), then by taking your earnings out at the end of each year, you'll have earned $10,000, a 100% return.

But, if you invest $10,000 for 10 years earning the same 10% for each year but roll over your returns instead of withdrawing them, then you'll have earned $25,930, a 159.30% return.

And, the beauty of compound interest is that it works for everyone, rich or poor.

But the principle of compounding can also be used in business if you know how to apply it. Just by understanding the power of compound interest you can invest in the stock market and never lose any money by using leverage. We will explain this when we get to the power of leverage.

5). Learn To Use Other People's Money. OPM IT!

The fifth thing is never spent lump sums of money. People of wealth will invest their money and use other people's money to gain the maximum return. They will place their money in the bank or Credit Unions and then borrow against their deposits. Most successful business owners will maximize their income by taking lump sums of money earned and put that money in a high interest Certificate of Deposit and getting a loan against the CD. Then they will repeat this process many times. Soon they have millions in CD earing high interest. Then they start a small Credit Union to loan money to those in their community. That's how you use other people's money.

You can do this with tax return money. I started using Other People's Money it with a $10,000.00 tax return check. I took my return to my local Credit Union and started a CD for 10 grand. I got a loan against the CD and paid my bills and other things of importance. Once I repaid the loan I did it again and again. Now my wife and I have several thousands in CDs. Using other people's money is a powerful way to build wealth.

Also use Credit Cards more than Debit Cards because Credit Cards is the banks money not yours. You can establish good credit by using secured credit cards. But once your credit scores and good enough get credit cards and use other people's money then save and invest your own money. This is a very powerful wealth secret.

6). Leverage

But the principle of compounding can also be used in business if you know how to apply it. Just by understanding the power of compound interest you can invest in the stock market and never lose any money by using leverage. I was taught by some very wealthy men how to use leverage when investing in the stock market and The S&P 500 Index or Standard & Poor's 500 Index. The principle is simple if you know that when the stocks go up the bonds go down you leverage one against the other and you will never loose money in these powerful investment entities. For example: if you invest 40% in the stock market and 40% in the bond market, then 20% a Money Market fixed account you will never lose money in your investments.

Rich men understand that to get really wealthy you have to learn to use other people's resources to gain greater returns.

Bill Gates leveraged IBM's marketing and distribution by licensing his Windows software to IBM's PCs, thereby gaining access to their customers as well.

Thomas Edison leveraged the brainpower of the country's leading scientists to come up with solutions for harnessing electricity and creating the light bulb, the phonograph, the alkaline battery, and many other inventions that we still use today.

Henry Ford is credited with creating the mass production system, which leveraged labor and technology to produce the Model T. His mass production system is still used by the big automakers today, as well as every other major manufacturing industry.

Starting now, the successful Start.

Incorporate positive leverage in your life so that you can gain greater returns in time, energy, and money — just like the rich.

7). Estate Planning: establish different types of Trust to become law suit and probate proof.

Transfer assets into a living Trust! Here are the benefits of a Living Trust.

1. Understand the benefits of a living trust. The primary reason to establish a living trust is to avoid probate.

By cutting out the legal process to recognize and validate your will, your assets can be distributed to your beneficiaries without the added time and cost of probate.

2. Categorize your property. Before you can transfer them to a living trust, you need to make a list of your assets and fit each into one of the four main categories. Each type of asset has a different procedure for transferring it into your trust.

Real property is the first category. This includes your residence, secondary homes, income property, and any other real estate where you hold a full or partial interest. This can include property you own in another state.

A second category is your cash accounts. This includes checking and savings accounts, as well as Certificates of Deposit and Money Market accounts.

Your next consideration is financial instruments including stocks and bonds in both privately and publicly held corporations.

The final category is tangible personal property. This can include your vehicles, boats, furniture, antiques, art, and other collectibles.

In conclusion a person can Maintain, Manage and Multiply their Assets for Greatness by understanding that assets put income into your accounts monthly. Start saving now and start your own home-based business. Study other successful business owners that are doing what you want to do. Build several streams of income. Maximize the power of never spending lump sums of money. Get Certificates of Deposit and borrow against them to increase your asset base. This is how you build leverage. Then protect all your assets with a powerful Living Trust. These are all powerful tools that any person can use to leave a legacy for their family. There is greatness in everyone. You can birth your greatness by developing personal affirmations that build positive thoughts that become reality. I will close with this. Here is the personal affirmation that I try to state every morning. Dr. Steven D. Davis, I AM HEALTHY! I AM WEALTHY! I AM HAPPY! I FEEL TRIFFIC! THIS IS GOING TO BE A PROSPEROUS DAY OF SUCCESS, INCREASE AND PURPOSE!

About Dr. Steven D. Davis

Apostle Dr. Steven D. Davis is a true marketplace Apostle and entrepreneur. He is the President/CEO and Presiding Apostle of The Cyrus International Network of Churches & Ministries, Inc, President/CEO, Senior Overseer of Greater Works Evangelism, Inc, President/CEO of JAH Financial Consultants, Inc., The Vice President/Executive Director of New Horizons Community Development Corporation. He is also an Adjutant Professor of Economics and Finance at Concordia University in River Forest, Illinois.

DR. STEVEN D. DAVIS

Apostle Dr. Davis has a Doctor of Theology in Biblical Counseling, a Doctor of Business Administration in Financial-Management, a Master of Arts in Education, and a Bachelor of Arts in Business Administration; he is a Certified Asset Management Specialist, Licensed Financial Professional, Licensed Life & Health Insurance Producer, Certified Estate Planner, and A Notary Public-National Signing Agent. He is a retired schoolteacher (fifteen years) from the Chicago Public Schools and an Operating Engineer (twenty-six years) from the city of Chicago and the U.S. Postal Service.

Most importantly, he gave his life to Jesus Christ in 1977 while serving in the U. S. Marine Corps. He became a Licensed Minister in 1981 at New Hope Baptist Church under Pastor Troy L. Kates Sr. Apostle Dr. Davis became an Ordained Minister/Evangelist in 1989. Later in 1997, he was ordained an Apostle by Apostle John J. Eckhardt at Crusaders Church.

Apostle Dr. Davis does Financial Enrichment Seminars that are designed to unlock the revelation knowledge of hidden treasures and wisdom keys that will challenge you to embrace a new economic reality and enable you to convert what you have learned into tangible, practical asset allocation and wealth acclimation. Apostle Dr. Davis is the author: of "Supernatural Soul Winning," How to Develop a Supernatural Soul Winning Team (SWAT) in the local church, and Solomon's Secrets of Financial Success, a financial manual teaching the wealth secrets of the wealthiest man that ever lived and "How To Build Self Esteem In Children. "He has written several articles and publications for Newsletters, with a book release set for November of 2023 entitled "Thirty-Three Things You Would Know About Money If Told You. Other books to come by 2023: "How to Enter into A Divinely Inspired Relationship," "How Can I be Proud," I've Got What You Need & You Don't Even Know It," "Kingdom Economics" and "Children of The Kingdom" God Doesn't Have Kids."

Apostle Davis lives in the Chicago land area with his wife, Apostle Valerie R. Davis.

You can contact Dr. Davis
Cell: 773-510-3424, Email: sdapostle@email.com
Mailing: 16140 Winchester Ave, Markham IL, 60428.

To send Tax Deductible Donations:
Cash App $jahman161
PayPal: https://www.paypal.me/greaterworkschurch

Websites: https://www.jahfinancial.com
https://www.greaterworkschurch.info

DR. SARITA GRAHAM

Finding Peace
By Dr. Sarita Graham

THE PROMISE OF GOD

My calling is leadership and ministries of help. At first, I could not identify why I was born, seeing I had so many gifts and experienced so much at the young age of 12. I can remember clearly watching Kathryn Kuhlman on TV one Saturday afternoon; for some reason, I began to weep. My mother came into the room and saw me weeping. She laid on the floor with me, holding and rocking me until I fell asleep. Under that anointing, my mother stated I laid there for about two hours. I never understood what transpired. When I relocated to Kansas City, Missouri, I had the opportunity to meet her niece, and she prayed in the facility and for me. I shared with her what I encountered at 12 years old watching her aunt. She stated that was a great calling on my life, and she said, "Make sure you answer the call."

TRYING TO STILL MY PURPOSE

Genesis 26:18-26
When I think about the story of Isaac, I think about myself. Before my father passed and the passing of my great uncle, both greatly encouraged me about having a relationship with God first and leaving an inheritance for your children's children, also in Proverbs 13:21-22.

Every vision that was given to me ended up in a quarrel. My first challenge was opening a bridal shop in Gladstone, MO. Very quickly, my business picked up with celebrities, judges, sports figures, and many more. There were two major incidents that basically closed me down. For example, a judge's son rented several pieces of merchandise from me and would not return them. When I inquired, he stated, "You don't know who I am and who my father is."

My second challenge was when a professional football player charged over $1,500 in products. Due to his status, he canceled his credit card and kept the merchandise.

My third challenge came when I began donating my time at a homeless shelter for youth girls to empower them with the message, "You are special," like the olden days when the older women sat in a circle to empower the younger women while knitting. So, I took that same concept of empowering young girls that they are special through creating in them a sewing skill while making a wedding dress. It became intriguing and even hit the newspapers. One evening before I left working with the girls, the director asked me if I could go tomorrow evening for dinner to share the empowerment tool that I was training the girls on. Well, that next evening, I went and shared the girls' accomplishments during our presentation and highlighted each dress that was made. After the presentation, we had to leave and could not stay for dinner. We went back to the room and ate ramen noodles.

That following week I was in a craft store, and the lady stopped me and asked if I was the woman that empowered the young girls with the wedding gowns. I said yes, and she began giving me accolades and shared with me that she had donated thousands of dollars on behalf of what I was doing. I volunteered my time, product, and service to empower young girls. I contacted the director to inform her I would not be returning as the dinner was fundraising for their organization. The fourth challenge was the one that almost bankrupted me – my financials, my integrity, and all my possessions. "For now, the Lord has made room for me, he has made me fruitful in many ways." Genesis 26:22

OUTLEARING THE WOLVES, by David Hutchins

As I survived and continued to live and exist through all of my disappointments, I questioned God, "Why?" I was doing well in business and had an opportunity where I was chosen by DeVos Urban Leadership Initiative, which invested in me for a 15-month leadership program. During the course, I gained practical skills and had to read first a short-page book "Outlearning the Wolves" which was a book that truly prepared me. I recognized later what it taught me. In 2004, my oldest daughter came in from Langston University to celebrate my graduation. She stated, "Momma, that was the best thing you could have done. I'm proud of you that the program gave you so much business knowledge, leadership, and awareness." Not quite a year later, September 2005, around 10:30 am, I received a call my daughter was found deceased in her apartment.

    At that time, I had a contract with the state ATR voucher program serving our community, allowing me to assist men/women with substance abuse and housing with the state vouchers program. At that time the majority of the certified organizations would use my services. There were two other agencies also chosen to assist the needy. I had to take a couple of weeks off to mourn before I could return back to work. While dealing with my loss, I received a phone call from the Department of Mental Health asking me to take over a transitional housing program. I told her I had just lost my daughter and was still grieving. She apologizes and states that she is sorry for my loss. She shared that she pulled my file, and saw that my vision was to open a transitional housing program. "Please call me back if you have any interest," she said. After I got off the phone, I called my mother and shared the information with her. She asked me what would "Princess," say? I cried and prayed, prayed and cried. A few days later, I returned the call and said yes. I met with the house owner to sign lease papers less than three weeks after moving in. There were six women, and in less than two weeks, there were 12. I took the insurance money, renovated the 12-bed transitional house, and named it after my daughter, "The Princess House." I could not believe how fast it grew. Within a month, I opened another 28 beds for men returning from prison and filled it up in three weeks with a waiting list. Next thing, all of a sudden, it felt like tigers, lions, and bears were attacking me. A client was at the woman's facility, and she called me and stated that a man and woman were there stating they were taking over the Princess House. I got in my car and proceeded and caught them coming down the outside step. I addressed them in a negative way. Read between the lines.

After that, it was one thing after another. The state voucher portal was taken, and the 28-bed facility could not get paid. I lost money and had to shut it down. Agencies stopped supporting me. I helped organize a coalition, which eventually became very politically unexceptionable. I remember going to Washington, DC, where I was on a panel with two other colleagues. We were chosen to speak. The other two spoke before me, and when I began to speak, the audience gave me a great response. All of a sudden, my colleagues snatched the mic from me. It happened so fast. There were over 100 people from around the US. What I brought to the table was what I learned from DeVos, the 5 Core Values. At the 10-minute break, so many people came up to me saying, "I'm so sorry – you were awesome. It was sad and rude to see him snatch your mic."

I was at the Princess House one morning, standing out on the patio, and I saw a man coming up the ally. As he approached, he threw several Molotov cocktails. But, God had me there to prevent a fire. God has blessed me with the Princess House, which was a historic Phyllis Wheatly House. It sat there for over seven years, boarded up, and no one pursued it. It seemed that once I obtained it, there were so many people trying all kinds of ways to take it. Everything attached to the ministry and that house they fought me tooth and nail. Another state leader asked me to do a partnership.

I shared with him my past experience, and he stated change is here. Well, I entered into the partnership. It was going well for a short time. All of a sudden, the vouchers stopped. I could not pay rent, lights, gas, and what it took to manage. I heard a knock on the door. It was the process server serving me an eviction notice. That was a big setup. The person that encouraged me came back apologizing. I went to court, and the judge stated I could not take anything out of the house, not even a can good. I remember I furnished a 42-bed facility. I never heard you cannot take the stuff you supplied. I shared with the judge that I had personal things of my deceased daughters inside. She told me to make a list and have it faxed by 4:00 pm the same day. I called a friend who had trucks and shared with her what happened. In less than an hour, she had eight trucks and 15 homeless manpower, and we made a list of all the stuff that I put in that house. Before the set time expired, I sent the list to the judge. I also was in a Coalition that I helped start, and an award ceremony was coming up in about a few months. Many wanted to give me an award for all the great things I had done. One morning I was having a staff meeting, and the phone rang. The person identified who both of them were. They said, "YOU STOMACH ME, AND I WILL MAKE SURE YOU WILL NOT RECEIVE THE AWARD OVER MY DEAD BODY NOR ANY SUPPORT FROM THE COMMUNITY."

PUZZLE PIECES - PUTTING MY LIFE BACK TOGETHER

Isaiah 54:17
As you look at a puzzle, you see it has many pieces. Those pieces during the span of my lifetime were pieces of disappointment, trauma, rejection, insecurity, and grief that had caused so much pain. I decided one day that I was going to forgive and put it all behind me. On October 21, 2021, I kneeled on the floor and began crying out to God and praying, Lord, help me! I cried so hard that I was almost going into an anxiety attack, then I got up off the floor and went to take a hot bath to calm me down. In the tub, I began praising and thanking God, then I began to relax, meditate, and said to myself, "It's over. Enough is enough." Then I proceeded to get out of the tub, and in the process, I heard an audible voice that spoke very loudly, "Every sword that came against me will come against them." That was an unbelievably frighting experience. I began to look in the room, and there was no one else in the room but me. It comes again, "Every sword that came against me will come against them." I ran to the room and began to write it down. While writing, it spoke again, "Every swear that comes against me will come against them." I begin weeping to know that the Spirit of the Lord heard my prayer. Enough is enough, and I begin to see things turn around just to let you know God is real, and He cares. Every piece of the puzzle during our lives, we will face many challenges, many circumstances, and many situations. BUT GOD is always there.

As I continue my morning prayer, GOD always shows up. One morning, rainbows appeared on both of my knees during my prayer time. I screenshot it to my husband. The next time I was sitting in my office with my grandson. He said to me, "Nanny, it looks like it is going to rain. Do you want me to close the windows?" I told him not yet. A little later, we both looked out the window and saw how dark it was, but then the sun proceeded to come out between the dark clouds. The sun began to be so bright, all of sudden, a beam from the sun came down, and the sun was on my face. My grandson began hollering, "Nanny the sun is on your face! The sun is on your face!" When the sun came on my face, it was a warm feeling that almost blinded me. I just held my hands up to surrender and begin saying thank you, Jesus. He keeps sharing with me, daughter, I see you, and I am with you.

DR. SARITA GRAHAM

About Dr. Sarita Graham

As servant leadership takes on its many forms, individuals harnessing intrinsic wisdom, personal ethic, and altruism remain at the heart of its intentional design. Displaying such intent with unyielding measure; is the prolific humanitarian, Dr. Sarita L. Graham.

Dr. Sarita L. Graham is a world-class facilitator, advisor, cleric, CEO, and Founder of **Sarita Lynne Ministries**, a multi-dimensional conglomerate servicing various communal and educational exigencies. In 2005, she brought life to **The Princess House**, a memorialized transitory housing haven named for her late daughter; committed entirely to the sole purpose of rehabilitation, homelessness prevention, and the overall safety of women. The quarterage proved itself quintessential, as its growing numbers led to more than two locations, including two male service-based wings; **Isaiah's Place**, in 2008 and **Joshua's Safe place**, in 2015, both designed to promote balance and responsible, independent living, by preventing relapse and recidivism. To date, Dr. Sarita L. Graham has served more than 15,000 men and women, helping them to transform their lives, obtain housing, a relationship with God, employment, and restoration.

Her mantra is clear: She was born to live out her faith in action, to serve humanity through acts of love, humility, and essential purpose.

Dr. Sarita L. Graham couples her assiduity in philanthropy with sincere regard for education, achievement, and communal involvement. She holds a Doctorate of Divinity, MA in Christian Counseling, a Ph. D in Bible Studies, and a BS in Religion. Adding to her educational procurement, Dr. Sarita L. Graham is a 2003 Graduate of DeVos Urban Leadership Initiative and holds more than ten certifications in diversified leadership and human service concentrations, such as **CRPR** (Certified Reciprocal Peer Recovery) **MARS** (Medication Assisted Recovery Specialist) **MAADC** (Missouri Alcohol and Drug Counselor) and more. Her appreciation for educational acquisition is clear, as she also founded **Royal Community Christian Community College, resting formally under the umbrella of Sarita Lynne Ministries.** Having a natural propensity for multi-functional leadership, Dr. Graham is often called upon for her expertise in various fields; ranging from her success as an orator and spiritual life coach to holding the chair as the **2012 SAMSHA Leadership Missouri Delegate**, and four yeas ago, **Vice-Chair of KCSATRSC** (Kansas City Substance Abuse Treatment and Recovery Supports Coalition).

Though displaying all the traits of a modern renaissance woman, from Grand Marshalling Super Bowl XVII with Jim Brown, NBA Cheerleading with the Detroit Pistons', coiffeuse artistry, and more, Dr. Sarita L. Graham has made her innate path clear through the vocation of serving others.

When Dr. Sarita L. Graham is not out serving the world, she is a true asset to her communal body and a loving member of her family and friendship circles.

Dr. Sarita L. Graham. Leader. Organizer. Humanitarian.

Sarita Lynne Ministries
Royal Community Christian College KC
https://www.saritalynneministries.com
royalswithcommunitychristiancollege.info
Sarita Lynn Enterprise, LLC
https://www.lynneenterprise.com

Email: saritagraham@aol.com, saritagraham15@gmail.com

THE GREATNESS IN YOU

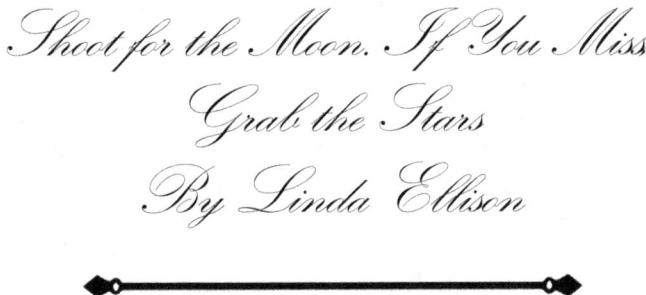

Shoot for the Moon. If You Miss Grab the Stars
By Linda Ellison

Just know that if it doesn't challenge you, it won't change you; therefore, as you begin reading this chapter, change is inevitable, but growth is a choice. I want you to find your story inside of my story. As I share, I want to remind you that your failures do not define you but simply refine you. Did you know that Thomas Edison attempted the lightbulb over 10,000 times before he was successful? This teaches us that we must obviously incorporate failure into our success stories. Right? Failures are inevitable. We cannot go through life and really believe that we will not experience failures. Truly, F-A-I-L stands for finding answers in learning! Failure is merely feedback on this journey that we call life. Realizing that we must incorporate failure into our success stories comes with experience as well as maturity. Setbacks are part of success, not the opposite. So, as I tell you my story, I want you to think about what you consider a major failure, no matter how big or how small. It could be divorce, college, a career, a business, family, or even your children. Whatever it may be, just think about what you may consider a major failure that may keep you up at night.

    I grew up in a little small town in Texas called Lamarque, and I am Clarence and Virginia's "baby girl" of four children. My parents have been married for 57 years now and are remarkable people, to say the least. My dad was employed at Texas City Refinery, and my mom was a stay-at-home parent. My siblings have all received certifications in their career fields now. Growing up, I was that eager little smart girl believing I was the real Lynda Carter, Wonder Woman! I was considered the "lucky one." I made A's throughout kindergarten all the way to high school and even into college. Being a gifted and talented student, which is what smart kids were called in my elementary years, on to being on the Dean's List in college. I was, of course, programmed in my mind to believe that because I was so smart, life was going to be a breeze. That is what we are taught by parents, teachers, and people alike, that our report card syndrome can dictate our future. We later learn that this simply is not true, as Bob Proctor explains.

I chose nursing as my career because I wanted to make a great difference in healthcare while making sure to treat people with compassion and a great attitude. So, as I entered the nursing program as an aspiring nursing student at the University of Texas Medical Branch in Galveston, TX, in 1993, I went straight into the program with no problem. I was so excited to get into this program. Then it happened; I had to "find answers in learning." Yes, I was unsuccessful and devastated about the program. But I am persistent. I picked myself up and just went to another nursing program at a different school. I was advancing fine with one semester left before graduation while now married and pregnant with my firstborn. Then what happened? Yep, I had to find more answers in learning. It was very tough for me to decide what to do next for my future.

My husband of 25 years, Sean, and I did what we thought was best at that time. I redirected my desire to receive degrees and certifications in various areas of the medical field. Now, as a mother of three (my oldest son, Sean Terry Jr., is 25 and now graduated from college in real estate and is married with his two sons and my two daughters. Alysse Gayle is 20 attending college, and now in child development. Ashlyn Kerri is 15 and is a straight "A" student who made nationals in track, and I have to mention my Lil' Yorkie, Diamond, that's 12 years old) living in two-story homes and driving Lexus cars; life is good. I became a stay-at-home parent like my mom with my third baby in 2007, and it's what many would call the American dream. But how many of you know you still have that burn just to know what could have been because you feel like something is missing inside?

Well, now it is 2015, and my son is starting college, and guess who is going back with him? Yes, me! Returning to school over 20 years later, I expected that I would have to take all my science courses over. However, my credits are good! I go straight into the nursing program. Grateful, I believe that this is really my time! I wish I could have said that the program was a breeze, but I did experience hiccups along the way. Nonetheless, graduation is now in view, and it is time for the final test. With that last test, do I have to revisit those past years of nursing results? I had to find more answers in learning. Sadly, this time it is different, though. Part of me dies in this program. My spirit is broken. Many will say you tried it, but you failed. Or Linda, it is only nursing, but you cannot let the opinions of others become your reality.

Overthinking, self-doubt, and self-sabotage had visited during those testing sessions. Those paradigms from the past had gotten me out of my "Wonder Woman" mindset. This moment even had me questioning my God because how many of you know that feeling of when you really believe it is your time? God had shown up so many times in my life during this nursing program, and I felt so connected to Him that this could not happen to me. Even before the program in 2001, when my firstborn baby girl was born with a rare condition, neonatal hemochromatosis, God brought her through with merely a chelation of vitamins when all but one of the doctors at Texas Children's Hospital in Houston, Texas, came to my husband and I telling us to prepare that my baby would not make it. She is now my strong-willed baby girl who has a certification as a home-based business owner and attending college. With such strong faith I had built in God, there was no way I could come so far not make it again. I believed. However, our dreams and plans are not always God's plans for us. One day you will look back and thank God that he gave you what you needed instead of what you wanted. Sometimes God drops us so that we can fly. As Art Williams stated, "There has not been a machine to measure the heart of a champion."

God opens doors no man can shut. The system will work if you work the system. You must live your desires, not your fears. Hidden belief lies in our subconscious that we are not aware are even there. But we will make some mistakes, learn what we can, and embrace the process. Just know that you must have goals in place other than the programming that we are accustomed to of going to college and then earning what the job tells us we are worth. You have to reprogram your mind without worrying about the "how." The setbacks we endure advance us to the place we are destined to achieve. We have to replace our mindset from fear and doubt to gratitude and forward momentum. It is easy to want goals and happiness for others and lose that same vision for ourselves, such as when we see our celebrities and those even close to us. But we have to get out of the box and into the now. We have to find a positive in every negative. We cannot let the outer world control us.

I listened to a motivational speech on gratitude about how that speaker was thankful that she did not get hired for a job that she felt she interviewed well for and qualified for. She was grateful that she was denied because afterward, she realized that it was a job she thought she wanted, but then after clearly thinking that she didn't really like all of the stipulations that the job had in place. She was later offered a job that did meet her desires and felt blessed. This is another example of how God's plan is not always ours, but we must trust the process.

You have to be able to overcome adversity by:
- Having determination
- Taking responsibility
- Treating negative feedback as an opportunity
- Focusing on your strengths
- Identifying new goals

You have to be able to fail forward with power and self-confidence in order to bounce back and get back in the game. Playing small will not allow you to pick up the pieces. Be willing to bet on yourself!

Our legend Les Brown always says that we will have to fail ourselves to succeed and that a setback is a setup for a comeback. I had to stand up inside of myself and redirect my desires so I could "re-spark" my fire. I had to become the CEO of my own life, realizing that life does not happen to you; it happens for you. Sometimes our feedback is not immediate; however, in my current career coordinating medications for the mental health community, I am receiving a larger salary than the average school nurse career I was pursuing! Now I am given the opportunity to be on stage with the great Les Brown with the Power Voice #4. Again, we must incorporate failure into our success stories. Then it did not stop there because I later found myself on the stage with Che Brown with the Comeback Champions, which led me to be a professional motivational speaker with Lisa Nichols, Kim Coles, R&B singers Tamika Scott X-Scape and Chrisette Michele, and all the other great speakers. I am now an international as well as an Amazon #1 best-selling author. Just know you cannot ever quit. Mr. Les Brown reminds us that we have to be HUNGRY! Les, Joyce Meyer (my spiritual mom for 25 years!) Steve Harvey, Oprah Winfrey, Jon Talarico, and the Obamas have shaped my faith to remind me that as long as there is still hope, there is still a victory. Anyone who has never failed has given up on trying, or they have never tried anything new. As Napoleon Hill stated, "Every adversity, every failure, every heartache carries with it the seed of an equal or greater benefit." You just keep going because we have greatness inside of us. Know that we cannot quit until we win. Now it is time to power up and continue to be great! The "L" in Linda is for learning always, and the "G" in Gail is for going to win! So, let's go out and double our failure rate as we fail forward. And remember to shoot for the moon because even if you miss, you'll land among the stars.

LINDA ELLISON

About Linda Gail Bates - Ellison

Linda Ellison is a travel entrepreneur to clients all over the world, helping them adventure financially and time freedom while traveling to places they love. She believes the key to every successful business is incorporating high standards and simple formulas and making each client the top priority.

Linda has been mentored by Les Brown and Jon Talarico on the Power Voice, where she has gained a high regard for her passion for speaking to motivate and inspire others. Linda is recognized as a reputable coordinator of helping the mental health community with great communication skills in support of their medication needs. She graduated with a Science and Arts degree and has a background in pharmacy. She is also a nutritionist and Life Coach. Linda was blessed with sharing the stage with Kim Cole, Lisa Nichols, Tamika Scott, and Chrisette Michele and was able to tell her story. She is also an international as well as an Amazon number one best-selling author

Website: www.thegreatlindagailellison.com
https://linktr.ee/Mrslindagail
https://www.facebook.com/linda.ellison.37625

What Will Your Story Be
By Dr. Shirlee Turner

The Dream
Psalms 37:4 Take delight in the LORD, and he will give you the desires of your heart.

It's Christmas morning, and there I sat, surrounded by everything that was on the list I sent to "Santa" several months prior. But even at five years old, my requests were never for toys with the sole purpose of mere entertainment. Each toy represented an entrance to a world about which I spent countless hours dreaming, one which I truly believed would manifest in the years to come. I held the microphone comfortably in my hand, familiar with its use from the innumerable times I had spoken at my church. I envisioned myself standing on massive stages, addressing millions of people across the world with messages of inspiration and hope. The record player was playing the background tracks and vocals during the "rehearsals" for my future performances with the likes of Aretha Franklin, Tina Turner, and the Supremes, naming a few. Through the lens of the camera I received, I produced the scenes that would play out on the big screens of Hollywood, making my mark in the movie industry, ultimately being awarded my own star on the Hollywood Walk of Fame. The cute little "high-heeled shoes" carried me down the runway as I accepted my crown for Miss America. And, of course, the doctor's bag contained all the necessary tools and gadgets, equipping me with everything I would need to assure that anyone that was hurt or sick would be well taken care of. Although I did not have a great affinity for dolls, those in my possession became the perfect subjects upon which to master my medical skills.

But then life unfolded. With each passing year, the expectations, beliefs, opinions, criticisms, and judgments of others slowly drained the power from those dreams like the fading bulb of a flashlight with a dying battery until they were but a distant memory. With good intentions, people inundated me with messages to be practical and to find a stable and financially secure career. Subsequently, the only reasonable choice out of my plethora of dreams was to follow the path of becoming a physician, right? It was a commendable profession held in high esteem, brought enormous prestige and admiration, and of course, produced an acceptable paycheck with a desirable lifestyle. Without hesitation, that's the path I chose, excelling each step of the way as I climbed the ladder of success in both clinical and leadership roles. I was held in high regard by patients and their families. Staff valued my natural ability to navigate difficult conversations and put others at ease. My experience and expertise proved to be a great resource to my colleagues, who sought my perspective on their most challenging patients and medical enigmas. And I gained great respect and admiration from those at the upper management levels.

I was living the dream, or so it appeared. But then it happened.

The Fall
Psalm 37:24 Though he fall, he shall not be utterly cast down; For the LORD upholds him with His hand.

There was nothing different about this particular day. In fact, all my days had become a repeat of the previous ones. Having grown accustomed to working twelve plus hours six to seven days a week, I effectually juggled the responsibilities of two, sometimes even three, different roles, spent countless hours in meetings, teaching and mentoring students, providing leadership to other providers, and most importantly, delivering compassionate support and care to dying patients and their loved ones. While relentlessly advocating for work-life balance for my staff, the boundaries in my own life became blurred to nonexistent. Nevertheless, I approached each day with optimism, hope, and the belief that at some point, something would shift, and my life would become, once again, manageable. This proved to be the day that a shift would occur, albeit not the shift I was expecting.

It was late into the evening when I finally left the office. Exhausted from chronic sleep deprivation, the emotional drain of holding space for the sundry feelings of those around me, and the unending frustration of trying to get someone to address my unreasonable workload, I aimlessly walked to my car for what seemed like an hour. Reaching for my car door, I was gripped by an indescribable sense that my life was collapsing beneath me. Tears began to fall down my cheeks as I wrestled with an overwhelming feeling of defeat. What happened to me? How did I get here? This was not at all the life I dreamed of. The sobs escalated as I placed my belongings in the back seat while scanning my surroundings to make sure no one was watching. I could no longer pretend that everything was ok. Every aspect of my life was disintegrating, leaving a trail of fragments that would never be able to reconnect to form the façade of perfection I had been living. I had fallen to the depths of darkness for which I could have never been more ill-prepared. I slumped down in the seat of my car and cried out, "I want this all to end." But by the grace of God, it did not.

The Awakening
Romans 12:2 And be not conformed to this world: but be ye transformed by the renewing of your mind, that ye may prove what is that good, and acceptable, and perfect, will of God.

Eventually, I was able to start the car and begin my drive home. During the ride, I replayed the reel of my life and took note of every event and decision that brought me to that point. As difficult as it was to accept, I uncovered an ugly truth. My life was a culmination of the aspirations of others, molded by their views and beliefs, and conformed to meet their expectations. Somewhere along the journey, I completely lost myself through my need to gain love, respect, and appreciation. My self-worth was tethered to someone else's approval of me, and I had sacrificed every part of my very being to obtain it. I discovered that my actions and behaviors were primarily a result of the belief that to be valued, you must prove yourself valuable. Hustling for my self-worth, I sought external validation in every area of my life, settling for whatever life offered and asking for no more. From this, the shell of my existence was created and took form to reflect the image of the world around me and not that which God had created in me. Placing my value on external acceptance resulted in me accepting that which I did not value.

I came to the realization that if my life was going to change, my thinking had to change, "For as he thinketh in his heart, so is he." Proverbs 23:7. Deep down inside, I knew that I was destined for greatness. And with God's help, I was going to rewrite my story.

The Revelation
Jeremiah 29:11 For I know the plans I have for you," declares the LORD, "plans to prosper you and not to harm you, plans to give you hope and a future.

For the first time in years, I felt a twinge of hope. I recognized God's greatest gift bestowed on mankind was the gift of choice. Through the words of Tony Robbins, "Where focus goes, energy flows," I was reminded that I could not control the people and circumstances around me, but I could control what I chose to focus on. And I made a choice to focus on myself. Not the chameleon me, who became so effective in masking who she was until she no longer knew herself. No, me that sat in the middle of the floor on that beautiful Christmas morning, seeing life's potential through the toys that surrounded her.

This journey would require that I first challenge all the limiting beliefs that stripped me of the opportunity to live authentically. Those beliefs suggested that I was not enough and that only through others would I find my self-worth. Acceptance of who I was required me to learn how to be comfortable in my own skin, with all of its flaws and imperfections. Equally as important, I had to make peace with my past, which included forgiving myself for the countless mistakes and bad decisions I made, as well as the betrayal of my core values, which led me to accept and tolerate actions, behaviors, and circumstances that almost destroyed me. And although life left its share of scars, those scars did not have to represent defeat but a map to my destiny.

DR. SHIRLEE TURNER

The Message
Romans 8:28 And we know that all things work together for good to them that love God, to them who are the called according to his purpose.

  Who you are today is a direct result of the choices that you have made. We often allow the negative circumstances of our past to continue to fuel the trajectory of our future. But when you recognize that you are the author of your own story, you can choose to rewrite the chapters, which can alter how your story will end. You do not have to remain in a story that does not serve you. Just by shifting your focus from the experiences of your past to the experiences you want to create, you unleash the seeds of greatness that lie within you. How you assimilate your past and navigate through life's defeats will have a profound impact on your future. You cannot control what happens to you, but you do have the power to choose how you respond. The words you silently tell yourself have power, and those words can impact the direction your life takes. Every day you get the chance to change your story. And in every moment of that day, you are afforded the opportunity to shift your perspective, choose your words, and determine the actions that will shape your destiny.

  As the author of your story, holding the pen that writes the narrative, what will your story be?

About Dr. Shirlee Turner

Dr. Shirlee Turner is a successful, accomplished physician with a medical career spanning 30+ years. In addition to serving her country as a Medical Officer in the US Navy, she has cared for patients along the entire life spectrum, experiencing the joy of hearing an infant's first cry to the sorrow of witnessing the last breath of a terminally ill patient. A recognized leader in the medical community, she served as Regional Medical Director for one of the largest healthcare companies in the US and is currently the Chief Medical Officer for the oldest and largest not-for-profit hospice in her region.

During the height of the pandemic, when the fragility of life became hauntingly apparent to her, the quintessential façade of success and happiness that Dr. Turner presented to the world developed a deep fissure through which she was able to see that inside, she felt utterly hopeless and defeated. Her passion and desire to meet the needs of everyone around her had caused her to lose the very essence of who she was, exacting a huge toll on her physical, mental, and emotional well-being. But through her experiences at the bedside of her dying patients, helping them navigate the complexities of their own lives fraught with broken relationships, lost hopes, and unfulfilled dreams, she began to find a path of healing for herself. Recognizing that if she did not dramatically change the direction of her life, her own last days would be filled with the same guilt, disappointments, and regrets shared by many of her patients. She realized that to transition from this life to the next with peace and gratitude, one must live an authentic life of purpose; and how one experienced their last days was intricately intertwined with how they responded to the experiences of the life they had lived.

Dr. Turner's mission is to help women who are broken, unfulfilled, and feeling defeated, to rediscover who they are, define and then build a life of purpose and meaning, allowing them to experience joyful living in the now so that when that time comes to reflect on their lives, they will have a story they are proud to tell.

A mother to an energetic and highly competitive adult son with Down Syndrome, when Dr. Turner is not working, you will likely find the two of them on some wild adventure, at the movies, enjoying outdoor concerts, or her sitting on the sidelines of a variety of Special Olympic Sporting Competitions unapologetically cheering him on.

Contact:
Facebook https://www.facebook.com/ShirleeETurner
Email: ShirleeTurnerMD@ShirleeTurnerMD.com

My Story
By Tonya Flowers

As I authored my story, I felt intimidated and weak, thinking I did not have anything to say. But God showed me that I do have a testimony. If God can do it for me, He can do it for you. I have confidence in Christ to do a great work in me. Here I will tell you a few traumatic situations that tried to knock me down, but I continued to get up. I'm praying that Jesus directs my path in this book. I went to Relentless Church with Pastor John Gray in Powder Springs and dropped my manual, in which I started drafting my book. I thought everything was lost, and I was defeated again. I did not let that discourage me, so I decided to get back up and write.

I was born in the early 70s to Nelson and Ann Flowers. They were very much in love and still are to this day. My father is a Vietnam veteran who was awarded three bronze stars. He also retired from the railroad and provided for his family. My father is an entrepreneur at heart and has many businesses. He is also a missionary traveling all over the world, assisting pastors as they preached the gospel of Jesus Christ. My lovely mother is a virtuous woman at heart. My mother raised her eight brothers and sisters while going to school. She has a heart for all people. Growing up, we did a lot of volunteer work. My mom's profession was nursing, and she was very capable of doing that. My parents always had my cousins in the house, so they were more like my brothers and sisters growing up.

I had the best upbringing until my dad moved us to Mississippi. This city girl was bullied and picked on. That's where I believe I lost my self-esteem. One thing I knew how to do was hide my emotions. I then turned into the girl that never said no. I was the shy people pleaser. I only had one friend, and her family started taking me to church. This church was different from the church my mom took me to. I went from a Baptist Church to a full Pentecostal, which showed me next-level spirituality. I received the gift of speaking in tongues.

I asked my parents whether I could move back to Erie, PA, which was called the worst place for a black person to live. But I wanted to be around the people I grew up with, and I wanted to go home. Now I was in my senior year of high school, I still went to church, and they noticed I spoke in tongues. At that time, people weren't speaking in tongues up north. So, then I was introduced to being in the ministry. In high school, I continued to do volunteer work, and I was able to share volunteer work with other high schoolers. I went to East High School, where a counselor told me I wasn't college material. This was another blow to my esteem, so I didn't tell anyone what this counselor told me. I then joined the military at the tender age of 17, and my grandmother had to sign off on the paperwork. I was in the delayed entry program while still in high school, but I was able to go to the reserve units on the weekends. I was attached to a military police unit which I loved. I thought about becoming a police officer because I love to help people, but then my cousin, who is like a brother to me, was in a tragic accident, and he lost his life. So, after that happened, I wanted to run away because Shawn was one of my protectors. Soon after his funeral, I enlisted on active duty and was sent off to basic at Fort Jackson Columbia, South Carolina.

While in the military, I was in and out of the church, more so in. I continued to do volunteer work and house homeless people in government housing. From a young age, my heart would hurt when I would see a homeless person, especially if they had kids. I would bring a lot of homeless people to my house to stay, but this one family stood out. One time, on a snowy day in Alaska, I picked up a single mother and her five kids and brought them back to my on-post housing. They stayed with me for about three months until my first Sergeant found out and told me they had to move out ASAP! I was able to find them shelter because I didn't want to get kicked out of the housing. That's when I went out and bought my first house in Anchorage, Alaska. Now I could help whoever I wanted to, and I did.

I have housed so many people in all the different states I've lived in due to military PC moves. I do not discriminate; I've shown love to strippers, people on substances, and people about to lose their minds. So, over the many years of me taking people into my private home, I talked to my parents about some business ideas and just talked in general as we do. We discussed starting a nonprofit to house homeless veterans because veterans are dear to our hearts, and eventually, we will open this to the public. My parents would worry about me giving rides to homeless people or hitchhikers or bringing people into my house that I didn't know. But I felt the tug of the Lord on me each time I did this. Recently I met a guy while in culinary school, and we became friends. He was going through a difficult time with his husband. While going through that difficult time, he began using drugs and alcohol. I was the one that got him into rehab with the VA Medical Center. I wrote to him, called him, got him whatever he needed, and was there for him. He spent a few months in rehab, and when he got out, he had nowhere to go. I allowed him to stay with me; he is now clean, sober, and working. It took three months for him to get his own place. I still check on him from time to time; he is still working and maintaining his apartment.

Nelsville Community, Inc's mission is to provide shelter and restore dignity and hope to our veterans who gave their lives and service to our country. Nelsville Community, Inc endeavors to strive to go above and beyond for our veterans no matter the challenge; we aim to deliver our absolute best work every single day across our services. Nelsville Community, Inc will accomplish this by collaborating with local government businesses, community organizations as well as other nonprofit organizations to build healthy relationships and obtain the resources needed to succeed. Our organization is committed to providing resources, knowledge skills, and other services revolving around veterans. Our goal is to help them regain stability in their lives but offering transitional or permanent housing and the delivery of critical social services. We strive to improve the quality of life for our veterans by increasing the number of homes and reducing the prevalence of homelessness among veterans. We desire to identify market-based growth opportunities in our veteran communities through our own research, education policy development, and programs that will lead to a paradigm shift in the veteran community. Nelsville Community, Inc is expanding and able to provide more critical programming and services to play a significant role in enabling veterans to reach their full potential and gain the confidence and resources they need to live the comfortable life they deserve.

As of January 2020, Mississippi had an estimated 1,107 experiencing homelessness on any given day, as reported by the Continuums of Care to the U.S. Department of Housing and Urban Development (HUD). Of that total, 76 families were households, 68 were veterans, 51 were unaccompanied young adults aged (18 to 24) and 146 were individuals experiencing chronic homelessness. This perpetual cycle of a lack of knowledge, resources, or opportunities will continue to affect the people in our communities unless they are given the opportunity to empower themselves. Organizations like Nelsville Community, Inc can provide these veterans with wrap-around services that offer both immediate and long-term advantages helping our community thrive and succeed.

According to the United States, an interagency council on homelessness, just over 9% of all adults experiencing homelessness in the United States are veterans of the United States military. This shows the need for our organization. We will offer many programs that provide all the assistance needed and provide veterans with homes and comfort. Nelsville Community, Inc brings the education aspect combined with the awareness to the people and other organizations in our community. Our ultimate goal of Nelsville Community, Inc is to increase participation in policymaking that results in equitable policies to improve the quality of life for all veterans in need of better living situations. Our goal is to not only assist with creating stable living environments for those in need but also equip them with the resources and skills necessary to empower themselves and rise above their misfortunes.

My email is tflowers@nelsvillecommunity.com,
My website is HTTPS://nelsvillecommunity.org
1" Mississippi Homelessness Statistics."

Acknowledgments

I have to start by thanking my parents, Nelson and Ann R. Flowers. They are prime examples of Godly people, humanitarianism, and entrepreneurship. They have paved a life full of fun and selflessness hard to compete with. Thank you for your love and guidance. My three sons, Altonio, Jhai, and Timothy Flowers. They are my three heartbeats who love and support everything I do. To Altonio my gamer, I love you, Son. To Jhai, my twin in everything just about, you are my ride or die, Son. Congratulations on being a YouTube sensation and starting your own business. You make videos for people and have a company building skateboard ramps. You can find Jhai Flow on all social media outlets and on eBay! To my miracle Baby Timothy, you are keeping me young. I had Timothy at 39 years old and had to undergo an emergency C section for a placenta abruption. Just wait; this kid will be great; he is here for a reason. Thank you, Keisha Williams, for being with me during this time of my pregnancy and birth. Keisha was a young Soldier in my platoon at the time. Now Keisha is a successful businesswoman owning a silent headphone party supplier, catering business, and cleaning business. Her websites are blackoutex.com; bpwcatering.com and ngaclean.com

Timothy Flowers timflowers7@hotmail.com, thank you for always being the best big brother a girl needed. We are going to build an empire together.

To the Chef who always inspired me, told all the corny jokes, and checked on me during an emotionally abusive relationship, Chef Paul Bodrogi at the Arts Institute of Atlanta pbodrogi@aii.edu, Thank you!

To Professor Ophelia M. Santos osantos@aii.edu, my instructor, who was always tough on me and did not let me turn in half-done assignments. I did many assignments more than twice, but you were always there to guide me, even with your hectic schedule. I will complete your class, I promise!

About Tonya Flowers

Altruism is a profound component nestled in the hearts of those called to servant leadership. Trailblazing this exact path, filled with the unsurpassable ethics of benevolence and intention, is the compassionate professional Tonya Flowers.

Tonya Flowers is an author, retired conscript, and CEO and Founder of Nelsville Community Inc., a nonprofit organization fashioned to meet the various needs of unhoused communal veterans. Having generously served more than two decades as Sergeant First Class in the military while enduring the unforeseeable events of tragedy, war, and mental anguish, Tonya found an innate purpose in serving humanity through the power of empathic diligence and benevolence.

Tonya's mantra is simple: She reasons to remain a beacon of light and hope for the broken, a helping hand for the lost, and a catalyst for communal change.

Combining an unyielding heart to serve others with a standard of personal excellence, Tonya Flowers shares sincere regard for education, achievement, and community service. She holds a bachelor's degree in culinary arts and an associate's degree in General Studies and retired from the U.S. Military Sergeant First Class. Prior to the development of her own nonprofit organization, Tonya has been often recognized for her devotion to service overall; whether in soup kitchens, shelters, and other communal efforts, she radiates the proverbial ethic of humanitarianism.

Inspired greatly by the legacy of philanthropy energized through her parents, it is Tonya's hope to expand her platform, create state-of-the-art resource facilities efficient enough to house as many unhoused veterans in Mississippi as possible and generate lasting revenue for her venture through the creation of diesel stations and African-American owned grocery conglomerates.

When Tonya is not out serving the global community, she is an asset to her local communal body and a loving member of her family and friendship circles.

Tonya Flowers. Leader. Organizer. Humanitarian.

STEPHON SUGGS

Recognize the Greatness in You
By Stephon Suggs

This chapter is dedicated to Indi and Stephon Suggs Jr. I want you to always know you can do ANYTHING! The sky. You are the gift from above, A ribbon in the sky. Be eagles not pigeons, you were born to fly!

Recognize the greatness in you.
As I strive to see the greatness in me.
When we get out of our own way,
How great could we be?
How far could we sail?
If we did not fear the sea?
How far could you soar?
With no fear of heights?
We worry so much about if the timing is right.
I been through the struggle; I stayed up all night.
When you get tired of the darkness, it's time to seek the light.
When all have greatness, first we must believe.
If you give it your all, who knows what you could achieve.
Never give up. We all have that choice.
I have a lot of things to say; it's time to use my voice.

I can recall being around 5 when I started to realize the conditions around me were not ideal. The household had little structure, positivity, or food. When you are young, and you see all these things go on around you that are outside of your control, you start to question the world and your role in it. You start to normalize and rationalize things that are far from normal or rational. You trick yourself into thinking that this is all life has to offer and that everyone around you is in a similar position, so there is no reason to complain. I was not in an environment that cultivated a growth mindset. This cause me to develop very low self-esteem and confidence in my abilities. Deep down I felt like

I was an eagle, but my reality had me training to be a pigeon. I was certainly buying into the mindset. I figured I would never fly, so why try?

I always had a passion for poetry and helping others. When I was in the 5th grade, I chose poetry as an elective class because of this very pretty 5th grader that also decided to join the class. I remember admiring her in class on the first day when suddenly I was interrupted by the instructor, Mr. John telling me to write something! I picked up the pen, and who knows exactly what I wrote. What I do know is Mr. John started to see something in my writing ability.

He would challenge me to write poems weekly and even gave me my first opportunity to perform on stage. As I reflect, he is the first person to ever encourage me to write more. Truth be told, at that time, I only wrote when prompted to. Even throughout high school, I would write occasionally but never consistently enough to gain traction. I was so consumed with all the issues in my life that it was hard to focus on anything that could change my future. Honestly, I was just happy to make it day by day. I continued even after high school, carrying this low confidence with me. If you knew me in my younger 20s, you might not have been able to tell. I wasn't even aware!

I can see now that I have always had this pattern of self-sabotage stemming from not truly believing I can have and be more. This toxic pattern, mixed in with a lack of quality role models, led to a lot of substance and sexual addictions for me. It was how I learned to cope with all the pressure. I played it safe and tried to stay out of the way. My mindset was so screwed that I legit thought that everything I experienced somehow disqualified me from living a fulfilling life. I started to make decisions that reflected a man who did not have long-term aspirations. I know what it feels like to lose hope and want to give up. I continued to go through the motions all my younger and mid-20s.

I welcomed my first child Indi into the world in April of 2014. I was determined to let this be a catalyst. All my life, I wanted to prove to my parents I could do better than them. This was my chance to show them! Or so I thought! Don't get me wrong, my daughter made me a better person, and it started to wake me up, but paradigms are so deeply rooted that I learned I didn't have as much power as I thought. Those first few years of being a father were tough. I made many mistakes, which did not help my confidence overall. I was humbled when it came to judging my parents for sure.

In December 2017, I got a call from my brother that really changed my world. As soon as I answered, it was like I knew what he would say before he said it. "Pops gone," he said with a cracked voice. I fell to the ground and started crying. I didn't always understand my dad, but I was not ready to lose him! I was only 26 and had many more questions about how to be a man. For some time, I felt evilness in my spirit.

The reason that my dad's death changed my world forever is that after losing him is when I started to seek something to heal my heart. I had no idea where to start, so I started finding YouTube videos on positivity. At first, I scoffed at the idea and thought a lot of it was corny. I continued to find messages that were starting to resonate with what I had gone through and was going through. I started to read scripture and listen to pastors such as TD Jakes, Dr. Dharius Daniels, and Steve Furtick. I started to tap into the mindset of motivational speakers such as Les Brown, the late great Dr. Myles Munroe, the late Bob Proctor, Tony Robbins, and many more.

I didn't recognize it at the time, but all along, I was planting seeds that would soon have a major impact on my life. Fast-forward to March 2020. It is a week before my 29th birthday, and instead of being happy, I am scared out of my mind. Not only was there a global pandemic that, at the time, no one really knew how it would end up but knowing that if I was to lose my life because of this virus, I had done very little to leave a legacy. Not because I did not have the talent, but because I did not have the courage to face my fears. That was a gut punch unlike any other.

For the first time in my life, I decided I would stand for something and not let my past define my future. I have been watching these YouTube videos, and my mind was expanding as far as what is possible. I knew it was time to take things to the next step. I knew I needed mentorship and a community of like-minded people if I was truly going to change my ways. Essentially, I needed to surround myself with eagles! I believe that whatever you are seeking is also seeking you. This theory was reaffirmed to me the moment I received an email from Les Brown's account. Months prior before the pandemic, I wrote a long email explaining that I would love to be mentored by him and sent it to his website. I thought nothing of it for months. In May of 2020, when I got a response telling me about a mentorship program he was launching, I knew this was something I could not miss out on.

In September of 2020, I gave my first virtual speech at Les Brown's Power Voice Summit! This meant so much to me because I went from listening to this guy to be able to work with him! I also got to read him two poems that I wrote for him. One was explaining his impact on my life, and the other wished him a wonderful birthday. Talk about dreams aligning with reality!

Over the last two years, I have had the pleasure of learning from the master of public speaking, in my opinion. Connecting with Les Brown has also led me to meet my coach Jon Talerico. I cannot put a price tag on how much I had grown over the past two years when I decided to act and reach out to other eagles. It is not easy, and to this day, I still have bad days. I have a community of people around that keeps me focused, motivated and hungry to share my talents with the world. In August of 2021, I welcomed my first son Stephon Jr into the world. My children are my legacy, and they motivate me to break these generational curses. I never want my son to have to google how to be a man. I have done it before. I recognize that my parents were not the enemy. They were just part of the cycle. One that I must break.

The power in my words is not what I have been through or anything I have done but, more importantly, what is upcoming. I made a pledge to use my gift of poetry and spoken word to be the missing void that connects those who need healing. I would not be in this position today if it weren't for others believing in me all that time that I did not believe in myself. That borrowed belief is what I use as strength to conquer obstacles that lay in front of me. If I can use my talents to restore balance, I must accept the challenge! We all have greatness in us. If you are like me, maybe, you did not grow up in a situation that gave you confidence. I get it. I promise you that I am living proof that confidence can grow.

You just must never give up and seek better because what you are seeking is also seeking you, whether you reach millions or just a few. Answer the call not for what it can provide you but because it is what you are born to do. I believe in you.

About Stephon Suggs

"Failure or success, it starts with a choice. I will not fulfill my purpose if I do not use my voice."

Stephon Suggs is a passionate speaker, poet, and author from Washington DC. Stephon uses his poetry and life experiences to connect with young men who struggle with confidence and other issues that plague our young men. Stephon has a goal to impact 1,000,000 men. His poetry has a way of catching the audience's attention and causes self-reflection.

In 2020 Stephon had the pleasure to be a part of the world-renowned Les Brown's Initial Power Voice summit, which was streamed on multiple streaming platforms. He received his speaking certification in August of that same year. After being

STEPHON SUGGS

mentored by Jon Talarico for the last two years, as well as being associated with the Million in You Network, Stephon is now ready to use his voice in a major way to inspire 1,000,000 people, one person at a time.

Contact Stephon:
https://www.facebook.com/sizzle.suggs

Perseverance During Uncertainty: Victory at the End
By Tara Nicole Green

As we walk out the journey of life, we respond to the essence around us. Our surroundings and the moments that we experience call out for our response. This response might be in the form of emotions, physical movement, or some form of action. Life is up and down, and some refer to it as a roller coaster ride. We all know life does not stand still. Life happens, and it continues regardless if we are prepared for the journey or not. Therefore, there is no way to avoid the ups and downs and uncertain times.

We all are unique in terms of how we all deal with unpredictable situations. Some of us respond by taking action immediately, others might ponder on thinking about the correct action and then respond, and many don't take action at all, becoming an emotional mess. Regardless of the response, the fact remains that you must go through the process to reach VICTORY. According to Dictionary.com (2022), the term victory is defined as "A success or triumph over an enemy in battle or war; an engagement ending in such triumph; the ultimate and decisive superiority in any battle or contest; a success or superior position achieved against any opponent, opposition, difficulty, etc." Regardless of the design of the obstacle you face, triumph is inevitable. Some say that things always seem to work themselves out. The fundamental attribute is TIME, and experiencing each stage of the process eventually gets you to the final stage of overcoming VICTORY.

Each circumstance encompasses six elements of stages that an individual might experience. First is the initial jolt of bewilderment. The second is acclimation to the circumstance. The third is an emotional release. Fourth, the coming to terms with what happened. Fifth, ask the question, WHY? Sixth, needing vindication or resolution and sometimes both. The last is moving forward in spite of the obstacle or challenge, during the process of moving to eventually propel and triumph over the circumstance. An individual eventually will try to deal with or manage the situation with the goal of reaching a resolution.

The six key elements combined together create perseverance. To persevere means "steady persistence in the course of action, a purpose, a state, etc., especially in spite of difficulties, obstacles, or discouragement. Continuance in a state of grace to the end, leading to eternal salvation" (Dictionary.com 2022). An individual would need to stay the course. At times "I quit" or "It is too hard" will surface in one's thoughts. Immediately countering those thoughts of negativity with words of power and positivity will allow one to overcome those feelings of doubt. James 1:4 states, "Let perseverance finish its work so that you may be mature and complete, not lacking anything." Understand that the obstacle pressing you should not feel good. The challenge is not easy. It is the pressing and stretching that reshapes you and makes you stronger. Romans 5:3 states, "Not only so, but we also glory in our sufferings, because we know that suffering produces perseverance." James 1:3 says, "Because you know that the testing of your faith produces perseverance." Keeping focused on your gain and not on how much it hurts minimizes the pitfalls of depression and losing the will to continue.

It is crucial to be careful of the thoughts you permit to dwell in your mind. Reject every thought that is not encouraging or inspiring. Pessimistic thinking and disallowing thoughts produce speech of the same kind. Actions soon follow, creating roadblocks in the journey. 2 Corinthians 10:5 (KJV) "Casting down imaginations, and every high thing that exalteth itself against the knowledge of God, and bringing into captivity every thought to the obedience of Christ."

It takes time to reach victory. The process requires commitment. Choosing to quit will only leave an individual stuck. Finishing strong empowers you to feel complete and accomplished. Your journey will not only empower you but others that will encounter the same obstacle as you did. Revelation 12:11

(KJV), "And they overcame him by the blood of the Lamb, and by the word of their testimony, and they loved not their lives unto the death."

Fasting is powerful while going through your journey. The sacrifice of fasting demonstrates your surrender to God, the willingness of a humble heart, submission, and repentance heart. The action of fasting weakens the flesh but strengthens the spiritual connection with God. Fasting is very important, along with prayer. They both coincide together.

Maintaining a posture of praying throughout the entire process is a commitment. Prayer sends our petition to God regarding our burden. An individual must present the request, get quiet, and wait on God's response. Prayer triggers the releasing of God's vision for our action that leads us to completion and overcoming to VICTORY. Vision is God-given. In the story of Nehemiah, through prayer, God responded, answering the petition of prayer and granting Nehemiah wisdom, strength, and favor. Through commitment, the walls of Jerusalem were no longer in ruins but were rebuilt by God, giving Nehemiah the vision and a plan. First, Nehemiah petitioned God regarding his burden of the ruined walls of Jerusalem. Nehemiah waited and then prayed to God before the process and throughout the process.

Seeking God each step of the way in your journey sets you up for the favor of God. Our Lord God responds by giving you the vision, direction, and wisdom you need to overcome to VICTORY. The story of Nehemiah demonstrates that God will not leave you nor forsake you. God will not abandon you. God will restore you and keep you. Our God works on our behalf behind the scenes just as he did with Nehemiah. God set Nehemiah up for VICTORY. God will set you up for VICTORY!

God will provide everything you need. Nehemiah cried out to the Lord regarding the walls of Jerusalem. God granted favor, and Nehemiah was able to get permission to leave his post and return to Jerusalem. Also, God granted resources; the wealth through the Persian Empire provided all the wherewithal needed for the rebuilding of the wall. God will give you the resources you need to get to VICTORY.

Give God the glory! As the story of Nehemiah demonstrates to us that there was a dedication of the wall after the wall was successfully completed. All came to give thanksgiving, singing with cymbals and instruments, choir singers, purification, and offering great sacrifices. All rejoiced for what God had done.

As you go through your journey, continue to praise God and be thankful. God will show up throughout the process. As you pray and seek wisdom, understanding, and direction, God works behind the scenes granting favor, moving things in place to work for your good, and working out logistics on your behalf. You may not always see God working, but continue to praise, having faith that he is working for you.

What if it does not look or feel like God is by your side and you are not making progress towards VICTORY? The journey to VICTORY is not the same for all. There may be times that you don't feel like things are working, and God may not feel close. Attention, please! God is always nearby. God will never leave you. Deuteronomy 4:31 (NIV) "For the Lord your God is a merciful God; he will not abandon or destroy you or forget the covenant with your ancestors, which he confirmed to them by oath." Continue the path and stand strong, speaking scriptures out loud. Psalms 23 (KJV) "The Lord is my shepherd; I shall not want. He maketh me to lie down in green pastures: he leadeth me beside the still waters. He restoreth my soul: he leadeth me in the paths of righteousness for his name's sake. Yea, though I walk through the valley of the shadow of death, I will fear no evil: for thou art with me; thy rod and thy staff they comfort me. Thou preparest a table before me in the presence of mine enemies: thou anointest my head with oil; my cup runneth over. Surely goodness and mercy shall follow me all the days of my life: and I will dwell in the house of the Lord forever. Also, speak out loud the scripture Psalms 91: 1- 16; it applies to you and your journey.

When the time of VICTORY has arrived in your circumstance, give God all the glory and praise for all that he has done. The uncertainty of circumstances is just that. You are not sure of anything. Applying the elements, praying, fasting, and acknowledging God in the process draws him near to you as well as keeps you focused on God and his sovereignty. 1 Thessalonians 5:18 (NIV) "Give thanks in all circumstances; for this is God's will for you in Christ Jesus." 1 Chronicles 16:34 (NIV) Give thanks to the Lord, for He is good; His love endures forever. God is in control. He is able to lead you and guide you through the process to reach VICTORY. James 5:11 (NIV) As you know, we count as blessed those who have persevered. You have heard of Job's perseverance and have seen what the Lord finally brought about. The Lord is full of compassion and mercy.

TARA NICOLE GREEN

About Tara N Green

Business professional with over 20 years of business management experience in Fortune 500 companies. Areas of knowledge- Finance and Accounting, Commercial Leasing Accounting/Finance, and Risk.

Adjunct Professor – Teach course subjects in Business, Professional Development, and Accounting/Finance.

Published Author – Award Winning, Best Seller

B.S. in Business Administration, Accounting from DeVry University, and dual master's degrees in Business Administration, Accounting, as well as a Master's Degree in Project Management from Keller University. Currently, she is pursuing a Doctorate in Business.

Dedication to inspiring others and making her community a better place by conducting empowerment workshops for young girls aged 6 to 18 years old on topics such as money, savings, budgeting, and goal setting.

Believer in the power of volunteerism and service. While serving as Chair from 2016-2019, raised over 46K for United Negro College Fund recipients.

Humble Servant and Worshiper of God. Faithful believer of the word of God.

Enjoys cooking, gardening, and watching movies with her husband.

Contact Tara:
https://www.facebook.com/TaraGreenthepinnaclestrategist

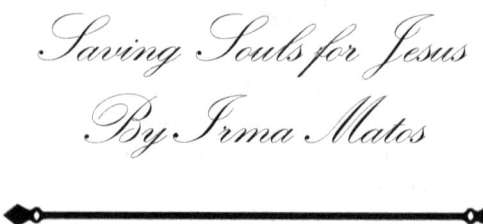
Saving Souls for Jesus
By Irma Matos

When I was a child in Cuba, I dreamed of doing big things. I felt I had greatness in me. I thought I would be an engineer or maybe even invent something that would change the world.

I used to write stories when I was a child, and I would read them to friends in the park at the corner of my house after school. I could feel greatness within me. Being dragged away from everything I knew and coming to the United States, that sense of greatness was stifled. Many years went by, and I started a business, but I didn't feel I had done anything extraordinary or great until I started serving at the Emmaus Retreat and the Mission. I felt I was making a difference in people's lives, and that was an incredible feeling. There was pure joy in helping the women that came to the retreat. I realized that I was the happiest when I was serving. Perhaps you, too, have felt a call of greatness but are unsure how to express it. I encourage you to tap into your spirituality. Look for ways to serve, teach, and share lessons learned with others.

Spirituality encompasses more than just our relationship with God. It is also reflected in how well we listen to our intuition, which is God whispering to us. Our interactions with others are also our way to be an instrument of God's love. My missions throughout the years have been filled with examples of this.

Early in my childhood, I served in my local church, providing necessary assistance to the priest, the nuns, and others. I felt a sense of accomplishment, a closeness to God and those who served him. Later, I realized that God was using those men and women to teach me valuable lessons about how to be an instrument in His service and how I could help others to have a deeper relationship with Him.

Once I moved to the United States, the church was not part of my life as much for a long time. Yet, I was still surrounded by people who demonstrated acts of service and kindness. My teacher and friend, Muskie, was one, my mother was another, and there were certainly others. Their examples built a legacy that I find myself still reflecting on today.

With all that motivation and inspiration to serve, I found myself in a unique position to take advantage of an opportunity to participate in a mission trip. These trips involved a small group of individuals who traveled to Tabasco, Mexico, providing practical assistance while encouraging them in their walk with God.

I met an older woman on one of my missions to Mexico, and she was very ill. She was thin, had no teeth, and was dealing with severe stomach pain. I asked her how old she was twice, and the reply was the same both times. "I am the youngest of three." She told us that she wanted to be baptized. The day that she was supposed to be baptized years ago, the woman who had volunteered to be her godmother never showed up. She still had the white dress she had bought for the occasion. I didn't understand how another opportunity did not present itself in all that time.

I heard the calling from God and volunteered to be her godmother, and she agreed. She was baptized, and also received communion, and was confirmed as well. Both of us were joyful on that day. It was very emotional for me. I remember that she told the priest, "Father, thank you for getting me out of purgatory." I had hoped to see her again, but she passed away six months later. Yet, despite not being able to see her again, I was happy to be the instrument God used to save her soul.

I learned from this experience to be aware of your surroundings. Listen to your intuition because it is God speaking to you through it, and perhaps He is looking to use you to bless someone else. You must be open to being an instrument of God. I never thought, in a million years, I would have a Mexican goddaughter much older than me.

One of the challenges of leaving Cuba was being disconnected from my spiritual community. I missed the church and my activities. I missed my friends and the nuns. In my new school and new city, I learned English and kept up with my studies. I was getting used to living with my mother's side of the family. I missed my paternal grandparents, who raised me, and my cousins on my father's side of the family. Also, my church and the park where I used to play with my friends had been just a block away, but in the United States, it was different. The whole shift was overwhelming, and I found myself drifting away from the church and the anchor it had always been in my life as I worked to acclimate to my new home.

Even though I was not involved in the church like before, God never left me. I felt his blessings throughout my life, in the friendships I cultivated, which I keep to this day, and in the way He always took care of me, even during times of loss, such as the death of my teacher and friend Muskie.

One day, a friend of mine spoke to me about the Emmaus Retreat. It is meant to be a very personal walk and encounter with Jesus Christ. Everyone who had gone through the experience came away enlightened and feeling a deeper spiritual connection. My friend could not stop raving about how much she enjoyed it. She was clearly impressed and recommended it highly. I asked her to tell me more about what happened during the retreat, but surprisingly, she got quiet. Then she told me that if she answered all my questions, it would spoil the experience for me. I had to live it and find out for myself.

Her responses and enthusiasm prompted me to sign up for the weekend retreat. I had not been to a retreat since I had left Cuba, and I missed them. It was the most fantastic weekend of my life. I had an encounter with Jesus Christ, and it transformed me. I have not stopped talking about how it invigorated me spiritually. In fact, I was so inspired and transformed that I ended up serving on the team that organized the retreat. I am still involved today.

Personally, I find that the Scriptures about giving and receiving apply. Even though I give of my time to these retreats and other activities related to the church, I get so much more back spiritually. I find that spending time with like-minded individuals who are also trying to live a life guided by God and His principles encourages me to keep on that path despite any challenge I might face.

I am the happiest when I am serving on the Emmaus Retreat. It is such a joy to see the women that come on Friday evening looking like they have the weight of the world on their shoulders and watch them leave the retreat on Sunday with a fresh sparkle in their eyes and joy in their hearts. What a transformation!

My involvement with the retreat also helped me to reconnect with my life of service from the early days in Cuba. I realize now that there is nothing like being of service to others. What a joy!

One aspect of the retreat that benefited me greatly was that I came out of my shell. I stopped protecting myself and became open and vulnerable, which led to more spiritual growth. I also began to learn a lot of things about myself, including things that I realized, were important to change.

Instead of being controlling, sure that I knew everything, I opened myself up to relying more on God. I began to be less arrogant and self-sufficient. Instead, I started to focus on being more aware and more compassionate, and I made myself available to serve.

After a meeting one night, an Emmaus sister named Connie told me, "You are in the wrong profession." I had written and given presentations for the retreat and wrote a couple of articles about my experiences as a missionary in Mexico. Those efforts had impressed her. I pondered what she said, wondering what profession would be best. Then I realized that changing careers would involve showing others how to live a life of humility and service, one that would lead to blessings.

The truth is that we all have opportunities and moments where we can teach and share our experiences with others. The wisdom of humanity is passed down from one generation to another through stories, advice, and values. Little did I know that my greatest achievement and the greatness in me would be demonstrated by the way I serve the Lord.

IRMA MATOS

About Irma Matos

Irma Matos is the International Best Selling Co-Author of Boss Your Lane and Women Of The Power Voice. Irma is the author of the upcoming book, *A Noble Profession: Life Lessons To Inspire Your Soul & Live In Abundance*, as well as an entrepreneur, property management consultant, real estate investor, life coach, speaker, and missionary. She immigrated to the United States from Cuba in 1970. After completing her formal education, Irma created a property management company, which she ran for 33 years. Today, she serves as a consultant for her former company and its clients. In addition, she is a Certified Life Transformation Dream Builder Coach and Life Mastery Consultant, guiding her clients in the fulfillment of their goals and dreams.

In 2006, Irma was honored to be invited to the President's Dinner in Washington D.C. as the Business Advisory Council Honorary Chairman. She received the Congressional Medal of Distinction from the NRCC in recognition of her Outstanding Meritorious Service. Integrity, honesty, and loyalty are three pillars that define Irma both personally and professionally.

She has traveled to Mexico as part of several missions. Her goal is to inspire people to live a vision-driven life and impart the many life lessons she has learned to others, including the importance of gratitude and service in order to live in abundance.

Today, she lives in Miami, where she continues to write, consult, coach, speak, and serve others.

CONTACT INFORMATION FOR IRMA MATOS:

Email address:	IrmaMatosAuthor@gmail.com
Website:	anobleprofessionbook.com
Facebook:	irma.matos.7

CPSIA information can be obtained
at www.ICGtesting.com
Printed in the USA
LVHW020921060922
727670LV00007B/285